EVERY DAY A
FRIDAY

ALSO BY JOEL OSTEEN

Your Best Life Now: 7 Steps to Living at Your Full Potential
Your Best Life Now Journal: A Guide to Reaching Your Full Potential
Your Best Life Now Study Guide: 7 Steps to Living at Your Full Potential
Daily Reading from Your Best Life Now: 90 Devotions for
Living at Your Full Potential
Your Best Life Begins Each Morning: Devotions to Start
Every New Day of the Year
Your Best Life Now for Moms
Become a Better You: 7 Keys to Improving Your Life Every Day
Become a Better You Journal: A Guide to Improving Your Life Every Day
Daily Readings from Become a Better You: 90 Devotions
for Improving Your Life Every Day
It's Your Time: Activating Your Faith, Achieving Your Dreams,
and Increasing in God's Favor
It's Your Time Journal: A Guide to Activating Your Faith,
Achieving Your Dreams, and Increasing in God's Favor
Daily Readings from It's Your Time: 90 Devotions for Activating Your Faith,
Achieving Your Dreams, and Increasing in God's Favor

EVERY DAY A
FRIDAY

HOW TO BE HAPPIER 7 DAYS A WEEK

JOEL OSTEEN

New York   Boston   Nashville

David J. Pollay's *The Law of the Garbage Truck* was used with permission by Sterling Publishing Co., Inc. Copyright © 2010 by David J. Pollay.

Scripture quotations noted AMP are from *The Amplified Bible.* Copyright © 1954, 1958, 1962, 1964, 1965, 1987 by The Lockman Foundation. All rights reserved. Used by permission. (www.Lockman.org)
Scripture quotations noted KJV are from the King James Version of the Holy Bible.
Scripture quotations noted NASB are from the New American Standard Bible®. Copyright © 1960, 1962, 1963, 1968, 1971, 1972, 1973, 1975, 1977, 1995 by The Lockman Foundation. Used by permission.
Scripture quotations noted NIV are from The Holy Bible, New International Version® NIV®. Copyright © 1973, 1978, 1984, 2011 by Biblica, Inc.™ Used by permission. All rights reserved worldwide.
Scripture quotations noted NKJV are from the New King James Version. Copyright © 1979, 1980, 1982, Thomas Nelson, Inc., Publishers.
Scripture quotations noted NLT are from the *Holy Bible*, New Living Translation, copyright © 1996, 2004. Used by permission of Tyndale House Publishers, Inc., Wheaton, Illinois 60189. All rights reserved.
Scripture quotations noted The Message are taken from *The Message.* Copyright © 1993, 1994, 1995, 1996, 2000, 2001, 2002. Used by permission of NavPress Publishing Group.

FaithWords
Hachette Book Group
237 Park Avenue
New York, NY 10017

www.faithwords.com

FaithWords is a division of Hachette Book Group, Inc.
The FaithWords name and logo are trademarks of Hachette Book Group, Inc.

The publisher is not responsible for websites (or their content) that are not owned by the publisher.

Printed in the United States of America
First Edition: September 2011

10   9   8

Library of Congress Cataloging-in-Publication Data

Osteen, Joel.
Every day a Friday : how to be happier 7 days a week / Joel Osteen.—1st ed.
p. cm.
ISBN 978-0-89296-991-3 (regular edition)—ISBN 978-1-4555-0731-3 (large print edition)   1. Happiness—Religious aspects—Christianity.   I. Title.
BV4647.J68O88 2011
241'.4—dc23

2011024932

This book is dedicated to Victoria, Jonathan, and Alexandra.
I cherish each of you. Your love, joy, and happiness brighten my
life, and I wake each morning looking forward to another day
spent with you. You truly do make every day a Friday.

CONTENTS

PART V
Laugh Often

PART VI
Be a Dream Releaser

PART VII
Celebrate Yourself

ACKNOWLEDGMENTS

It is fitting that this book is called *Every Day a Friday* because I've learned that every day brings a deadline when you are writing a book. Thanks to many talented and hardworking people, we met all of our deadlines and produced an inspiring and uplifting book that I am very proud to offer.

As always, God guided me through the process with help from my editor Rolf Zettersten at FaithWords/Hachette and Hachette Chairman and CEO David Young, along with leadership team members Chris Murphy, Martha Otis, and Harry Helm.

I am grateful also to my literary agents, Shannon Marven and Jan Miller Rich at Dupree Miller & Associates, who once again proved invaluable throughout the entire process.

Special thanks go to Wes Smith, a true wordsmith, whose speed at the keyboard is matched only by his strong work ethic and good humor.

In this book I offer many stories shared with me by friends, members of our congregation, and people I've met around the world. I appreciate and acknowledge their contributions and support. Some of those mentioned in the book are people I have not met personally and, in a few cases, we've changed the names to protect the privacy of individuals. I give honor to all of those to whom honor is due. As the son of a church leader and a pastor myself, I've listened to countless sermons and presentations, so in some cases I can't remember the exact source of a story. Thanks to all who have touched my life with their own. My intention in writing this book is to pass on the blessings, and to God be the glory.

I offer special thanks also to all the pastors across the country who are members of our Champions Network, especially that group's chairman, Pastor Phil Munsey, and his wife, Jeannie, of Life Church in Irvine, California.

I am indebted to the amazing staff of Lakewood Church, whose service to God's house makes every day a joyous one for me. I am grateful to the loyal members of Lakewood whose stories inspire me, whose lives bless me, and whose loyalty humbles me. I express my sincere appreciation to the thousands of selfless individuals across America and around the globe who generously support our ministry and make it possible to bring hope to a world in need. And I am thankful for the millions of fine people worldwide who watch our services on television, via the Internet, and through the podcasts. I consider each of you to be a valued part of our Lakewood family.

I am blessed to have a supportive family of wise and talented people who help keep our ministry humming along, including my brother Paul and his wife Jennifer, my sister Lisa and her husband Kevin, and my brother-in-law Don and his wife Jackelyn. Inspiring and out-working us all is my mother, Dodie Osteen, who serves as a wonderful example of someone who finds happiness and joy in each and every day.

PART
I

Don't Give Away
Your Power

CHAPTER ONE

Make Every Day a Friday

John was ninety-two years old and blind, but he was just as sharp as could be when his wife, Eleanor, went to the Lord. He didn't feel he should live alone, so John decided to move into a nice seniors' home. On the morning of the move, he was up and fully dressed by 8:00 a.m. As always, the elderly gentleman looked impeccable, with his hair perfectly combed and his face neatly shaven.

A cab picked him up and took him to the seniors' home. John arrived early, as was his habit, and waited more than an hour before a young aide, Miranda, came to show him to his new room. As John maneuvered his walker through the hallways, Miranda described his room in great detail. She said sunlight came in through a big window, and there was a comfortable couch, and a nice desk area.

Right in the middle of her description, John interrupted her and said, "I love it. I love it. I love it."

Miranda laughed and said, "Sir, we're not there yet. You haven't seen it. Hold on just a minute, and I'll show it to you."

John said, "No, you don't have to show it to me. Whether I like my room or not doesn't depend on how the furniture is arranged. It depends on how my *mind* is arranged. Happiness is something you decide ahead of time."

As wise old John understood, happiness is a choice. When you wake up in the morning you can choose what kind of day you want

> *Happiness is a choice.*

to have. You can choose to be in a good mood, or you can choose to be in a bad mood.

Choose Happiness

My purpose in writing this book is to help you arrange your mind so that you choose happiness each and every day. Whatever challenges you may face, whatever circumstances are weighing you down, you can choose your response. How you live your life is totally up to you. It's not dependent on your circumstances. It's dependent on your choices. Abraham Lincoln said, "Most people are as happy as they've decided to be."

Honest Abe would have enjoyed a recent study that found happiness increases 10 percent on Fridays. Why is that? People are excited about the coming weekend, so they decide to be happier. They make up their minds on Fridays to enjoy their lives more.

I challenge you to let every day be a Friday. Give yourself permission to be happy every day. Not just on the weekends. Not just when you have a special event. Not just when you're on vacation.

If you have the right mind-set, you can be just as happy on Monday as you are on Friday. The Scripture doesn't say, "Friday is the day the Lord has made." It says, "*This* is the day the LORD has made" (Psalm 118:24 NKJV; emphasis added).

This means Monday, Tuesday, Wednesday, and every other day of the week. You can be happy even when it's raining, when you have to work late, or when you have to do the dishes.

Why don't you make up your mind to be happy every day? You've heard the saying "TGIF. Thank God it's Friday." For you and me it also should be, "TGIM. Thank God it's Monday."

"TGIW. Thank God it's Wednesday."

"TGIS. Thank God it's Sunday."

Another study said there are more heart attacks on Monday than any other day. So many people just decide that Monday is a stressed-out day. They suffer the Monday morning blues.

When you wake up on Monday morning, don't accept those negative thoughts that come knocking on your door, saying, *It will be a hard day and a long week. Traffic will be bad. I have so much work to do. I just need to make it through the Monday morning blues.* Don't buy into those thoughts.

Instead, say, "Thanks, but no thanks. I've already answered the door and almighty God, the Creator of the universe, has sent me a hand delivery of joy. I know this will be a great day!"

Decide that for you, there are no Monday morning blues. Instead, choose the Monday morning *dos* by saying, "I do have a smile. I do have joy. I do have God's favor. I do have victory."

Yes, I know some days are more difficult than others. But if you program your mind in a positive way, you won't have to drag through certain days just hoping to get to Friday so you can finally enjoy life.

Faith is always in the present. Your attitude should be: *I'm excited to be alive at this moment. I'm excited to be breathing today. I'm excited about my family, my health, and my opportunities. I have plenty of reasons to be happy right now.*

Happiness Is Your Right

According to the authors of the Declaration of Independence, our Creator gave each of us the right to life, liberty, and the pursuit of happiness. Even the British prime minister David Cameron recognized this recently when he proposed polling all residents each year to measure their GWB—General Well-Being.

"Well-being can't be measured by money or traded in markets," he said in an interview. "It's about the beauty of our surroundings, the quality of our culture, and, above all, the strength of our relationships."

A researcher in Australia found that life goals and choices have as much or more impact on happiness than our body chemistry or genetic makeup. Another study found that half of our happiness is determined by factors other than biology. Ten percent is connected to "life circumstances" and the other 40 percent is dependent on our life decisions.

It is your choice to be happy. Make up your mind to enjoy this day, to have a blessed, prosperous, victorious year. You may have some setbacks and your circumstances may change, but don't let that change your mind. Keep it set on happiness.

It's not what happens to you or what you have or don't have that is important; it's how your mind is arranged and the choices you make. When our daughter, Alexandra, was just a little baby and I'd get her out of her crib in the morning, she'd be so excited to hear me coming, she'd start jumping up and down. She'd give me a great big, full-body hug with her arms and legs, then a big kiss.

Why was she so excited? She was just happy for the dawning of a new day. Alexandra was excited to be alive to have another day to enjoy. That's the excitement God has placed inside every one of us. We should never forget how to celebrate each day. But so often as we get older, we let the challenges of life push us down and sadden our spirits.

We have to realize every day is a gift from God. Once this day is gone, we can never retrieve it. If we make the

> We have to realize every day is a gift from God.

mistake of being negative, discouraged, grumpy, or sour, we've wasted the day. Some people squander year after year, being unhappy because somebody is not treating them right, or because they are not getting their way, or because their plans are not working out as quickly as they would like. I've made up my mind to not waste any more days. I'm celebrating each as a gift from God.

Prepare for Victory

We prepare for victory or defeat at the very start of each day. When you get up in the morning, you have to set your mind in the right direction. You may feel discouraged. You may feel the blahs, thinking, *I don't want to go to work today.* Or *I don't want to deal with these children.* Or *I've got so many problems.*

If you make the mistake of dwelling on those thoughts, you are preparing to have a lousy day. You're using your faith in the wrong direction. Turn it around and say, "This will be a great day. Something good will happen to me. God has favor in my future, and I'm expecting new opportunities, divine connections, and supernatural breakthroughs."

When you take that approach, you prepare for victory, increase, and restoration. God says to the angels, "Did you hear that? They're expecting

My goodness. They're expecting to prosper in spite of the economy. They're expecting to get well in spite of the medical report. They're expecting to accomplish their dreams even though they don't have the resources right now."

When you begin each day in faith, anticipating something good, God tells the angels to go to work and to arrange things in your favor. He gives you breaks, lines up the right people, and opens the right doors.

That's what allows God to show up and do amazing things. Sometimes you will see major improvements in your life if you just make that minor adjustment. You would not only have more energy, you would also have a better attitude, and you would be more productive. You would see new doors open. You would meet new friends. You would get some of those breakthroughs you've been praying for if you would just get up in the morning and, instead of preparing for defeat, prepare for victory. Prepare for increase. Prepare for God's favor.

You have to set the tone at the start of each day. If you leave your mind in neutral, the negative thoughts will start to come just by default.

Have you ever been lying in bed in the morning and out of nowhere you're reminded of all the mistakes you made yesterday and all the problems in your future? That's the enemy trying to set your mind for a negative, defeated, lousy day.

Don't fall into that trap. The Scripture says, "Set your minds and keep them set on what is above (the higher things)" (Colossians 3:2 AMP). Be proactive. Take the offensive. When you get up in the morning, say along with David, "This is another day the Lord has made. No matter how I feel, no matter what the economy looks like, no matter what the medical report says, I am choosing to rejoice. I choose to live this day happy."

Do you know what you're really saying when you take that approach? You are proclaiming: "I will not allow anyone to steal my joy today. I will not allow disappointments and setbacks to discourage me. I will not focus on my problems and my mistakes. I've made up my mind to enjoy this day."

I have a friend being treated for cancer. He's a young man, very talented, very athletic. If he had not told me, I would never have known anything was wrong in his life. I've never once heard him complain. He's always friendly, upbeat, and enjoying life.

I asked him the other day how he could keep such a good attitude during such a difficult time. He said, "When I get up in the morning I ask myself, 'Do you want to be depressed today, or do you want to live happy?' and I choose to live happy."

If you want to be happy, you have to be happy on purpose. When you wake up in the morning, you can't just *wait* to see what kind of day you'll have. You have to *decide* what kind of day you'll have. The Scripture says in Psalm 30:5 that joy comes in the morning. When you wake up each morning, God sends you a special delivery of joy. When you get up in faith and make the declaration "This will be a good day," you answer that knock at the door. You receive the gift of joy God sent to you!

The problem is, some people never answer the door. The knocking has not been answered for months and months, years and years: "Come on! Let me in! You can be happy! You can cheer up! You can enjoy your life!" I don't know about you, but I've made up my mind to answer the door. I'm waking up every morning and saying, "Father, thank You for another beautiful day. I will be happy. I will enjoy this day. I will brighten somebody else's life. I am choosing to receive Your gift of joy."

You Have What You Need to Be Happy

I've found that most of the time we have what we need to be happy. We just don't have the right perspective. For instance, you may not be happy with the job you have right now. But if you lost that job and went months without any income, you probably would be very happy to win it back.

> *We have what we need to be happy. We just don't have the right perspective.*

You see? You had what you needed to be happy. You just didn't realize it. I know people who are perfectly healthy, but they're never really happy. There's always something bothering them. They want a bigger house or a better job. But if they were to lose their health and then regain it, I'm sure they would be thrilled. They have what they need to be happy.

I hear women complain and complain about their husbands and men complain and complain about their wives: "[He or she] is just too much of this" or "not enough of that." But if their spouses were suddenly gone and they were lonely month after month; if they didn't have anybody to talk to; if they had nobody to eat dinner with, they might be happy just to get back their "old goats," I mean, their *husbands* or *wives*.

Keep your life in the right perspective. Every one of us has something even right now to be happy about: our health, our jobs, our families, or an opportunity.

I know this couple who were constantly complaining about their house. It was too small and too far out in the country. It was a source of frustration year after year. But when the economy went down, unfortunately, their income went down as well, and they came very close to losing that house. Just before the bank foreclosed on it, they were able to refinance so they could keep their home.

Do you know they now think that house is the greatest thing in the world? They show it off like it's brand-new. What happened? They changed their perspective.

I hear people say, "Well, I've got to go to work today."

No, the right attitude is to say, "I *get* to go to work today. I have a job. I have an opportunity. That's reason enough for me to have a smile on my face."

"Well, I've got to clean this house. It's so much work."

No, "I *get* to clean this house. I'm strong. I'm healthy. On top of that, I have a house. I'm not living under a bridge somewhere."

"I've got to take care of these children. All I do is cook and clean and do the laundry."

No, "I *get* to take care of these children. They're a gift from God. They're a special treasure."

I've found there are very few things in life that we have to do. "I've got to pay my taxes." No, really, you *get* to pay your taxes. The fact that you have taxes due means that you've made money. That tells me God blessed you with opportunity.

"Well, I've got to go to the grocery store today."

No, that means you're healthy enough to eat. "I *get* to go to the grocery store."

"Well, I've got to drive in traffic."

No, that means God has blessed you with a car. "I *get* to drive in traffic."

"Well, I've got to buy my wife a Valentine's Day gift."

No, that means God has blessed you with a wife. You don't have to buy her a gift. You *get* to buy her a gift. And if you don't, you will be unhappy, because if Mama is not happy, nobody is happy!

Happiness Is Based on Your Perspective

I read about these two men who'd been bricklayers for more than thirty years. They were working on a huge skyscraper downtown. One man was always negative, discouraged, constantly complaining, and dreaded going to work. The other man was just the opposite. He was excited to show up each day and had an attitude of faith and enthusiasm about life.

One day a friend came by the jobsite and asked them separately what they were doing. The first said, "Aw, we're just laying brick. We've been doing this for thirty years. It's so boring. One brick on top of the other."

Then the friend asked the second bricklayer. He just lit up. "Why, we're building a magnificent skyscraper," he said. "This structure will stand tall for generations to come. I'm just so excited that I could be a part of it."

Each bricklayer's happiness or lack of it was based on his perspective. You can be laying brick or you can be building a beautiful skyscraper. The choice is up to you. You can go to work each day and just punch in on the clock and dread being there and do as little as possible. Or you can show up with enthusiasm and give it your best, knowing that you're making the world a better place.

I've found we create much of our own unhappiness. We see what's wrong rather than what's right. We look at what we don't have rather than what we do have. We don't celebrate each day and appreciate the gift that God has given us.

Years ago, a man traveling by train met a very successful couple. The lady was wearing expensive clothing and jewelry. This couple was obviously well-to-do. The traveler shared their first-class cabin, which was very comfortable. But from the start the lady did nothing but complain. She complained that the temperature wasn't right, complained that there wasn't enough light, complained that the food wasn't good, and complained that her seat was dirty. She made everyone miserable.

During the journey, the traveler struck up a conversation with her husband. He asked what kind of business he was in. He said he had been in the car industry and God had blessed him in a great way. But he added; "Now my wife, she's in the manufacturing business."

The traveler thought, *That's kind of odd. I mean, she's so dignified and dressed so properly. That just doesn't seem like it fits.*

He asked very curiously, "What does she manufacture?"

"She manufactures unhappiness," the husband said. "She's unhappy everywhere she goes."

You may need to change businesses, not physically but mentally. Get out of the business of manufacturing unhappiness. Quit dwelling on what's wrong. Quit seeing the faults and start seeing the good. Start being grateful for what you have. Appreciate the gift of today.

Keep a Song in Your Heart

As I walked out of the house early one recent morning, I heard all these birds singing and singing so loud and so cheerful. Little birds were chirping and chirping. Big birds were making a melody. It was like they were having a big party. I wanted to say to them, "Hey, birds. Have you read the newspapers lately? Did you see the stock market last year? You're not supposed to be singing, enjoying life. What's wrong with you? You're acting like everything will be all right."

What was it with those birds? They know a secret. They know their heavenly Father is in control. They know God has promised to take care of them, so they go through the day singing and enjoying life, regardless of the circumstances.

That's how to start off each day. Get up in the morning and have a song of praise in your heart. Put a smile on your face. Go out into the day and be determined to enjoy it. The apostle Paul wrote: "Be happy [in your faith] and

> *Get up in the morning and have a song of praise in your heart.*

rejoice and be glad-hearted continually (always)" (1 Thessalonians 5:16 AMP).

How long are we supposed to be glad-hearted? How long are we supposed to have a smile on our faces? As long as people treat us right? As long as we feel okay? As long as the economy is up? No, the Scripture says, "Be glad-hearted *continually (always)*." That means in the good times and in the tough times, when it's sunny and when it's raining.

When dark clouds are over your head and you feel like life is depressing and gloomy, always remember that right above those dark clouds the sun is shining. You may not be able to see the sun in your life right now, but that doesn't mean it's not up there. It's just blocked by the dark clouds. The good news is, the clouds are temporary. The clouds will not last forever. The sun will shine in your life once again.

In the meantime, keep your joy. Be glad-hearted continually. Don't let a few clouds darken your life. The rain falls on the just and the unjust. That means we all face disappointments, unfair situations, tests, trials, and temptation. But know this: Right past the test is promotion. On the other side of every difficulty is increase. If you go through adversity with a smile on your face and a song in your heart, on the other side there will be a reward.

But so often in the tough times we become discouraged. "I'm down today because business is slow." "I'm upset because I got a bad medical report." Or, "I'm worried about this legal situation."

Human nature tends to turn negative in difficult times. But the Scripture tells us to do just the opposite: "Count it all joy when you fall into various trials" (James 1:2 NKJV). That doesn't seem to make sense to some people. "You mean we're supposed to be joyful and glad-hearted in the middle of tough times?" they ask. Yes, that's right, because when you lose your joy, you lose your strength.

You need your strength more than ever in the difficult times, and your strength is dependent on your joy. When you're facing a financial crisis, dealing with an illness, going through a breakup in a relationship, or raising a rebellious child, you need your strength. If you go through those challenges feeling negative, bitter, and discouraged, you will not have the vitality to stand strong and fight the good fight of faith.

You can keep your joy by knowing that on the other side of each test is promotion. On the other side of every setback is opportunity. On the other side of every offense is growth. The difficulties you face are not there to defeat you. They are there to increase you.

Just keep reminding yourself, *Even though this is hard, even though I don't understand it, even though it's not fair, I'll keep a good attitude and stay full of joy, knowing that this is not setting me back. It is setting me up for God to bring me through to the other side of this in an even better position.*

The Key to Handling Adversity

If you complain, you will remain. You'll stay right there. If you become negative and soured on life, you won't pass the test. There was promotion available. There was opportunity for new growth, but because you didn't count it all joy, you missed out. The good news is this: God will give you another opportunity. He can still take you where you need to be. For instance, when someone offends you, your attitude should be, *I won't be upset. I'll count it all joy. I know this is simply a test, and on the other side of this challenge I'll be promoted.*

When business is slow, instead of griping, count it all joy. Tell yourself, *This, too, shall pass. I know God is supplying all of my needs.* Or when you face a disappointment, your negative emotions will tell you to be down and discouraged. You'll feel self-pity trying to set in. But instead of submitting to those negative emotions, encourage yourself: *Get up. Be strong. There are good days up ahead.*

That's how you pass the test. That's how you count it all joy.

In the tough times, don't be surprised if you feel that spirit of heaviness trying to overtake you. Don't be surprised if you hear those thoughts telling you, *It will never work out. You'll never get well. It's over. It's done.* Don't believe those lies. You don't have to be guided by your emotions. They're not in charge. You're in charge. Instead of letting your negative emotions talk to you, talk to yourself.

When you wake up in the morning and that negative thought comes to your mind saying, *It's a lousy day*, don't just agree and say, "Yeah. It's a lousy day, I feel terrible." Instead, turn it around and talk to yourself.

Make a declaration of faith out loud: "This will be a great day. I will get well. God will restore health to me."

Put Your Hope Back in the Lord

This is what King David did. He put his hope in the Lord. That spirit of heaviness tried to steal his destiny. He became depressed and very discouraged during those dark times. But David said, "Why are you cast down, O my soul?... Hope in God" (Psalm 43:5 NKJV).

He was asking himself, *David, what's wrong with you? Why are you discouraged? Why have you lost your joy? God is still on the throne. God still has good things in store. Put your hope back in the Lord.*

When that heaviness tries to come on you, do the same thing. Look in the mirror and say, "Listen here, self. Cheer up. Put on a new attitude. We're not staying down. We're not staying defeated. We're putting our hope in the Lord."

There is so much doom and gloom in our world, so many negative news reports. If you are not careful, you'll find it sinking in. The spirit of heaviness will overcome you, stealing your enthusiasm and draining your joy.

"Oh, but it's just so bad," you might say.

The Scripture tells us what to do when this happens: Put on "the garment of praise for the spirit of heaviness" (Isaiah 61:3 NKJV). When you feel that heaviness is trying to overtake you by telling you, "There's nothing good in your future. You've seen your best days," the first thing to do is take off the old coat of heaviness. Throw away the coat of self-pity. Get rid of the coat of discouragement and put on a new coat of praise.

Thank God for what He's already done in your life. Thank Him for the victories in your past. Thank Him for how far He's already brought you. And then take it one step further. Thank Him in advance for the victories He has planned ahead for you. Thank Him for the new doors He's opening. Thank Him for the situations He's turning around. Thank Him for the favor He has in your future.

You cannot give God thanks and stay down and discouraged.

If you do that, you will feel a new joy rising up on the inside. You will feel your faith increase. You won't have that victim mentality; you will have a victor mentality. One thing I've learned is you cannot praise and stay defeated at the same time. You cannot give God thanks and stay down and discouraged.

Put on the Garment of Praise

When you put on the garment of praise, that spirit of heaviness has to go. Sometimes you won't feel like doing it. You won't feel like having a good attitude. You won't feel like being grateful. That's why God says to offer up the sacrifice of praise. God knew it would not always be easy. You will have to dig your heels in and say, "God, I don't feel like doing this. It doesn't look like it will ever work out. I'm tired, lonely, discouraged. But God, I know You're still on the throne. I know You are good and You are good all the time, so I choose to give You praise. I choose to give You thanks anyway."

When you offer up that sacrifice of praise, supernatural things begin to happen. Scripture tells us the story of the apostle Paul and his companion Silas. They were imprisoned for sharing their faith. They had been unjustly beaten earlier in the day. What were they doing at midnight in their jail cell? Complaining? Having a pity party? Saying, "God, it's not fair. Where were You today?"

No, they were singing praises and giving thanks to God. They were saying, in effect, "God, we know You're bigger than our problems. We know You're still in control. You are well able to get us out of here." Sure enough, at midnight there was a great earthquake. The prison doors flew open. The chains fell off, and Paul and Silas walked out as free men.

What started it? Their offering up the sacrifice of praise.

Really, anyone can have a good attitude when everything is going well. We can all celebrate and be grateful when we're on the mountaintop, but where are the people who give God praise even as the bottom falls out? Where are the people who rise up each morning and prepare for victory and increase in spite of all the news reports predicting doom and gloom? Where are the people who say, "God, I still praise You even though the medical report wasn't good" or "God, I still thank You even though it didn't turn out my way"?

I believe you are one of those people. I believe you are of great faith. Your roots go down deep. You could be complaining. You could be discouraged. You could have a chip on your shoulder, but instead you just keep giving God praise. You've got that smile on your face. You're doing the right thing even though the wrong thing is happening.

That's why I can tell you with confidence that you are coming into greater victories. Enlarge your vision. Take the limits off God. You have not seen your best days. God has victories in your future that will amaze you. He will show up and show out in unusual ways. You may be in a tough time right now, but remember this: The enemy always fights you the hardest when he knows God has something great in store for you.

You are closest to your victory when it is the darkest. That is the enemy's final stand. Don't be discouraged. Don't start complaining. Just keep offering up that sacrifice of praise.

The Voice of Gladness

The Old Testament prophet Jeremiah wrote, "[There shall be heard again] the voice of joy and the voice of gladness, . . . the voices of those who sing as they bring sacrifices of thanksgiving into the house of the Lord. . . . [God] will cause the captivity of the land to be reversed and return to be as it was at first" (Jeremiah 33:11 AMP). I particularly love two words in that verse; *reversed* and *return*. God is saying when you stay full of joy, when you learn to offer up the sacrifice of praise, God will turn things in your favor. He will reverse negative situations. He will return, or restore, what's been stolen.

But notice that restoration doesn't come from complaining, being negative, or being sour. Restoration takes place when you have the voice of gladness, the voice of joy. That means you get up in the morning with a song in your heart. You go out each day with a smile on your face. Things may not always go your way, but you don't become discouraged. You shake it off and count it all joy.

When you live that way, you might as well get ready. God will be reversing and restoring. He will reverse finances that have been down. He will reverse a struggling business. He will reverse a legal situation in your favor. He will reverse a health issue to heal you.

Not only that, God will restore what should have been yours. He will restore the years you lost because somebody did you wrong. He will restore a relationship that's on the rocks. Restoration will occur because you have the voice of joy, the voice of gladness, and you keep offering up that sacrifice of praise.

Learn to count it all joy. Don't be determined to never have problems. Be determined to stay full of joy in the midst of your problems. Arrange your mind in the right direction.

And no matter what comes your way, don't lose your joy. Learn to offer up that sacrifice of praise. If you keep the voice of gladness, the voice of joy, you cannot stay down and defeated. God has promised He will reverse and restore. Not only that, but because you have joy, you will find the strength to outlast every attack, to overcome every obstacle, to defeat every enemy. You will become everything God created you to be, and you will have everything God intended for you to have.

CHAPTER TWO

Don't Give Away Your Power

Every day we have plenty of opportunities to be upset, to be frustrated, and to be offended. Maybe the day's plans didn't work out, or somebody was rude at the office, or a job that should have taken one hour took three. Life is full of inconveniences. There will always be interruptions and difficult people. We can't control all our circumstances, but we can control our reactions.

> We can't control all our circumstances, but we can control our reactions.

I've heard it said that life is 10 percent what happens to you and 90 percent how you respond. Go into each day positive, hopeful, and expecting God's favor. But at the same time be realistic, knowing that most days will not go exactly as you planned. If you become stressed because you are off schedule, frustrated because someone offended you, or upset because your child wouldn't eat breakfast, you are giving away your power.

It's good to have plans, but at the first part of every day submit those plans to God and just say, "God, this is what I would like to accomplish today. But I know You're in control, so I submit my plans to You. And I've decided in advance that no matter what comes my way, I will stay in peace, knowing You are directing my steps and that all things will work together for my good."

But too many people these days have the wrong approach to life. They think they can't be happy unless they control all their circumstances and everything goes their way. But that's not realistic. You have to come to the place where you can say, "I don't have to have my way to have a good day. My plans don't have to work out for me to be happy. Everybody doesn't have to treat me right for life to be enjoyable. I have already made up my mind: No matter what does or doesn't happen, I will stay in peace and enjoy this day."

The Scripture says that "no one will take away your joy" (John 16:22 NIV). No circumstance can take your peace. No interruption can take your enthusiasm. You have to give it away. The next time you're tempted to be upset and frustrated, ask yourself, *Is this worth giving my power away?*

Or, *This man is rude to me on the phone. I don't even know him. Is it worth giving him my joy?*

Or, *This co-worker left me out of a meeting; is it worth giving away my peace?*

You may not have the victory, not because you can't, but because you keep giving it away. Life is too short to be upset and offended. If you allow your circumstances to control your joy, there will always be some reason to be discouraged.

"It's the economy."

"It's the stock market. That's why I'm so down."

Quit giving away your power. God is still on the throne. The economy in heaven is doing just fine. As long as you're connected to Him, everything will be all right.

"Well," you say, "I had to cancel my vacation this year."

Or, "My boss sure is hard to get along with."

"This neighbor, he really gets on my nerves. I've been praying and asking God to change him."

One thing I've learned is to never pray for God to change somebody else without first saying, "God, change me."

Even if that offensive neighbor were to move away, if you don't learn this principle—to never allow others to steal your joy—two more just like him will move back in.

You Have to Be the Change You Seek

Jesus put it this way: "Stop allowing yourselves to be agitated and disturbed" (John 14:27 AMP).

Notice it's a choice we have to make. He didn't say, "I will make sure your circumstances are perfect. That way you can be happy."

He said, in effect, "The things upsetting you right now don't have to upset you. The people aggravating you, even if they don't change, they don't have to aggravate you." If you'll make adjustments and change your approach to life, you can be happy in spite of those circumstances.

I'm asking you today to stop allowing negative people and disappointments and inconveniences to steal your joy. You have to put your foot down and say, "This child gets on my nerves—I love him—but I will rise above it. I won't let this control me." Or, "This grumpy boss jumps down my throat for no reason, but I'm not letting him ruin any more of my days." That's what it means to not give away your power. You have to be determined to enjoy your life.

A woman once told me about her husband's very obnoxious relative who repeatedly made cutting and demeaning remarks to her. Every time they were at family get-togethers, invariably, this man would say something that offended her. She would become upset and it would ruin the whole trip. She reached a point where she didn't want to even go to her husband's family events. Finally, she told her husband, "You've got to do something about that man. He's your relative."

She was expecting the husband to say, "You're right, honey. He shouldn't talk to you like that. I'll go in there and set him straight." But the husband did just the opposite. He said, "Honey, I love you, but I cannot control him. He has every right to his opinion. He can say what he wants to, but you have every right to not be offended."

At first she couldn't understand why her husband wouldn't really stick up for her. Time and time again she would feel upset. If her husband's relative was in one room, she would go to another room. If the man was outside, she would make sure she stayed inside. Her whole focus was avoiding this man. Eventually, she grew weary of allowing him to have such an impact on her life. One day it was like a light turned on. She realized that no one took this man seriously and that she was giving away her power. She was allowing one person who had issues of his own to keep her from becoming the woman she was meant to be.

When you allow what someone says or does to upset you, you're allowing that person to control you. When you say, "You make me so mad," what you're really doing is admitting that you're giving away your power. As long as the person knows they can push this button and you'll respond this way, and they can

> *When you allow what someone says or does to upset you, you're allowing that person to control you.*

make that remark and you'll get upset, and they know if they go outside you'll go inside—as long as you keep responding the same way—you are giving them exactly what they want.

People have a right to say what they want, to do what they want, as long as it's legal. And we have a right to not be offended. We have a right to overlook it. But when we become upset and angry, we change. If somebody walks into a room and we grow tense, it's because we're putting too much importance on what that person thinks about us.

What a person says about you does not define who you are. His or her opinion of you does not determine your self-worth. Let that bounce off you like water off a duck's back. This person has every right to have an opinion, and you have every right to ignore it.

I've found that some people feel it's their calling in life to point out what others are doing wrong and where others are missing it. They're constantly critical, always finding fault. There is nothing they love more than keeping someone upset, and arguing, and always on the defensive.

Rise above that. You don't need them to agree with you. You don't have to win their approval. Let that go, and just be who God made you to be.

Even the great leader Moses had to deal with relatives who didn't like the woman he'd chosen to marry because she was of a different nationality. They criticized Moses publicly, saying, "We don't agree with this. We refuse to approve of this marriage."

But deep down, Moses knew he was making the right decision. He didn't argue with them. He didn't become upset. He didn't criticize them. He just kept his peace. As it turned out, the person who was the most vocal critic of the bride contracted leprosy and was soon no longer around.

You don't have to respond to every critic. You don't have to prove yourself to them. Just stay on the high road and let God fight your battles for you. Some who will cross your path simply don't want peace with you. No matter what you say or do, they will not be won over. Even if you were to change, they would still find some reason to be critical. You have to accept the fact that no matter what you do, some people will never be at peace with you.

I had a real nice sports car when I first dated my wife, Victoria. I was in my early twenties and wanted to impress her, so I kept that car spotless. There wasn't a scratch on it. Then I was driving home from Victoria's house late one night and I had an accident. I was proceeding through an intersection. The light was green. Another car going the same direction turned right from the wrong lane and hit the back of my sports car, spinning it around.

After taking a few moments to calm down, I stepped out of my car. I knew the accident wasn't my fault. And I'm naturally easygoing. There is not much that upsets me. I checked my spotless car. The back end was totally destroyed.

About that time the other driver climbed out of his car. It was very dark, but I could see he was probably in his fifties. He started ranting, raving, and cursing, and then he said, "Kid, learn how to drive. I am so mad at you."

I thought to myself, *I'm the one who should be upset. He just turned from the wrong lane.* He was about thirty yards away. I could see he was working up his anger. Then he started running toward me like he wanted to fight.

My first thought was, *Do you want some of this?*

You know that's not true. My real first thought was, *How big is he?*

When he came within fifteen yards, I saw he was twice my size. Right then and there I had a revelation: This was not a battle worth fighting.

I went around to the other side of my car.

You say, "Joel, you mean you were a chicken?"

No, I just wanted to live!

He fit into that category of people who will never be at peace with me.

When Jesus sent His disciples out into certain homes, He told them to speak peace over each person in each house. And He said, in effect, "If they don't receive it, then the peace you're offering them will come back to you" (see Luke 10:5–6).

That tells me if you do your best to be at peace with people—even if they won't take your peace—the good news is that peace will just come back to you anyway. You'll not only enjoy your peace, but you'll be given their share as well. When you do the right thing when the wrong thing is happening, God sees it and He rewards it.

Two friends walked into a corner store to buy a newspaper and the store clerk treated them rudely. One of the friends, after paying, smiled at the clerk with a grin and said: "I hope you have a great day today."

As they were leaving his friend said, "Is that clerk always that rude?"

"Every single day," the other said.

"Well, are you always that nice?"

"Every single day."

This puzzled his friend so he asked why.

"I've made up my mind that I'm not allowing one person to ruin my day," was the answer.

He had decided not to give control of his mood or attitude to anyone else. That store clerk had every right to be rude and obnoxious, but everyone he mistreated also had the right to go right on being happy, kind, and friendly.

Strength Under Control

When you encounter people who are poisoned inside, don't let it rub off on you. If you sink down to their level and you're cold and rude back to them, you've allowed them to contaminate you. Rise above that. Be a part of the solution, not the problem. You overcome evil with good. If somebody is rude to you, just bless them, smile, and keep moving forward.

Jesus put it this way: "Blessed are the meek, for they will inherit the earth" (Matthew 5:5 NIV). When we hear the word *meek*, many times we think of someone who is weak, shy, and reserved; just a fearful little person. The image is that meek people can't stand up for themselves and everyone runs over them. That's not meek at all. Meekness is not weakness. It's strength under control.

Meekness is like a wild stallion that has been tamed. The horse is still strong, still powerful, and has just as much speed as before he was tamed. The only difference is, now that strength is under control. You can walk up to the horse, pet him, lead him around, probably get on him and ride him. But don't be fooled. He has the same power, the same tenacity; he's just learned how to control it.

When you're a meek person, you don't go around trying to straighten everybody out. You don't respond to every critic. People may be talking about you, but you don't let it bother you.

Keep your strength under control. It's not how proud you are, or how many people you straighten out, or how you can prove yourself. If you argue with a critic and try to prove yourself, all you're doing is sinking to his or her level. Don't fall into that trap. You are an eagle. You can rise above it.

You may have the power to straighten out your critic. You may feel like giving them a piece of your mind. Your emotions may tell you, *Get in there. Pay them back. Get even.* Instead, listen to what the apostle Paul told his protégé Timothy: "Be calm and cool and steady" (2 Timothy 4:5 AMP). He was saying, in other words, "Don't give away your power. Keep your strength under control."

A guy was eating a burger in a little country diner when a motorcycle gang came in. These bikers were big and tough and mean. Just to show who was in charge, one of them came to the guy's table, knocked his hamburger onto the floor, picked up his water, and poured it on top of the guy's head.

"Oh, I'm sorry. It was an accident," the biker said sarcastically.

He was trying to pick a fight. The guy sat calmly, took out his napkin, wiped off the water, stood up, and walked out of the restaurant. The biker shook his head and said to the waiter, "Not much of a man, is he?"

The waiter said, "No, and not much of a driver either. He just ran over twelve choppers with his car."

That's strength under control.

If you are easily upset, don't continue year after year that way. If you allow little things like long lines, the weather, a grumpy salesman, or an inconsiderate receptionist to steal your joy, draw a line in the sand. Say, "You know what? That's it. I'm not giving away my power anymore. I'm staying calm, cool, and collected."

David J. Pollay, author of *The Law of the Garbage Truck*, was in a New York City taxicab when a car jumped out from a parking place right in front of it. His cabbie had to slam on the brakes, the car skidded, and the tires squealed, but the taxi stopped an inch from the other car. The driver of the other car whipped his head around, and honked and screamed in anger. But David was surprised when his cabbie just smiled real big, and waved at him.

David said, "That man almost totaled your cab and sent us to the hospital. I can't believe you didn't yell back at him. How were you able to keep your cool?"

The cab driver's response, which David calls "The Law of the Garbage Truck," was this: "Many people are like garbage trucks. They run around full of garbage, full of frustration, full of anger, and full of disappointment. As their garbage piles up, they look for a place to dump it. And if you let them, they'll dump it on you. So when someone wants to dump on you, don't take it personally. It doesn't have anything to do with you. Just smile, wave, wish them well, and move on. Believe me, you'll be happier."

Successful people don't allow garbage trucks to unload on them. If somebody dumps a load on you, don't be upset. Don't be angry. Don't be offended. If you make that mistake, you'll end up carrying their loads around and eventually you'll dump them on somebody else.

Keep your lid on. Sometimes you may need to have a steel lid. These days, though, so many people are dumping out poison through criticism, bad news, and anger, you'll need to keep | *Keep your lid on.* | that lid on tight. We can't stop people from dumping their garbage, but by keeping our lids on, we can tell them to recycle instead!

Right after the 9/11 terrorist attacks, I was invited to a local television station to be interviewed on a news program. I had to be there early Monday morning around six thirty. I was already tired after our Sunday services and weekend events. The day was cold, and raining, and still dark. I didn't really feel like being on television, but I had made the commitment, so I was on my way. They had told me beforehand to park right up front in this special lot reserved for the people on the program. And so when I arrived, I pulled in there. But when I parked my car, a woman security guard rushed at me like I had just committed a major crime. She was not friendly at all. In fact, she was downright rude.

"Sir, what do you think you are doing?" she said. "You cannot park here. This is reserved for our special guests."

I wanted to say, "Lady, you can't get any more special than me."

I had to bite my tongue.

"Well, ma'am, I am on the program today and they told me I could park here," I explained.

"Oh, they don't know what they're talking about," she said. "I run this lot. You have to park outside the gate."

I returned to my car. I couldn't find anywhere to park. I had to go into a little neighborhood far away, and it was still raining. I didn't have an umbrella. And as I ran to the station, with every step I thought, *This is not right. I need to tell somebody about that parking lot lady. I should get her straightened out.*

I was about to give away my power, but I walked into the building and forgot all about it.

A couple of hours later, after the show, I walked out and the sun was shining. Do you know the same security guard came up and she was like a different person?

"Oh, Pastor Osteen," she said. "If I had known that was you, I would have let you park there."

I was so glad I bit my tongue. She went on to say, "Do you think you would have time to pray for me?"

I wanted to say, "I would if I didn't have to walk so far."

Make up your mind that you will not accept other people's garbage. They may dump it, but you don't have to receive it. Keep your lid on.

Emotions Are Controlled by Circumstances or Character

A small pot boils the quickest. You can tell how big a person is by what it takes to get him upset. Your emotions will be controlled by either your circumstances or your character. If someone is rude to you, your emotions will tell you, *Pay them back. Get even.*

That doesn't take any discipline. When your strength is under control, when you've developed your character, you realize, *I'm bigger than this. I will not let them pull me down. I have places to go, goals to accomplish, dreams to realize.*

I think it's interesting that the apostle Paul never prayed for people to be delivered from their problems. He prayed that God would give them the strength to go through challenges with a good attitude. At times we think, *God, if You would just change these people who are aggravating me; God, if You'd just make my child straighten up.* Or, *God, if You'd just move my boss to another planet.* Or, *God, if You'd deliver me from these people, I could be happy.*

But the truth is, those people may never change. I hope they do, but even if they don't change, *you* can. If you make an adjustment, they won't upset you anymore.

You have the power right now to live a joy-filled, faith-filled, peace-filled life. But you must say, "God, even if it never changes, it will not steal my joy. I know You hold me in the palm of Your hand. I know You have my best interests at heart, so God, I'm totally trusting You."

The enemy can use against you anything you feel you "have to have" to be happy. If you think you *have* to be married to be happy, the enemy can use that against you. If you think your boss *has* to change before you can enjoy your work, you'll go year after year dreading it, thinking that's why you can't be happy.

It's good to have hopes and dreams. It's good to wake up each day believing and expecting. But don't wait for those things to come before you enjoy your life and find happiness. This is the day the Lord has made, not tomorrow, not when all your dreams come to pass, not when all the negative people are changed, but *today.*

Understand, God has you exactly where He wants you. If you'll learn to be happy where you are, God will take you where you want to be. He's promised He will give you the desires of your heart. If there is something you really want, I would encourage you to put it on the altar. Just say, "God, I would really love to have this. God, You know the desire You put in me. I would love to be married. I'd love to see my spouse change. I would love to be promoted. But God, I'm not waiting on that to be happy. I'm happy right where You have me."

That's the kind of attitude God is looking for.

Change for the Good

I know a man who struggled in his marriage for years. He and his wife did not see eye-to-eye on many issues, and she would not come to church with him. For the longest time this left him feeling down and discouraged. Then, I saw him awhile back and asked how everything was going. He seemed to be very upbeat. He said, "Everything is great. I'm really enjoying my life."

I thought for sure that he and his wife were getting along better and they had resolved all those issues. But he said, "No, my wife is just the same. We still don't see eye-to-eye. She still won't come to church with me."

Then he said something very interesting.

"She hasn't changed, but I've changed. I don't let our differences upset me anymore. I don't let them steal my joy."

Find out what is stealing your joy. Take inventory of your life. What are you allowing to upset you? What's causing you to stress out all day? Identify what it is, and then make a decision to change your approach in that area. After all, being upset will not make the situation any better. If someone is rude to you, being rude in return will only sour your day. If your plans don't work out, stay in peace. Instead of being upset, know that God is still directing your steps. He's still got you exactly where He wants you.

I was driving in a crowded parking lot and finally saw a space, but another driver got in there before I could, even though it was obvious I was waiting. I made this decision: "I'll give him the parking spot, but I will not give him my joy."

> *It's liberating when you understand you don't have to give away your joy.*

It's liberating when you understand you don't have to give away your joy. Sometimes we blame other people or other things for problems that we've created for ourselves. We don't realize that our refusal to change is causing the same problem again and again. I heard about this man who had not been feeling well. He went to see his doctor. The doctor said, "What's wrong?"

He said, "Well, Doctor, lately I've been dizzy and I'm seeing white spots."

The doctor examined him and put him through some tests. Several days later, he called the ailing man back and said, "Sir, I hate to tell you this, but you've got a rare disease and we think you only have about six months to live."

The man quit his job and set off to travel the world and do all the things he'd always hoped to do. He spent more time with his family, and he bought a new sports car. One day he was driving by this famous clothing shop and decided to go in and buy a tailor-made suit.

The tailor came in and measured his arm length: "Thirty-three inches." Then he measured his waist: "Thirty-two." Next was his pant length: "Thirty-four." And finally the tailor measured his neck and said, "I'm making you a size sixteen-and-a-half shirt."

The man said, "No, I wear a fifteen-inch shirt."

The tailor measured his neck again very carefully.

"No, sir," he said. "Look, you wear a sixteen-and-a-half-inch shirt."

The man was very adamant. "No, sir. I wear a fifteen-inch shirt," he told the tailor. "I've worn that size my whole adult life. I want you to make me a fifteen-inch shirt."

The tailor said, "Well, fine. I'll make you a fifteen-inch shirt, but it will be so tight it will make you dizzy and you'll see white spots."

Often, people become set in their ways and refuse to change even when they are hurting. If you are willing to change, if you will make adjustments, many times you will see your "white spots" disappear. You will see your frustrations go away.

Recognize the real source of the problem. If it's you, make a change. If it's someone else, don't let him or her steal your joy. Don't give away your power. Keep your lid on. When somebody tries to dump their garbage on you, just smile, wave at them, and move on. If you'll learn this principle to not give away your power and focus on developing your character, you will enjoy life much more.

CHAPTER THREE

Express Your Joy

I went for barbecue one day and the drive-thru lady was very grumpy. She jumped down my throat before the first part of my order was out of my mouth.

"Hold on! I'm not ready," she barked.

Then I made the mistake of asking her what the side dishes were. You might have thought I'd asked for her favorite child.

She screamed the complete list of sides at me.

I had to keep reminding myself to stay calm: *You're the pastor of a church. Keep your joy. Don't let her affect you. Infect her instead.*

You have to talk yourself down in the heat of battle. Giving her a piece of my mind would have been easy. I'd just repent later. Instead, I remembered that dealing with challenging people helps build character.

I placed my order as nicely as could be at the drive-thru speaker. I said "Please" and "Thank you" and tossed in a "Have a good day!" at no extra charge.

Then when I drove up to her window, I put on the most fake smile you've ever seen.

"Good to see you," I said, as chipper as I could muster.

I was really thinking, *You need counseling!*

Grumpy turned from the register, looked at me, and did a double take.

"Pastor Joel, I watch you all the time!"

I wanted to say, "Do you ever listen?"

Then, instead of my barbecue, she handed me one of my books. (I'm positive she hadn't read it yet!)

"Would you sign this for me?" she asked, a little nicer but not much.

I opened it and thought about underlining all the lessons on joy.

Instead, I signed it, "Keep smiling that beautiful smile, Joel Osteen."

The Oil of Joy

Hebrews 1:9 says, "God has anointed You with the oil of gladness more than Your companions" (NKJV).

You and I are supposed to be happier than the average person. God has anointed us with the oil of joy. You can't let anyone's bad attitude ruin your good one. Instead, infect them with a smile and a kind word. God knew you would have to deal with negative people. That's why He said, "I've given you an advantage; I've anointed you with the oil of joy so you can be happier than those around you."

Tap into that joy and don't hide it. It should be seen.

Studies have proven that a smile on your face is good for you and everyone around you. In one test, people were asked to show facial expressions for fear and anger. Their bodies responded just as if they were really feeling those emotions, triggering increased heart rate, raising their skin temperature, and making them sweat. Those same people were then asked to smile, and their heart rates settled down, their temperatures dropped, and they didn't sweat so much. They said they felt happy.

Our Creator knows all this, of course. God refers specifically to our "countenances" more than fifty times in the Scripture. You see the word *rejoice* again and again. To rejoice doesn't just mean to sing. It also means to brighten up, to put a smile on your face, to be cheerful. When you go through the day with a smile, you are rejoicing. By having a cheerful countenance, being friendly and fun to be around, you are giving praise to God.

Too many people drag through the day with long faces. Some don't smile for months. Then they'll come up with those same sour faces after a service and say to me, "I've got the joy of the Lord."

I'll think: *You should notify your face!*

The Bible says to be sober-minded, not sober-faced. You receive back what you project. If you're sour, grumpy, and unfriendly, then others will be sour, grumpy, and unfriendly back to you. Misery loves company.

> *The Bible says to be sober-minded, not sober-faced.*

If you look miserable, you will attract defeat, negativity, gloom, doom, and discouragement.

But when you smile and project an aura of warmth, kindness, and friendliness, you will attract warmth, kindness, and friendliness. Happy people will be drawn to you.

If you're not receiving what you like, check what you're sending out. No happy person wants to be around an old stick-in-the-mud. Anyone who is going places will avoid the company of people wallowing in the pits. Your happier friends might pull you out of the pit a few times, but eventually they will find more upbeat people with whom to share their lives.

You may have many challenges. I'm not making light of your circumstances, but Jesus said, "In the world you have tribulation and trials and distress and frustration; but be of good cheer" (John 16:33 AMP). I've found that sometimes you have to smile by faith. Instead of being depressed, discouraged, or worried, say, "I'm not moved by what I see; I'm moved by what I know, and I know this is the day the Lord has made. I'm choosing to be happy."

When you smile, you send a message to your whole body that says, *God's in control; everything is all right. This will be a good day.* Don't wait to see how you feel before you express your joy. Put a smile on your face first. Then the joy will come.

Smiling improves your attitude. You see life in a different light. It's difficult to smile and be negative. It's hard to stay in a bad mood if you act cheerful and friendly. One expert says smiling tricks the body into feeling good. That's the way God created us. Smiling resets your mood.

Smile Power

Our church in Houston receives many visitors who are undergoing treatments from a major cancer medical center nearby. I have been inspired to meet many of these patients who have smiles in spite of their condition.

They are at peace. They are still joyful because they understand this principle: When you brighten up and wear a cheerful countenance, your body is assured that everything will be okay.

Smile and you will have more energy, improve your mood, and get well more quickly. But if you wear a long face and you're sad and depressed, your body will feel tired and run-down.

My sister Lisa experienced this during difficult times years ago. For months she had no joy. She was so depressed she wouldn't leave the house. Lisa prayed for happier, healthier times. She knew all the Scriptures. Her friends and family did their best to cheer her up, but nothing seemed to help.

Lisa's problem was that she was waiting to feel better so she could cheer up. But she had it backward. First you have to cheer up, and then you'll feel better. Lisa put on a smile out of sheer determination. She smiled by faith. She chose to wear a cheerful countenance.

And her step of faith was the turning point. She broke free of the chains of depression. If Lisa had not smiled by faith, she might still be praying for happiness to find her. She tells this story in her book *You Are Made for More*.

Have you heard the saying "You've got to fake it till you make it"? You may have to wear a fake smile, but if you keep at it, God will turn it into a real smile. Lisa won back her joy and God paid her double for her trouble. My sister came out of hard times even better than before. Her comeback began when she chose to smile by faith.

We all can find some reason not to smile, whether it's high gas prices or low income. But your response should be, "I'm too blessed to be stressed. My future is so bright, I need sunglasses." Or, as one person told me, "If I was doing any better, I'd be twins."

Put on a Happy Face

Scientists say that humans are programmed to mirror the facial expressions of others they encounter, so your smile is contagious. Make a habit of smiling. Scripture says, "In [God's] presence is fullness of joy" (Psalm 16:11 NKJV).

When you lack joy, you are disconnected from God's presence. When you're sad and frustrated and wear a chip on your shoulder, you've detached yourself from favor, blessing, healing, and promotion. Your happiness supply line has been disconnected.

You have joy deep within you, but sometimes you must push it up higher where we can all see it and share it. Professors at Yale University did a study on how appearance, personality, and attitude influence others. After much in-depth research, they concluded that the single most powerful force of human influence is not looks, height, or personality. Instead, your *smile* is your most powerful tool for influencing others in a positive way.

That explains the saying "If you're not smiling, you're like a person with a million dollars in the bank and no checkbook." Studies have shown that people who smile frequently are promoted more often and end up with higher-paying jobs. Why is that? Don't you prefer being with those who are happy, good-natured, and friendly? Of course, we all do!

I'm known for smiling a lot. My brother, Paul, says I was born with my Happiness Meter set on 98. His was set on 10, but he's working on it. My earliest baby pictures show me smiling. My mother says for the longest time she wondered if I was up to something, but she finally decided it was just my nature!

Years ago, I was in the mall with Victoria and she had picked out an outfit to buy. She was still shopping, though, so I offered to take it up to the line at the checkout counter. When I stepped in front of the salesclerk I smiled and said hello, just being friendly.

The checkout lady smiled back. She was about to ring up the clothes when she stopped and said, "Hang on, I'll be right back." She went into the sales office and came back and said, "This is going on sale this weekend, and I have permission to give you the sale price right now."

I smiled even bigger.

"Thank you so much," I said.

As she was folding the clothes to put them in the bag, she noticed this little part of the inside lining of one item had come undone.

"This looks like a problem. Do you see that?"

"Oh, yeah, that looks really bad," I said.

"Let me see what I can do," she said.

She headed back to the office and in a few minutes came back.

"Okay, I can cut the price to half the sale price."

I thought, *Man, if I keep smiling, they may owe* me *money!*

Victoria said I should shop with her more often after that. I told her it all started with a smile. If I'd stood at the counter looking like an old grouch, I don't believe the clerk would have gone out of her way to be good to me.

Add a Smile to Your Résumé

I can still remember the first time Victoria ever smiled at me. I walked into her mother's jewelry store and didn't see her right away. I was looking at the watches, but then I looked up and Victoria flashed a 10-carat smile. Within a short time, she had a ring to match. (Well, almost!) I know smiles are contagious because she's kept me smiling for more than twenty-five years.

Wearing a smile can work wonders whether you are the buyer or the seller, including when you are selling yourself. I read that the Holiday Inn hotel chain was looking to fill five hundred new jobs. They interviewed five thousand people. They automatically disqualified any applicant who smiled less than four times during the interview.

Another study on smiles found that seeing a friend's happy face has a greater impact on our moods than receiving a five-thousand-dollar raise. Did you know your smile is worth that much? After I read the results of that study I went around the church office smiling at the staff. "There's *your* raise," I said. "And there's *your* raise, and there's *your* raise."

Can you believe they told me they preferred cash? Even so, smilers are workplace winners.

> *Smilers are workplace winners.*

When Alexandra was born, I'd just stepped up to pastor our church and Victoria was helping me with all sorts of responsibilities. We needed a babysitter to help us take care of Alexandra during the day. Victoria and I talked with a half dozen candidates. Some were very qualified, with great referrals and strong credentials. We didn't hire any of them.

Instead, we hired a sixty-year-old woman without great referrals or an impressive résumé. She simply was as warm and sunny as a spring morning. She had a great smile and she flashed it throughout our interview.

She was one of the best hires I've ever made. Over the years she filled our house with joy and laughter. She thought everything Alexandra did was funny. I thought I knew a thing or two about the power of a smile. She taught us even more. She taught us that a smile invites what it expresses: kindness, respect, friendliness, and caring.

God gave us all a smile. Are you using yours? Is your joy being fully expressed? How much favor would you experience if you unleashed your full potential for happiness and joy?

Light the World

The Scripture talks about believers representing God here on the earth. We are Christ's ambassadors. If we're to represent God properly, we should do it with joy, with enthusiasm, with a smile. People of faith are supposed to be the lights of the world. I believe the switch that turns on the lights is a smile. Some who lack faith may not want to listen to what we believe, but they certainly watch how we live. We are living epistles read by all men. Some may not read the Bible, but they're reading our lives. As the saying goes, "Preach at all times; use words only when necessary."

When people see you, what kind of message are they getting? Are you friendly, happy, good-natured? Do they want the life you have? Or are you uptight, on edge, stressed, and so grumpy that people run from you?

One of our church members known for her radiant smile and personal warmth was shopping one day when the salesclerk casually asked her how she was doing.

"I'm doing great," she said with a smile. "I'm blessed and I'm believing to have a fantastic year."

The clerk smiled back and asked, "Do you go to Lakewood?"

Our member replied yes.

"I should have known," the clerk said. "Everybody who comes in here with a smile like yours is from Lakewood."

What a great testimony! Yet some critics give me a hard time because

I smile so much. You would think they'd be happy that I'm happy. A reporter asked me one time if I was offended because some call me "the smiling preacher."

"Not at all," I replied. "I take it as a compliment. I'm guilty of being happy. I'm guilty of enjoying my life. I'm guilty of living with enthusiasm."

This world needs more joy. If I feel it, I want to share it.

But when you express your joy and live cheerfully, don't be surprised if people are suspicious of you. They'll look at you as if they're thinking, *Why's he so happy?* Or, *She must be doing something wrong.* Or, *He must be high.*

Yes, I'm guilty; I'm high on the Most High. I'm happy, I'm excited, and I'm full of hope. I want my joy to be seen.

A Legacy of Laughter

Smiling comes easy for me because I was raised by a happy family. My grandmother's smile is one of my favorite memories. Every time I walked into a room and saw her, she would send a smile my way. Sometimes I'd run out of the room and come back just for another helping. She was full of joy, and she passed it on to me.

My father was the same way, except he expressed his joy by whistling, too. All day long we could hear him whistling away. My mother sometimes said, "John, would you quit whistling for a while?"

"Dodie, I'm just happy," he would reply. "I'm giving God praise."

"That would be fine, John, but you're whistling the tune to *The Andy Griffith Show*, and I'm not sure God watches much television."

I don't know either, but I do know that people who watch television are more likely to tune into a smiling face than any other. In 1983, I launched the television ministry for my father. The first year we had a veteran consultant come in to help us. He taught me something I've never forgotten.

We were watching Dad's sermon in the control room, and the consultant had us turn down the volume. He said the key to learning how to communicate in television is to turn down the sound and observe the speaker's facial expressions and body language and then to note the feelings they stir in you.

We tried this with several ministers. Some appeared very passionate, but without the sound they came off as angry and intimidating. You didn't want to watch them very long. The ministers who smiled and had a pleasant, unthreatening demeanor were more likely to draw you in even without sound.

Pass It On

People write me all the time and say they can't remember the sermon's message, but they were touched by the joy in my face. They felt love coming through on the screen. The same principle applies in life. When you are kind and friendly, you will be more effective in most situations, and your smile will spread joy all around you.

Let your joy be seen and pass it on. Be friendly. Smile on purpose and without condition. Smile at the police officers even when they are writing your ticket. Smile at the grumpy salesclerk. Smile at the boss who just asked you to work on your day off.

When things are difficult, smile by faith. Don't wait until you feel better. Smile, and the feelings to support that smile will catch up. Remember, you've been anointed with the oil of joy. You can live happily even when those around you are discouraged.

> *When things are difficult, smile by faith.*

If you develop a habit of smiling, God will reward you with His favor. You'll not only feel better, you'll also earn better breaks. You will see increase and promotion. People will be drawn to you, and I believe and declare you'll live that life of victory God has in store for you.

CHAPTER FOUR

Bloom Where You Are Planted

I was walking through the woods awhile back and came to this big open area full of large, tall weeds. For acres and acres, as far as I could see, there were these dead, dried-up, brown, ugly weeds. As I walked through the open field, about a hundred yards in, I saw this beautiful flower. It was so bright, so colorful, so refreshing. It had bloomed right there in the middle of acres and acres of old, ugly, dried-up weeds. And I thought, *Really, that's what God wants us to do. Just bloom where we're planted.*

You may work around a bunch of weeds, but that doesn't have to stop you from blooming. You may be married to an old weed. But the good news is, you can still bloom.

Too many people are negative and discouraged because they don't like where they are. They don't like their spouses. They don't like their jobs. Co-workers are hard to get along with. They don't like where they live. That's not where they want to be.

If negative people have to work late, it sours their day. They are always fighting against something. They are always trying to go somewhere else. But I've learned that God is more interested in changing me than He is in changing my circumstances. As long as I'm sour because I'm not getting my way, discouraged because I'm single and I want to be married, upset because the business isn't growing, that attitude will keep me right where I am.

If you want to see change, if you want to see God open new doors, the key is to bloom right where you're planted. You cannot wait until everything becomes better before you decide to have a good attitude. You have to be the best you can be right where you are.

Sow a Seed for God

Put a smile on your face. Be good to people even if they're not good to you. Be grateful for where you live even if it's not where you want to be. When you bloom where you're planted, you're sowing a seed for God to do something new.

The Scripture says, "The steps of a good man are ordered by the LORD" (Psalm 37:23 NKJV). That means as long as we're in faith, where we are is where we're supposed to be.

"That couldn't be right," you say. "I'm uncomfortable. I'm not in a good place. Somebody is not treating me right."

It may be difficult, but God will not allow a challenge to come into our lives unless He has a divine purpose for it. I've found that nothing happens *to* us; it happens *for* us. If we keep the right attitude, God will always use it for our good.

That person who is hard to get along with? He's not happening *to* you, he's happening *for* you. God is using him to grow you up. You're developing character. You're learning to be good to people who are not being good to you. God uses difficult people, like sandpaper, to rub the rough edges off us. The next time you see that person, instead of being upset and all stressed out, just smile real big and say, "Thank you so much for everything you have done for me."

Then you may have to help pick him up off the ground.

If God removed some of the challenges in your life right now, you would not be prepared for what He has in store. When tough times come your way, instead of being negative and complaining, say: "God, I may not like this, but I know I'm here in Your divine plan and You would not have allowed it unless You had something good for me to get out of it. It may not feel good right now, but I know it's helping me to grow and become all that You created me to be."

You Can't Fight Your Way to Happiness

So often we find ourselves fighting our way to happiness. We're always trying to reach somewhere else to be happy. "If I could just find something bigger than this small house." Or, "If I could just move to a better job or at least change departments." Or, "If I could just meet some new friends."

That sort of thinking will only hold you back from happiness. A better approach is, "This is where God has placed me right now, and until He moves me, I'll be happy where I am."

If I'm stuck in traffic, "This is not where I want to be, but this is where God has me so I'll relax and stay in peace."

If I have to work late, I'm not discouraged. "This is where God has me, so I'll be happy and enjoy it."

If somebody is mistreating me, I won't allow it to sour my day and steal my joy. Instead, I'll say, "This is where God has me for this season, so I will rise above it and be happy anyway."

That's what I mean when I encourage you to bloom where you are planted. Wherever you are, know that God has put you there for a reason. When you understand that, your mood won't go up and down depending on

> *Wherever you are, know that God has put you there for a reason.*

your circumstances or depending on how somebody treats you. You will be stable. You will be consistent. You will always wear a smile, be in a great mood, and be friendly. That's the sign of a mature person.

Take Responsibility

What I love about this approach is that it takes away our excuses and puts the responsibility to be happy on us. I know too many people who don't like their jobs. They dread working. They dread driving to work. They dread dealing with the people at work.

What a shame to be somewhere forty hours a week and not enjoy your work. "Well," you say, "you don't know these people I work with. You don't know how miserable it is."

Scripture says God has given us the power to enjoy our work. Quit telling yourself, *I can't be happy here. I don't like my job. I don't like the people. I can't wait till God opens up something new.* You are making yourself miserable.

Start telling yourself, *I have the power to enjoy this job. I'll have a great day. I'll enjoy the people. I'll be productive. I'll bloom right here where God has planted me.*

Sometimes the reason you are not happy on the job is that you are being asked to do things you don't want to do. But this is important: The person paying you may like things done a certain way. You may not agree. You may think you can do something better another way, but since the boss is approving the check, you'll need to do what the boss wants you to do. You have to be big enough to submit to the authority and do what you are asked with a good attitude, without always questioning, without walking away mumbling under your breath, "They just don't know what they're talking about."

Be Faithful Where You Are

I worked for my father at the ministry for seventeen years. I was in charge of the television production. We would do these big television specials and big concerts and all kinds of exciting things that I really enjoyed. But toward the end of my father's life, he didn't want to do so much. One time I had all these radio stations lined up to carry my father's broadcasts. I had worked long hours on this big deal. I asked my dad to come down for an hour a week to record his part and we would create the openings and the closings. But he said, "I don't want to do that. I'm seventy-five years old. I just want to relax and pastor the church."

I was so disappointed. I thought, *God, I'm young. I don't want to do less. I have big dreams. I want to do more.*

I considered leaving to pursue my own opportunities. When I searched my heart, I felt staying with my father was what I was supposed to do. I made the decision: "This is my father's vision. He's been here for forty years. He founded the place. He has a right to do what he wants. And so I won't lose my joy and pack up and leave just because I'm not getting my way."

I kept being my best day in and day out. Two years later my father went to be with the Lord. I realize now God put those dreams in my heart for my own ministry. It just wasn't the right time. But had I not been faithful where I was, had I not honored and submitted to that authority and done the right thing even though I didn't feel like it, I would not be standing here today.

When you pass that test of blooming where you're planted and keep a good attitude even when you don't feel like it, and stay calm when you don't get your way, and honor authority even when you don't agree, you are sowing a seed for God to take you where He wants you to go.

"My boss is difficult. My co-workers get on my nerves. They're negative. They complain. I've been praying for three years for God to give me another job. Why is it taking so long?" you might say.

Have you ever thought that God may have you somewhere on purpose so you can be a good example? God may want your light to shine, to brighten the days, to make a difference where you are. Why don't you take a different perspective?

If you pass that test and bloom where you are planted, God will open new doors. But as long as you are negative and complaining, nothing will change. You are not in position for God to promote you if you are not the best you can be right where you are.

When you are in an uncomfortable situation, realize that either God is doing a work in you or He is using you to do a work in someone else. There is a purpose. There is nothing wrong with asking God to change a situation. But until it happens, you have to trust that where you are is where you should be.

I've found that sometimes God has us endure a difficult season to help somebody else. We have to sow a seed and be uncomfortable, treated unfairly. We have to be extremely patient and kind and overlook things just so another person can become what God has created that individual to be.

God Will Use You for the Good of Others

Many unfair things happened to Joyce when she was growing up. Her first marriage to an abusive, unfaithful man didn't last. She married a second time and made her husband miserable. She wasn't trying to be a bad wife, but she had just been through so much pain. She was hurt and messed up.

She couldn't trust anybody. She was very negative, critical, and hard to get along with. Her second husband, Dave, wanted to leave her a thousand times. He had every right to walk away. Nobody would have blamed him. But deep down he knew he was supposed to stay. It was the most difficult thing he had ever done. Month after month, even year after year, he was uncomfortable.

His situation was unfair and difficult, but Dave kept blooming where he was planted. He just kept being his best: kind, forgiving, patient, overlooking things. He felt like he gave and gave and never received; all sowing and no reaping.

I'm happy to tell you that today it's a different story for this couple. Dave paid the price. He stuck with her. And now, thirty-five years later, he's reaping great rewards. That lady, his wife, is Joyce Meyer. She's not only healthy and whole, but they have a ministry touching people around the world.

Joyce and Dave are incredible people. Good friends whom I love and respect. Joyce once asked, "What if Dave would have been like my first husband and taken the easy way out? What if he had not stuck with me and paid the price?"

Sometimes God will ask us to put up with things to help another person. Where are the people unselfish enough to say, "God, I trust You. It's uncomfortable. It's not fair. I'm not doing it because I want to. I'm not doing it because I feel like it. But God, I'm doing it unto You"?

God rewards people like that!

The apostle Paul put it this way: "I have learned to be content whatever the circumstances. I know what it is to be in need, and I know what it is to have plenty. I have learned the secret of being content in any and every situation, whether well fed or hungry, whether living in plenty or in want" (Philippians 4:11–12 NIV).

He was basically saying, "I just bloom wherever I'm planted. I'll be happy and have a good attitude knowing that God is directing my steps. He's in complete control. And it's all a part of His divine plan for my life."

Be a Rose Among Thorns

Like Dave, you don't have to allow a bad environment to affect your happiness. Don't focus on the weeds. You may be spending all your time, so to speak, trying to pull up the weeds. In other words, trying to fix everything in your life, trying to make people do what's right, trying to straighten out all your co-workers.

You can't change people. Only God can. If somebody wants to be a weed, no matter what you do, they will be a weed. Spending all your time and energy trying to change them will keep you from blooming. One of the best

> *You can't change people.
> Only God can.*

things you can do is just bloom bigger than ever right in the middle of those weeds. Right in the middle of those negative and critical co-workers, put a big smile on your face.

Be kind. Be friendly. When they complain, don't preach a sermon to them. Don't try to stop them. Your job is not to pull up the weeds. Your job is to bloom. Just have a good report. The more they complain, the more grateful you should be. The more they talk defeat, the more you should talk victory.

If your co-workers come in one morning being sour and rude to you, don't be offended and think, *Well, I'm never speaking to them again*. That's the time more than ever to bloom. Put a smile on your face anyway. Have a good attitude in spite of that.

You Are Responsible *to* People, Not *for* Them

We are responsible for helping and encouraging others, for guiding them further along. But we are not responsible for their choices. You cannot force a good attitude upon someone. If they want to live in the pits, unhappy, discouraged, and in self-pity, that's their choice. Do not allow them to drag you into the pit with them.

If you spend all your time trying to encourage others, trying to make them do what's right, trying to keep them cheered up, they'll drain all the life and energy out of you. You cannot bloom if you spend all your time trying to keep others happy. That is not your responsibility.

I learned long ago that not everyone wants to be happy. Some people want to live in the pits. They like the attention it brings them. Make the decision to say: "If you don't want to be happy, that's fine, but you can't keep me from being happy. If you want to live in the pits, that's your choice, but I'm not diving in there with you. If you want to be a weed, you can be a weed, but I'm a flower. I'm blooming. I'm choosing a good attitude. I'm smiling. I'm happy despite my circumstances."

When you bloom in the midst of weeds, you sow a seed to inspire and challenge the people around you to come up higher, and that's a seed for God to take you higher.

You may be in a negative environment right now. The people in your life may not be going places. They may lack goals, dreams, vision, enthusiasm. You may not see how you could ever rise above. It might be easy to just accept and settle where you are and think this is your destiny.

Let me challenge you. This is not your destiny. You were made for more. God has incredible things planned for your future, but you have to do your part and bloom where you're planted. What does that mean? Develop your gifts and talents. Whatever you do, whatever your occupation is, do your best to be the best. Improve your skills. Read books. Take training courses. Go back to school if you need to. But don't you dare just sit back and think, *I'll never rise any higher. I'll never get out of this neighborhood. I guess this is just my lot in life.*

Your lot in life is to excel. It's to go further. It's to make a difference in this world. Take a stand and say, "I will not settle where I am. I was made for more. I'm a child of the Most High God. I have seeds of greatness on the inside. So I am rising up to be the best I can be right here, knowing God will take me where I'm supposed to go."

God Will Show Up

When you do what you *can* do, God will show up and do what you *can't* do. He will give you breaks that you don't think you deserve. He will cause people to be good to you for no reason. He will open doors that no man can shut. That's His favor shining down on your life.

Juan Rodriguez grew up in extreme poverty in Puerto Rico. His family had hardly anything to eat. Their home was nothing more than a shack. At seven years old, he was working in the sugarcane fields, carrying water to the workers. It didn't look like he had much of a future or that he would ever escape poverty.

But near his house there was an old run-down, beat-up golf course where he took a job as a caddie at the age of six to earn extra money. Soon, Juan was hooked on golf. He couldn't afford clubs, so he began playing with a stick. He used tin cans as golf balls. All through the day he would play rounds on his makeshift golf course.

When one of the local golfers saw how interested Juan was in the game, he helped Juan get a job on the course, making thirty-five cents a day. Whenever Juan wasn't working he was playing golf, perfecting his swing, mastering his putting, being the best he could be right where he was.

At twenty-one years of age, he was hired as a full-time caddy at a golf course in Puerto Rico. One day a professional golfer came through and saw how talented Juan was. This golfer took Juan under his wing and started working with him, teaching him, training him.

Today, many years later, Juan Rodriguez is better known as Chi Chi Rodriguez. He won eight tournaments on the PGA Tour, and twenty-two tournaments on the Senior or Champions Tour, where he was once named Senior Player of the Year. He started the Chi Chi Rodriguez Youth Foundation to provide role models and assistance for troubled and abused children.

Bloom where you're planted. Don't make excuses. Don't go through life thinking, *I've got a disadvantage. I've got too many obstacles. I'm the wrong nationality. I come from the wrong family. I don't have the connections. I could never get out of this environment.*

You may not see how you will rise above, but God sees. He already has a way. Your destiny is not determined by how you were raised, or by your circumstances, or by how many odds are against you; your destiny is determined by the Creator of the universe. And if you take what God has given you and make the most of it, like Chi Chi did, God will open doors. He will give you good breaks, and He will place the right people across your path.

Get rid of your excuses. Quit waiting for things to change. Sow a seed and be happy right now. When you're in difficult times, remember: Either God is doing a work in you or He's using you to do a work in someone

> *Either God is doing a work in you or He's using you to do a work in someone else.*

else. As long as you're in faith, where you are is where you're supposed to be.

Quit fighting to go somewhere else. Be the best you can be right where you are. If you make this decision to bloom where you're planted, you pass the test. God promises He will pour out His blessings and favor. You'll not only live happy, but also God will take you places you've never even dreamed of.

CHAPTER FIVE

Enjoy the Journey

A friend of mine received an invitation to visit the White House and meet with the president. He was very excited about this great honor. But then his son's basketball team won their division and they kept advancing to higher levels. And it just so happened that the state championship was on the same day my friend was supposed to go to Washington. So he had to decide whether to stay and see his son play or to meet with the president of the United States.

He could have thought, *Well, I can watch the game later by video. I can call and get updates. I can probably hear it on the radio.*

Instead, he didn't think twice. He had his staff inform the president's office that he would not be able to attend. He went to his son's game and it turned out to be a very exciting and very close match. The two teams exchanged the lead several times throughout the game, and with just a few seconds remaining his son's team was down by one point. It looked like they would come up short. But in the final seconds his son hit the game-winning shot, and they won the state championship.

Afterward, my friend said, "I would not have traded that moment for anything in the world, not even a meeting with the president."

Life is not really about getting to a destination. It's about how we live along the way. It's easy to become so goal-oriented and so focused on our dreams that we overlook the simple things we should be enjoying each day. Life is a journey. There is no such thing as the finish line. Once we accomplish this dream, God will give us another. When we overcome that challenge, there will be another. There is always another mountain to climb.

If you make the mistake of living just for the destination, you will look up one day and realize you've missed out on the biggest part of life. Most of life is routine. Most of us get up every morning, go to work, come home, eat dinner, go to bed, and then do it all again. There are very few mountaintops; you graduate from school, you get married, you have a child. The high times are few and far between.

But many people live only for the mountaintops. They're so focused on earning promotions, they work night and day. They don't really enjoy their families. They're so stressed raising their children, they don't enjoy their children. They're so caught up in solving daily problems, they don't enjoy the best moments of each day.

Slow down and enjoy the journey. This is what I had to do. Before I was married I traveled overseas with my father a couple of times a year. I lived for those big trips. I couldn't wait. When one trip was over, I immediately started counting down the months, the weeks, and hurried through the days to get to the next trip.

One day I realized I was hurrying through life just trying to get to my big events. Of course it's good to have things to look forward to. It's good to have goals in front of you. But don't put your life on hold until those things happen. Enjoy each day along the way.

Former football star Deion Sanders had a dream to win the Super Bowl. That's what he wanted more than anything else. He trained and trained, year after year, working tirelessly. One day his dream came to pass. His team, the San Francisco 49ers, won the Super Bowl after the 1994 season. After the big celebration, he was so disappointed. *Is this all that it is?* he thought. *I've worked and reached the pinnacle of my career. I thought it would be different. Yes, I'm happy. Yes, God has blessed me. But it's just not what I thought it would be.*

Some spend their whole lives trying to reach a goal, only to find out it's not what it was all cracked up to be. My friend, the real joy is in the simple things. It's in being with your family, getting up early and seeing the sunrise, taking a walk through the park, taking your daughter to lunch, going on a bike ride with your spouse. Of course, the goals and accomplishments bring us a sense of satisfaction, but they're only temporary.

You Can't Live Off Your Super Bowls

You can't live off your big events because after you savor them for a moment, God will birth a new dream in your heart, something new to look forward to.

I've talked to many people who have made it to the very top in their fields. The one common regret I hear is that they succeeded, but at the expense of their families. They say, "If I could do it over again, I would take time to stop and smell the roses. I would be there for my children's Little League games. I wouldn't live so stressed and uptight, thinking, 'If I could just get to the next level, then I'll slow down and enjoy my life.'"

Slow down and enjoy the journey right now. Take time for the people God has put in your life. They won't always be there. The Scripture says in James 4:14 that our lives are like a mist. We're here for a moment and then we're gone.

Every day, tell your spouse, your children, those who mean the most to you, how much you love them. I told Victoria the other day how much I appreciate her coming and listening to me speak every service. Awhile back we were out of town holding services. Then

> *Every day, tell your spouse, your children, those who mean the most to you, how much you love them.*

we returned to Lakewood Church and did three services on the weekend. And I figured she had heard my same message eight times in a row. Listen, after eight times I'm even tired of it. But she sits there, three services every week, and she laughs at my same jokes each time, as though it's the first time she's heard them. I know she's faking it, but at least she's faking it to make me feel good.

I don't take that for granted. Make sure the people in your life know how much you appreciate their sacrificing and supporting you. After all, you wouldn't be where you are if somebody wasn't paying the price to help you move further down the road.

My mother is another great example of this support. Every service when

I'm preaching I hear her egging me on from the front row. Under her breath she's constantly whispering, "That's good, Joel." It doesn't matter what I'm talking about. I'm her son. She thinks everything I say is great. Why, I can say to the congregation, "You may be seated," and my mom will say, "Oh, that's excellent today, Joel."

I wouldn't be where I am today without those who have sown into my life. I'll never take for granted those closest to me—my family, my friends, my co-workers—all of those making sacrifices so I can fulfill what God has put in my heart.

Focus on What Is Truly Important

Many people these days are making a living, but they're not really making their lives. They're working all the time, living stressed-out, bringing the tension home, too busy to enjoy what God has given them. Understand that when you come to the end of your life, most likely there will still be work to do at the office. Your in-box will still be full. Your work will never be finished.

If you don't make your family and those you love a high priority to enjoy, to spend time with, to invest in, then you will miss out on what matters most. In your final days here on this earth, the job won't keep you company. Your family will. But if you spend all your time just investing in a career, giving the best of your life and energy to build a business, then your lack of investment in what matters most—your family—could leave you a very lonely person.

It's good to be focused and driven. It's good to be a hard worker. But it's important that you know how to put your work aside, walk away, and say, "You know what? This work will still be at the office tomorrow. So I'll do my best today. I'm working hard, but I'm also playing hard. I'm enjoying my family. I'm having fun with my children." If you don't make this decision, your family will have only your leftover time and leftover energy. They deserve better.

If you take the stress from the office home with you, the whole house will tense up. Don't let mistreatment at work or what you didn't get done sour your day so badly that you take it out on your family. Leave that at the office.

I don't know about you, but I would rather make less money and enjoy my life and enjoy my family than to be so overworked I never have any extra energy. There are plenty of opportunities I decline because I don't want my life to go by in a blur. I don't want my children to grow up without knowing me. I don't want to be so busy that I can't come home and work out or take a walk through the park or stay up and look at the stars or get up early and hear the birds singing.

Please realize that I am a very goal-oriented, disciplined person, and I do just what I'm asking you to do. I have trained myself to slow down and enjoy the journey.

Zigzagging Through Life

As a teenager, Frank Lloyd Wright, who became a famous architect, was walking through a snow-covered field with his uncle one day. They were headed to a house. But along the way Frank veered off and stopped by a barn to see the animals. Then he went over to a pond and took a look at that. Then he saw a fort off in the distance. He went out of his way to see that.

When he finally caught up with his uncle across the snow-covered field, his uncle said, "Now, Frank. I want to teach you a lesson. Look back at our footsteps in the snow. Mine came straight here. I never ventured off and I arrived here much quicker than you. But Frank, look at yours. You zigzagged all over the place and wasted so much time stopping all along the way."

Frank Lloyd Wright said that was one of the best lessons he ever learned. But he took it in just the opposite way from what his uncle intended. His philosophy was, "I still arrived at the same destination, but I enjoyed all the sights along the way."

There should always be a balance between working hard, being focused, accomplishing dreams, and taking time to stop and smell the roses. Appreciate and enjoy the great things God has placed in your life. Some of you are all work and no fun. If you change your approach, slow down, and enjoy the journey, you will still arrive where you're supposed to be, but your life will be so much more fulfilled.

I learned a lot of this from Victoria's side of the family. They love to laugh. They love to have fun. They enjoy one another. At dinner they can sit there and talk for hours. I can eat in ten minutes and I'm done. I'll think, *Let's get busy. Let's go do something. We've got goals. We've got dreams.*

Recently Victoria's mom, brother, and other family members came over after church for a late lunch. After I finished eating, I went to another room and watched a football game. Two and a half hours later I returned and they were still sitting at the table, in the same seats, laughing, talking, having fun. I was so amazed. I said to Victoria, "What are you all talking about?"

She said, "Oh, nothing."

Let me tell you, they can talk about nothing better than any folks I know. Why is that? They enjoy one another. They've taught me how to take time to smell the roses.

Think about this: God gives us a sunrise every morning. Do you ever enjoy it? He gives us stars every night. Do you ever look up and appreciate them? Maybe you have your mom and dad living close by. Do you ever stop by and spend time with them? Do you ever call them and talk about nothing?

God has blessed many with beautiful children. Do you enjoy them, or are you so busy raising them and cooking their dinners, making sure they're doing their homework and making sure they're cleaning their rooms, that you don't really appreciate the gift God has given you? I know most parents love their children. No doubt about it. But many don't really enjoy their children. Some parents let the pressures of raising them rob them of all the joy their children have to offer.

Some Things You Can't Get Back

When our daughter, Alexandra, was about three years old, she used to wake up at night and come down the stairs into our room. Of course, we would have to take her back to bed. For a few months she was waking up two or three times a night and coming down.

This was not long after I took over for my father and started pastoring. I was learning to minister, and there was a lot of stress and change just with that, so I wasn't sleeping much. One time I was telling Victoria, "We've just got to do something about Alexandra. She's coming down so much. You know, I'm just so tired. I'm not getting enough sleep." On and on.

Victoria said something I'll never forget. She said, "Joel, just remember, twenty years from now, you'll give anything to hear those little footsteps coming down the stairs. You'll give anything to have her wanting to come into your room."

That changed my whole perspective. I began looking forward to it. I treasured those moments that we could spend together. Your children may be a lot of work right now, but make sure you're enjoying them. They won't always be in the house with you.

You have to realize there are some things you cannot get back. Your children will be home for only so long. Take time for the people in your life. Don't rush out of the house without giving your spouse a hug. Don't be so busy that you can't go on that promised date with your child. Don't come home so tired that you can't go to the park and watch your teenager skateboard.

Make memories together. Twenty years from now you will look back and say, "Remember when our baby woke us up every night? Remember when our child made the game-winning shot? Remember when I'd take you to the park and chase you around? Remember when we'd sit around the dinner table and laugh and tell stories?"

Don't take now for granted. Your family needs what you have. They need your smile, your encouragement, your support, and your wisdom. They need to know you care and that they mean the world to you. It's important

> *You are living in tomorrow's good old days.*

not to just be *in* the house. Don't just show up. Be involved. Be engaged.

I heard someone say, "It's not the time we spend together. It's the moments we ignite to make memories."

I know plenty of people who live in a house full of family but they're very lonely. Everybody is busy. Everyone is doing his or her own thing. Nobody is stepping up to say, "You know what? We're a family. We take time to sit together at the dinner table and catch up. We enjoy the ball game or a dance recital and cheering on family members. We lift up one another when we're falling. We're enjoying what God has given us."

It's easy to be too busy. It's easy to become disengaged. But if you want the most out of life, draw the line and say, "I'm slowing down and enjoying the journey. I'm not taking for granted what God has given me. I'm not being a workaholic, and I'm not missing the years when my children are growing up. I'm not living so stressed out that I can't appreciate the simple things in life."

Don't Miss Everyday Miracles

A few years ago I was rounding everybody up at our house to leave for church, and we were running late. I was in a big hurry, all stressed out. Our son, Jonathan, was about eight years old. Somebody had given us a label maker, one of those little machines that you can type a message on and print out a label with a sticker on the back. Jonathan was by the back door typing in a message.

"Jonathan, put that up," I said. "We're late. We've got to go right now."

He said, "Hang on, Dad. I just need another minute, just another second."

I said, "Jonathan, we don't have another second. We'll be late for church. You've got to put it up." I was getting more and more stressed out.

About that time he printed out the message and handed it to me.

"You're the best dad in the world," it said.

I thought, *Well, maybe we can stay here a little longer, and print out a few more of those.*

Sometimes we become so caught up in our goals and so focused on the end result that we miss the miracles all along the way. Take time to smell the roses. Enjoy the different personalities God has put in your life.

I've found it's the simple things that mean the most. You don't have to take an expensive vacation to make a memory. You can create a memory sitting at the dinner table. You can experience a memorable moment watching your children play in the backyard, or rising early with your spouse and taking in a beautiful sunrise.

Some of my best childhood recollections were created when all of us kids—there were five of us—would sit with my father early in the morning and drink coffee by the fireplace.

My father would take his first sip of coffee then let out a long "Ahhh."

All of us kids, from four to fourteen, would do the same thing. We would have a contest to see who could do the best "Ahhh."

We laughed and had so much fun together. My brother Paul says his children still drink coffee early in the morning, sip it, and say their "Ahhhs."

I don't drink coffee anymore. I'm a little bit holier than he is!

Our family didn't have a lot of money when we were little, but my parents were very innovative. Occasionally they would drive us to the nearby airport when it wasn't busy, and we would ride the shuttle train together. That was free. We loved it. You would have thought they were taking us to an amusement park. We would go back and forth between Terminal A and Terminal B for an hour or two.

I'm sure people thought, *That family is so lost. They don't know what they're doing.* You know what we were doing? We were making memories. We were having fun together as a family.

Life Is What We Make It

When our children were younger we took them to Disneyland. Alexandra was about five years old. It was very much a struggle getting there that day. There was a lot of traffic. We were in a rental car, and we had difficulty finding a place to park. There was a long line just to catch the tram to the park. By the time we finally arrived in the park, I was very stressed out. We weren't there fifteen minutes when little Alexandra said, "Daddy, I want to go back to the hotel and go swimming."

I said, "No, no, no, Alexandra. We can swim anywhere. We can swim at home. We're at Disneyland, the Magic Kingdom."

"Daddy, I don't want to be at Disneyland," she insisted. "I want to go swimming."

I tried to win her over by saying we might see Mickey Mouse or Snow White. I promised her that so much fun awaited us.

"I don't want to have fun here," she said.

I finally had to say, "Listen, Alexandra. I paid fifty bucks for your ticket. You'll have fun whether you like it or not."

Seriously, it doesn't take a lot of money to have fun. Many times it's the simple things that we remember the most. Like the hotel swimming pool!

Casey was a huge baseball fan, and for his son's eighth birthday he bought him a baseball autographed by all of the New York Yankees. They had just won the World Series. He paid major money for it.

Casey was sure his son, Logan, would treasure it for years to come. But when he gave the ball to his son, the boy wasn't excited about it at all. In fact, he just looked at it and put it off to the side.

Casey was so disappointed.

"Logan, don't you like the ball?"

"Yes, Dad. But I'd like it a lot better if somebody hadn't written all those names on it."

Like little Logan, we must learn to enjoy the simple things in life. Today, everything is so complicated. We have five hundred channels on TV, the Internet floods us with information, and now we can access all these distractions on our cell phones and iPads and other devices. We can never escape from our work or our diversions.

If you are not careful, you will fall into the trap of thinking that you should always be busy, and that you must always be involved in something big and exciting. Slow down and enjoy the simple things. Turn off the TV and spend more time with your family. Take a walk. Go for a bike ride. Play games together. Do those special things that you don't need to pay for, no ticket required.

Growing up, we played a family game of hide-and-seek. My mom and dad would let us hide and then they would track us down and chase us all through the house. Playing that game with them was a highlight of my childhood days. My favorite memory is the time my sister Lisa became stuck in the dryer.

Thank God we had her on permanent press!

Simple Pleasures Are the Best

You can have great wealth and be miserable and lonely. Or you can have very little and still be happy and fulfilled. It's all in your approach to life.

A wealthy father decided to show his seven-year-old son how the "poor people" lived. They drove from their big home in the city to a little farm in the country where this friend and his "poor" family lived.

They spent the night with the family in their little wood-framed house. They had no television, no fancy furniture, and no carpet. Since there was no entertainment in the house, this family sat out on the front porch, where they sang, told stories, and laughed together.

After being there two nights, the wealthy father and son headed back home. The father was very curious to see if his son had learned his intended lesson. So he asked him how he liked it.

The little boy said, "Oh, Dad, I really loved it."

"Well, son, do you see how poor people can be?"

"Yes, Dad. I do."

"Tell me, what exactly did you learn?"

"Well, Dad, I learned that we have one dog at home, and they have four. We have a swimming pool in the middle of our backyard, but they have a stream with no end. We have fancy lanterns on our house, but they have the stars. We watch TV by ourselves at night, but they sit around as a family and have fun."

His dad shook his head, knowing that his plan had backfired.

But then his son added: "Dad, thank you so much for showing me how poor we really are."

Value What Matters to You

If you have people in your life to love, you are rich.

If you have your health, you are rich.

If you can hear your little girl's footsteps coming down the stairs, you are rich.

If you can talk with your family about nothing, you are rich.

> *If you have people in your life to love, you are rich.*

Maintain the proper perspective. Slow down and enjoy the simple things in life. Take more walks through the park. Look at the stars at night and think about God's goodness.

When you wake up in the morning, don't just drink your coffee. Sip it and say, "Ahhh." Ignite that moment. Slow down and enjoy the journey. There will always be another dream, another goal, and another challenge. Take time for what matters most.

Don't let yourself become so focused and driven, so busy with what you have to do each day, that you miss the miracles along the way. Imitate Frank Lloyd Wright and start zigzagging. Start enjoying the different things God has put in your life.

Someone said, "It's not that life is so short, it's that we wait so long to begin."

Why don't you begin today? Hug your children before you leave each day. Give your spouse a kiss. Call your parents and tell them how much you love them. Go visit those relatives you've been meaning to see.

We're not here forever. It's good to work hard, but learn how to turn it off. Stay in balance and play hard as well. If you'll make the decision to slow down and enjoy the journey, you will experience the fullness of what God has in store for you.

When you come to the end of your life, you'll have no regrets. You'll be able to say, "I made the most of my time here. I enjoyed my family. I enjoyed my friends. I finished my course with joy."

PART
II

Know What to Ignore

CHAPTER SIX

The Right Perspective

It's easy to focus on what's wrong in your life, what you don't have, and how big your obstacles are. But if you are not careful, you will lose sight of all the good things God has done for you. Don't take for granted the family, friends, and opportunities He has blessed you with. If you're in such a hurry and so stressed that you fail to appreciate the gift of today, you'll lose your joy and your ability to be happy every day of the week.

It's all about keeping things in perspective. Business may be slow, but it's the wrong perspective to think, *I'll never make it.* The right perspective is to think, *God is supplying all of my needs.*

If you are going through a disappointment, the wrong perspective is, *I should have known this would happen. I never get any good breaks.* The right perspective is to believe that when one door closes, God will open another.

You can put two people in the exact same circumstances and one will be complaining, negative, and just enduring life, while the other will be happy, grateful, and enjoying life. What's the difference? Their perspectives. It's how each chooses to see the situation.

We all have burdens that can steal our joy and cause us to be sour. But if we're to live life happy, we need the foundation of a grateful spirit. I've learned that seeds of discouragement cannot take root in a grateful heart. If you are unhappy today and you've lost

> *Seeds of discouragement cannot take root in a grateful heart.*

your enthusiasm, the quickest way to turn that around is to be more grateful. Instead of looking at what you don't have, thank God for what you do have. Instead of complaining about what's wrong, thank God for what's right.

I've talked to many people who have gone through disappointments. They've lost their jobs, their marriages, or their health. It's difficult for them to see any reason to be grateful. But really, it's a matter of perspective.

I heard of a man who complained he didn't have any good shoes until he met a man who had no feet. His perspective changed then and there.

He thought, *You know what? Maybe I don't have it so bad.*

The truth is, somebody in the world would gladly trade places with you. Somebody would love to be able to breathe like you. Somebody would love to be able to walk like you. Somebody would love to be living where you live. Have you thanked God lately for your family, your friends, your health, and the opportunities He's given you?

You Complain, You Remain

If you're complaining about where you are, you won't get where you want to be. If you're complaining about what you have, I believe God will not increase you with more.

Complaining about your old car, your small house, or your spouse won't get you anywhere. Remember this phrase: *If you complain you remain, but if you'll praise you'll be raised.*

To keep your life in perspective, try making a list of all the things you are grateful for. Write down ten things that God has blessed you with and put the list on your bathroom mirror. Every morning read over that list two or three times. Do the same every night before you go to bed.

Meditate on the good things God has done. Write down the times God showed up at the midnight hour and made a way where there was no way. Write down the time He protected you from that accident, the time He had you at the right place and you were promoted, the time the medical report said you wouldn't make it but your health suddenly turned around. Write down the fact that you have healthy children, a roof over your head, and a loving spouse.

When you meditate on the goodness of God, it will help you have the right perspective, and release your faith, too. When your faith is released, God's power is activated. You will see Him show up and give you something else to put on your list.

A middle-aged man named Nicholas was very down and discouraged so he went to his minister.

"Nothing in my life is going right," he said. "I have no reason to be excited, no reason to be thankful."

"All right, let's do a little exercise," the minister said.

He took out a legal pad and drew a line right down the middle.

"Let's list all your assets on this side, all the things that are right in your life," the minister said. "On the other side we'll list all your challenges, all the things that are bothering you."

Nicholas laughed.

"I have nothing on my asset side," he said, hanging his head.

"That's fine, but let's just go through the exercise," said the minister, adding, "I'm so sorry to hear that your wife has passed away."

Nicholas looked up abruptly.

"What are you talking about? My wife didn't pass away. She's alive and healthy."

The minister calmly said, "Oh," and then wrote down under assets "Healthy wife."

Next the minister said, "Nicholas, I'm so sorry to hear your house burned down."

"My house didn't burn down," said Nicholas.

Again, the minister calmly said, "Oh," and added "Place to live" to the list of assets.

The minister was on a roll.

"Nicholas, I'm so sorry to hear that you were laid off from work."

"Pastor, where are you getting all this nonsense?" he said. "I have a good job."

The minister wrote "A good job" on the list of assets.

"Can I see that list?" Nicholas asked, finally catching on. After looking it over, he added a dozen more assets that he'd been taking for granted instead of being grateful for them. Nicholas left the minister's office with a much different attitude.

Recognize Your Gifts

What was Nicholas's problem? He just needed to change his perspective. When he began to focus on the good in his life, he got his happiness and joy back.

If you struggle with staying encouraged and staying grateful, make a list of everything God has blessed you with. If you have your health, write it down as an asset. If your vision is good, write it down, too. The same with your job, your family, your friends, your children, and all your other blessings. Make that list and then go over it throughout the day. That should get you thinking in the right direction.

You have to realize that every day is a gift from God. What a shame to live this day or any other day defeated, depressed, negative, complaining, and with no enthusiasm. We all have obstacles. We all have things to overcome, but our attitude should be: *I know God is still on the throne. He's in complete control of my life. He's said His plans for me are for good and not evil. I'm not living this day defeated, depressed, or focused on what I don't have. I'm changing my perspective. Thank God I'm alive. Thank God I'm breathing. Thank God I'm healthy. Thank God for my family. I'm living every day to the fullest.*

Some people feel burdened by their duties and responsibilities, but those, too, are gifts. They complain because they "have to go to work" or they "have to take care of the kids." You don't *have* to do anything. You *get* to do all those things. God gives you breath. You couldn't go to work, take care of the kids, or mow the yard if God didn't give you the strength. You couldn't go to work if He didn't give you the opportunity.

Change your perspective. You don't *have* to go to work; you *get* to go to work. You don't *have* to take care of your children; you *get* to take care of your children.

Do you know how many people would give anything to have children? Some couples spend thousands of dollars and go through painful medical procedures in their efforts to have children. They would give anything to be cleaning up after their own kids. Thank God every day for blessing you with children. They are a gift from God.

Don't take anything for granted, not even the fact that you were able to get out of bed this morning without any help. When you opened your eyes, you could see. When you told your legs to walk, they obeyed. When your spouse said, "I love you," you could hear it. When your child gave you a hug, you could feel that embrace. When you ate breakfast, you could taste the food.

If you're to have the right perspective, appreciate the simple things God has blessed you with.

Take Nothing for Granted

A congregation member told me that his mentally challenged sister couldn't talk or walk or feed herself. She needed constant attention. Growing up, he and his other family members helped take care of her. They learned to distinguish among their sister's cries, which were her only way to communicate. There was a hunger cry and a cry for when she wanted to get up and a cry for when she wanted to go to bed, and another cry for when she was thirsty.

The most difficult cry was the sound she made when she had an itch. You see, she couldn't tell them where she felt the itch, so they would go all over her body scratching and scratching, trying to alleviate that itch.

Living with his handicapped sister helped this man appreciate the simple things in life that so many of us take for granted. Scratching an itch is no big deal, until you can't. Then it becomes a very significant matter indeed. It's a big deal that we tell our arms to work and they work. It's a big deal that we open our eyes, and without even thinking about it, we see.

When you get up in the morning and you're tempted to dwell on your problems—how you don't want to go to work and how life's not been fair to you—why don't you turn that around? Instead, thank God that you can scratch your itch. Why don't you thank God that you have no problem breathing? Why don't you look out the window and appreciate the simple things like the sun coming up, the birds singing, and the flowers blooming?

Sometimes we think, *My life is so routine, I just get up and go to work and come home. Nothing exciting is happening. I just do the same thing again and again.* But we should be thankful for routine everyday life. There's nothing ordinary about getting up and going to work. There is nothing ordinary about being able to see, having friends, or having family. Those are gifts from God.

Too often we don't realize how great we have it until something is taken

Too often we don't realize how great we have it until something is taken away.

away. I used to play basketball with a young man named Matt until he started having a problem with his eyes. He had always been very healthy and very active, but his eyes kept bothering him so he went to the doctor. After several tests they told Matt that he had cancer of the eye. The doctor said there was a very good chance he would lose his vision.

Matt was so distraught and upset. He went in for an operation, and, to the doctor's surprise, they discovered Matt did not have eye cancer. Instead, they found an unusual fungus behind his eye that was affecting his eyesight. They removed it and saved his vision.

When Matt woke up from the operation and heard that his vision was restored, he said, "This is the greatest day of my life."

Think about it. He didn't just win the lottery. He didn't just buy a big new house. He didn't just get a promotion. He simply got the news that his vision was back to normal.

After his eyesight was restored, Matt told me, "Every day I get up in the morning and on purpose I look around. I stare at my children and my wife. I go outside and look at the trees. I bend down and pick up an acorn on the ground."

Because Matt almost lost his vision, being able to see normally has taken on a whole new meaning for him. He will never again take his eyesight for granted. He will be forever grateful for the gift of sight.

How things changed for Matt when he thought he might lose something as "routine" and "normal" as vision. You and I should never take for granted what God has given us. If you can see, if you can hear, if you can walk, if you've got good health, family, friends, and a good job, learn to appreciate each of those gifts.

In Everything Give Thanks

Don't you dare go around complaining about all that's wrong. Change your focus. I understand you may not have your health, but you do have your family. You can be grateful for that. You may not be able to walk, but you can see. Thank God for your sight. You may not have a job right now, but your mind works, your arms work, your legs work. We all have something to be grateful for.

Keep the right point of view. If you have a hard time getting to sleep at night, think about all the homeless people without beds. If you are stuck in traffic, think about all the people who can't afford cars. If you have a bad day at the office, think about all those who are unemployed. If you have to walk three blocks to church, thank God that you are healthy and able to walk. If your hair is turning gray, be grateful it's not turning loose!

Being grateful is a key to staying happy. That's why King David said, "I will bless the Lord at all times; His praise shall continually be in my mouth" (Psalm 34:1 AMP). Notice how often he will praise the Lord? Continually! David knew a secret. You can't praise and complain at the same time.

If you're constantly thanking God for what He's done and praising Him for His blessings while meditating on His goodness, you won't have time to focus on what's wrong or to complain about what you don't have.

We all are tested every day. In your difficult times, when somebody is rude to you, when you go through a disappointment, when you get a negative report, when your child acts up, what will you say?

"Poor old me. I can't believe this is happening"? Or will you say, "Father, I want to thank You that I'm more than a conqueror. No weapon formed against me will prosper. You always cause me to triumph. I want to thank You that I'm not only making it through, but I'm making it through better off than I was before."

The Scripture says in 1 Thessalonians 5:18, "In everything give thanks" (NKJV). It doesn't say to give thanks for everything. We don't thank God for our troubles, for sickness or accidents. But we do thank Him for the trouble we're coming out of. We thank Him in the difficulty He's turning around. We thank Him for bringing us increase and promotion in a slow economy.

Any time you have an opportunity to complain, let that be a reminder to give God praise. Just turn it around and thank Him for working in your life. Remember, complaining only delays better days. But when you praise, God steps in to fight your battles for you!

Number Your Days

I read recently that more than a million people die every single week. Think about it. You made it another week! You're better off than a million people. You can thank God that you're alive.

The article also said that if you have a roof over your head, you are better off than 75 percent of the world's population. And if you have fifteen dollars to your name, you are in the top 8 percent of the world's wealthiest people—fifteen dollars!

Keep the right perspective. I read a poem that said, "I am thankful for the taxes I pay each year because that means I have a job. I am thankful for the mess I have to clean up after the party because that means friends have surrounded me. I am thankful for the lawn that needs mowing, the windows that need cleaning, and the gutters that need repair because they mean I have a home. I am thankful for sore muscles and for weariness at the end of the day because it all means I was able to work hard. I am thankful for the lady behind me in church who sings off-key because that means I can hear. And I am thankful for the alarm that goes off early in the morning because that means I'm still alive." It's all in your perspective!

Twenty years from now we will look back and remember these as the good old days. Let me encourage you to enjoy the moment. Make memories with those you love. Take time for the people God has given you. Look around at all the incredible blessings He's placed in your life.

Moses prayed to God: "Teach us to number our days" (Psalm 90:12 NKJV). He was saying, "God, help us to realize that every day is a gift. Help us to deal with stress and everyday challenges while still appreciating the gift of each and every day."

Let me ask you: If you had only an hour to live, who would you call? What would you say? And what are you waiting for?

Don't take for granted the people God has put in your life. They won't always be here. You and I will not always be here. Yet sometimes we act and live as if we're invincible. But life is like a vapor. We're here one moment and gone the next. I heard somebody put it like this: "We forget how fragile life is. We wait for Thanksgiving to give thanks. We wait for Christmas to give gifts. We wait for Valentine's Day to show love to those we hold dear. We say to ourselves,

Today is just an ordinary day. So we wait, and while we wait the clock ticks. Precious moments pass by. But in reality there is no such thing as an ordinary day."

Every day is a gift, unique and irreplaceable. Its hours may be used or misused, invested or wasted. God, teach us to number our days.

My prayer is that you will keep the right perspective, focusing on the good, not taking things for granted, and recognizing that every day is unique and irreplaceable. Slow down and appreciate what God has given you. Be thankful for the simple things, even the fact that you can scratch your own itch. Hug your children every day. Take time for the people you love. Find some reason to be grateful.

Look at what's right, not what's wrong. Remember, the seeds of discouragement cannot take root in a grateful heart. If you'll keep the right perspective and like David continually give praise, God promises that when you praise you'll be raised. He'll pour out His blessings and favor!

> *God promises that when you praise you'll be raised.*

CHAPTER SEVEN

Know What to Ignore

Not long ago, a reporter asked me what I thought about two men he named. I said I didn't know who they were and I had never heard of them. The reporter laughed and laughed. He thought that was so funny.

"Well, who are they?" I asked.

"They are your two most outspoken critics," he said. "They're always talking about you."

He couldn't believe that I had never heard of them. But I've learned this principle: I don't waste time engaging in conflicts that don't matter to me. I've learned that the critics cannot keep me from my destiny. What they say about me doesn't define who I am.

Whatever your critics say about you has no bearing on your worth. You are a child of the Most High God. The Creator of the universe breathed life into you. You have seeds of greatness on the inside. You've been crowned with favor. God has already equipped and empowered you with everything you need. Don't waste your valuable time trying to play up to people, trying to win over all your critics, or trying to prove to someone that you're important.

Accept the fact that some people will never celebrate you. They will never recognize your gifts. That's okay. Don't be distracted. God has already lined up the right people to celebrate you, the right people who will cheer you on and help you fulfill your destiny.

If you want to live in victory, you have to be very careful with your time and attention. You have to know what thoughts to ignore, what comments to ignore, and, I say this respectfully, what people to ignore.

If someone at work is always on your nerves, making sarcastic comments, you could try to straighten them out, but you'd be wasting valuable time and energy that could be spent pursuing your dreams. Don't be distracted. Ignore such people.

If a family member never gives you any credit, either you can let that upset and frustrate you or you can dismiss it and say, "No big deal. I don't need their approval. I have almighty God's approval."

You don't have to straighten people out. You don't have to pay somebody back. You don't have to be offended because of what someone said. You can ignore it and live happily. I'm convinced we would enjoy life a whole lot more if we would get good at knowing what to ignore.

Stay on the High Road

According to Mark 3:1–5, Jesus was in the temple on a Sabbath, the day of rest, when He saw a man with a withered hand. Jesus simply said, "Stretch out your hand" (v. 5 NIV), and immediately the man was healed. The religious leaders, the Pharisees, were there and they didn't like Jesus. They didn't understand Him. They got together and said, "Yes, Jesus did do something good. He did heal a man. But you know what? He did it on the wrong day. He shouldn't have been working on the Sabbath."

Like those Pharisees, some will condemn you no matter what you do. Even if you changed and did everything they asked of you, they would still find fault. You could buy them new Cadillacs and hand them the car keys. They would say, "You know what? We really want Lexuses."

Let me pass on a secret to save you heartache and pain: Ignore your critics. You don't need their approval. Stay on the high road. The more they talk, the more God will bless you. They may try to take you down. God will take you up.

I talked about this with a minister friend who has been around a long time and is well respected.

"If you had it to do over again, what would you change? What would you do differently?" I asked him.

Without missing a beat he said, "I would ignore a lot more. I wouldn't respond to every critic. I wouldn't waste time arguing about things that didn't matter. I wouldn't spend so much energy trying to make everybody understand me and make everybody accept me."

I believe many of us would see our lives rise to higher levels if we just ignored our critics.

Many years ago a young man named Saul was chosen to be the next king of Israel (see 1 Samuel 10). The prophet Samuel blessed him and called him up in front of the people and said, "He will be our next king."

Most of those present were very excited and they congratulated Saul. But when he returned home, many longtime friends ridiculed him.

"Saul is not our king. He's not a leader. He doesn't have what it takes."

They were actually jealous of Saul. They were so insecure, so intimidated, they had to try to push Saul down so they would look bigger.

Remember this phrase: "When people belittle you, they are being little themselves." Small-minded people won't celebrate you. Small-minded people will be jealous. They will gossip to make you look bad.

But they are not going where God is taking you. My friend, you are called to be an eagle. You are called to soar, to do great things. But we all have some crows squawking at us, some chickens pecking at us, some hawks attacking us. They are trying to bait us into conflict. Don't get drawn into those battles.

You have an advantage. You're an eagle. You can fly at heights to which no other birds can soar.

Crows love to pester eagles. The eagle is much larger, but the crow is more agile so it can turn and maneuver more quickly. At times the crow will come up behind the eagle and dive-bomb the big bird. But the eagle knows this secret: It can fly at altitudes that the crow cannot fly, as high as twenty thousand feet.

So instead of bothering with the pesky crow and its squawking, the eagle simply rises higher and higher and eventually the crow is left behind.

Do the same when someone is pestering you out of jealousy or spite. Soar above. Leave them behind.

God Will Make It Up to You

God hears what your critics say, and if you stay in faith, He will make it up to you. Use your energy to improve your skills, to be the best that you can be. And God will bring others across your path who will celebrate and encourage you.

> *Use your energy to improve your skills, to be the best that you can be.*

Saul could have easily lost his focus and wasted time defending himself. Many had contempt for the new king: "They despised [Saul], and brought him no presents" (1 Samuel 10:27 NKJV).

What did he do?

Saul ignored them. One translation says, "Saul paid them no mind" (v. 27 The Message).

Follow Saul's wise approach. Pay no mind to jealous people or those who try to bring you down. They don't control your destiny; God does. They are simply distractions. Just stay focused and do what God has called you to do.

After all, when you come to the end of your life, you won't have to give an account of it to your critics. Instead, you'll stand before almighty God, the Creator of the universe. You will hold your head high and say, "God, I did my best. I ran my race. I finished my course. I became who You created me to be."

That's true fulfillment. That's when you will be rewarded.

Don't Be on Edge

These days it seems we are all touchy and on edge. A member of our congregation told me recently, "I quit coming to church for two months because everybody was talking about me. Everybody was against me."

I didn't say it, but I thought, "Ma'am, *everybody* doesn't know you."

We have a big church. With seats for nearly seventeen thousand people, the odds of everybody picking on one person are slim.

This woman was on edge, like so many people today. She fell into a trap of creating conflict where there was none. As a result, she stayed home, missed church, and hurt only herself. The funny thing is, our church ser-vices seemed to be just as good as ever—matter of fact, a little bit better than normal—in her absence!

Maybe worse than being on edge is holding a grudge. What a waste that is! What's in it for you except stress and anxiety? I was leaving the mall with a friend a few years ago when he stopped near the exit doors to the parking lot. Our car was only about fifty feet outside the doors.

"Let's go another way," he said.

"Why?" I asked. "Our car is right here."

"I don't walk by that store," he said. "They did me wrong."

I might have laughed, but he was so serious and dramatic, I thought maybe they'd accused him of shoplifting or something worse.

"What happened?" I asked.

"They wouldn't take back a pair of shoes when I was in high school."

Twenty years ago? I thought. *I'd imagine that store manager is dead and gone by now, or retired to Florida.*

I wanted to say, "Just let it go. I'll buy you some new shoes!"

My friend had been carrying that grudge around so long that he'd probably worn out ten pairs of shoes due to the excess weight of it.

Are you on edge, carrying a grudge, or fighting battles that are not important but consume your time and energy and keep you from pursuing what's really important—your God-given goals, your God-given dreams?

You have only so much energy. If you become caught up in things that don't matter, when a real threat comes along—a real Goliath battle that might make a difference in your drive toward your divine destiny—you may not have the energy to win that battle.

People Pleaser

In my early days as a pastor, I had difficulty ignoring my critics. I wanted everybody to like me. I'd stepped in after my father's death in 1999, and his were big shoes to fill. He had led his church for forty years.

One of my problems was that I tried to keep everyone happy. I didn't want to lose anybody. I finally decided, *I will just be myself and do it the way God is leading me.* Ninety-nine percent of the congregation was behind me and very loyal. But there were a few who were not supporters. Some didn't like the way I ministered, and some didn't like the way I was leading the church.

I felt pressured to fit into their mold and become who they wanted me to be. But you are anointed to be you. When you let people squeeze you into their mold and you bow to pressure by trying to please all the critics, you lose your identity and uniqueness. It lessens God's favor.

So, I stepped into my own anointing. I made some changes and a few didn't like them. Some of the disgruntled members had been with the church a long time. They criticized me, but I did what I'm asking you to do. I ignored the criticisms. They didn't celebrate me, but I paid them no mind.

I didn't lose any sleep. I didn't try to win them over. I didn't say, "Just hear my heart." I just ran my race with purpose, with focus, and with integrity. I saw God give me His favor more and more. Eventually the critics left. But God brought me a lot more people, some forty thousand more. When you do things God's way, you never lose out.

After years of wasting my time and energy trying to win over my critics, I decided to focus on pleasing God and those who encourage me and love me. I accepted that some people would never come around to the wonder of me!

So I became a professional ignorer, and, I must say, I'm very good at it. I'm all for treating every person with respect, kindness, and consideration. But I no longer try to appease or please my critics.

From Mother Teresa to Nelson Mandela, from the Wright brothers to Steve Jobs; every person who has achieved great things has had critics. You will have yours, too. I've heard this said: "If you get kicked in the rear, it means that you're out in front."

The front-runner is always the focus of those who trail behind. The more success you have, the more opportunities there will be for distractions. The higher you go, the more haters will come out. When you reach a new level

> *Don't be a people pleaser, be a God pleaser.*

by pursuing what God has put in your heart, the jealous, critical people and the small-minded people will come out of the woodwork. But don't be a people pleaser, be a God pleaser.

The Fight for Approval

I met a couple years ago and tried to be a good friend to them, but they never seemed to warm up to me. They would greet me and act cordial enough, yet they kept a distance. I just could not understand that. I went out of my way to win their approval. I introduced them to my friends. In fact, one of those connections led to a business partnership for them. Still, they were not receptive to my offer of friendship.

Eventually, they relocated to another city. Don't ask me why, but I found people to help them move. I even gave them a gift for their new home. Despite all those efforts, this couple remained cool to me.

A few years after they left town, I heard that they'd said unkind things about me. They thought I hadn't done enough for them, and here I'd gone out of my way and bent over backward to help them.

I recently saw an interesting set of statistics on friendship. Researchers found that 25 percent of the people you meet will not like you. The next 25 percent won't like you but could be persuaded to. Another 25 percent will like you but could be persuaded not to, and the final 25 percent will like you and stand by you no matter what.

If you take those statistics to heart, you should feel free of any acceptance anxiety. Just realize that some people won't like you no matter what you do, so don't waste your time and energy trying to win them over. You could compliment some people every hour, send flowers every day, mow their lawns every week, but still they will never like you.

That's what I decided about that couple I'd done so much for. I realize now they're just among the 25 percent who will never like me. I wish I had known back then what I know now. I wouldn't have wasted my time trying to win them over.

If someone doesn't want to be your friend, just consider it that person's loss. *Too bad for you; you don't know what you're missing.* When I quit fighting those battles for approval and acceptance as a young man, God began to bring people into my life who celebrated me. Not long after, I met Victoria. She celebrates me. I celebrate her.

Do not waste your valuable time and energy playing up to anyone who snubs or slights you. Such people are merely distractions. One friend of mine calls them "background scenery in the story of my life." You don't need their approval to be who God made you to be. You don't need their acceptance. You are one of God's children.

Let go of their disapproval and know that God will send people who celebrate your talents, your personality, and your accomplishments. With them, you can just relax and be who God made you to be. Whatever you do, they'll think you're the greatest thing in the world.

In my grandmother's eyes I could do no wrong as a boy. Once, when someone ate her homemade chocolate-chip cookies before dinner, I was not even a suspect. Who was it?

"Not my darling Joel," she said. "It may have been one of his sisters, but I know Joel would never do that." My three sisters would be so aggravated. They'd say, "Grandmama thinks Joel is a saint."

I can't help it. I had favor even back then. That's the kind of people God wants to bring you, people who believe the best of you.

Take on this attitude: *I have something great to offer. I am one of a kind. I have a great personality. I have the right looks. And I will not waste time trying to make people love me. I will let that go and trust God to bring me divine connections, people who celebrate me just as I am.*

When Nehemiah was rebuilding the walls of Jerusalem (see Nehemiah 4), there were two men at the bottom of the mountain named Sanballat and Tobiah. They were his biggest critics, and the whole time he was up there working they were hollering things like, "Nehemiah, come down here and fight with us. You will never finish that wall. You don't have what it takes."

I love the fact that Nehemiah was focused. They were making a lot of noise, threatening him, calling him names, but he recognized there was no benefit to fighting with them.

When God puts a dream in your heart, there will always be the Sanballats and the Tobiahs trying to engage you in battles that don't matter. They may talk mean and say things behind your back. They'll try to lure you into strife. But be disciplined. Recognize when it's a battle that's worth fighting.

Be Your Best, Let God Do the Rest

A reporter asked Bill Cosby the secret of success. He said, "I don't know the secret of success, but I do know the secret of failure, and that is to try to please everybody." You have to accept that not everybody will support you. Not everyone will like you. Not everybody will understand you. That's okay. Be the best that you can be, and God will take care of your critics.

You don't have time to come down off that wall. You don't have time to convince your critics. You don't have time to argue. You have a destiny to fulfill. You have an assignment to accomplish. Learn to ignore the Sanballats and the Tobiahs. Before long, like Nehemiah, you'll complete your wall and your actions will answer your critics.

Stay focused on the main goals God has put in your heart. He will do amazing things. Like David, you will defeat your giants. Like Nehemiah, you will complete your walls. Ignore the distractions, and you will accomplish your goals all the quicker.

Choose Your Battles

Many of the challenges that may come your way are simply distractions meant to lure you from your destiny. When you are tempted to vent your emotions because someone has hurt or angered you, it is best to ask yourself, *Is it worth it? Even if I win this battle, what is the prize? What will lashing out accomplish?*

You may miss out on God's best while distracted by battles that don't matter. Maybe you are trying to prove your worth, trying to win over your critics, or playing for approval. Those are all needless distractions. Choose your battles wisely.

> *Choose your battles wisely.*

In the early years of our marriage, I had a pet peeve. If Victoria didn't turn off all the lights when she left the house, I'd get uptight.

"Victoria, be sure to turn off all the lights!"

A few hours later, I'd come home to an empty house with all the lights on. I would tell her once again we were paying too much on our power bills.

I knew she didn't leave the lights on intentionally. She just left without thinking to turn them off because she had other things on her mind. I'm more of a details person. Victoria is more of a big-picture person. We just have different personalities and different strengths.

I harped at her for about five years before I put that pet peeve down.

After all that time bringing tension into the house, getting uptight, it finally dawned on me, *Joel, this is not a battle worth fighting. If it costs you an extra ten dollars a month in electricity, it's well worth keeping the peace in your home.*

The lower power bills were not worth the higher stress and heartache. Learn from my mistake. How much tension are you bringing into the home unnecessarily? You may win a victory, but will it be worth the stress?

Have you ever heard the saying "A bulldog can whip a skunk any day of the week. But sometimes even a dog realizes it's just not worth the stink"?

Winning isn't everything.

Being Right Isn't All It's Cracked Up to Be

I've found it's easy to start a fight, but it's hard to end one. The best strategy is to take a step back, draw a deep breath, and say, "What truly matters here?"

Proverbs 20:3 says, "Avoiding a fight is a mark of honor" (NLT). If you want God to honor you, if you want to enjoy your life, be a peacemaker. Be the kind of person who avoids an unnecessary fight, a fight that carries no real rewards.

Your home needs to be a place of peace. You and your spouse need to be in harmony. You are stronger together than you are apart. Not only that, your children need to see a good example. They will treat their own spouses the same way they've seen their parents treat each other.

Fight mode should not be your daily setting. You likely have friends, family members, or co-workers who constantly run hot. They are always aggravated at a spouse, a neighbor, or someone in the office. Anger consumes their time and energy. They don't know when a battle is not worth fighting because there are no spoils. Even if they win, they'll be no further down the road toward happiness or fulfillment.

If you make the mistake of engaging in every potential battle that comes along, and you are constantly defending yourself, proving your point, straightening out others, then you probably won't have the energy to fight the battles that do matter. Be a warrior, but even a warrior knows when to sit one out. He saves his energy for the battles that mean something; those that move him closer to his God-given destiny.

First Samuel 17 tells the story of David and Goliath. As a shepherd boy, David was asked by his father to take meals to his brothers on the battlefield. They had much more prestigious positions as warriors. David was stuck tending the family flock. When he went onto the battlefield on his errand, he heard Goliath taunting his people. David asked the men standing around, "What is the prize for the man who defeats this giant?"

"The reward is one of the king's daughters in marriage and no more taxes," they replied.

David saw great value in fighting this battle. There were serious spoils. When David's older brother Eliab heard David talking about fighting the giant, he tried to embarrass him in front of the other men.

"David, what are you even doing out here?" he asked. "And what have you done with those few sheep our father left you with?"

Eliab tried to make David feel small.

I love the way David responded. The Scripture says that David turned and walked away from Eliab. David had feelings just like you and I have. I'm sure he wanted to say, "Oh, Eliab, you think you're something great. You're nothing at all."

He could have chosen to take on his brother. But he didn't take the bait. He focused on what was truly important. Had David wasted his time and energy on his brother, who knows if he would have defeated Goliath?

You have to ask yourself, *Are the battles I'm engaged in worth fighting? Do they have any rewards? Are they furthering me toward my God-given destiny?*

If a battle doesn't stand between you and your God-given destiny, simply ignore it. If somebody doesn't want to be your friend or treats you rudely, that's not worth a war.

When you are swept up in petty battles, you risk missing the Goliath put in your path by God to help you fulfill your divine destiny. The battles that do matter will come. Save your strength and energy for what's really important.

> *If a battle doesn't stand between you and your God-given destiny, simply ignore it.*

Disarm the Arguers

Right after I began ministering, this older gentleman came up to me in a serious state of mind.

"I need to know what you believe about the second dispensation of the Spirit," he said.

I thought, *Dear God, I must have missed the first one.*

My usual tactic in these cases is blatant honesty.

"Sir," I said, "I don't know about that at all."

This approach hardly fazed him. He wanted to debate, and since I didn't jump in, he went right ahead expounding on his own.

"Well, Joel, I believe this... and this... and this."

I kept my cool.

"You know what? I think you're right," I said. "I agree with you."

My refusal to take the bait finally gave him pause, but not much pause.

"Yeah, but I believe this, and this, and this," he said.

"I agree exactly," I said.

His face reddened. I was confusing him with my sinister affability.

"Yeah, but I believe this and this and this and this."

This poor fellow had won the argument three times, but he wasn't happy. He wasn't satisfied. He wanted to keep arguing. He was in fight mode.

Finally, he seemed at least halfway convinced that I agreed. He walked away. One. Two. Three. Maybe ten steps before I said, "Excuse me, sir. I'm not sure I agree with... that one thing."

He whirled around.

"I'm just kidding. Just playing with you," I said.

Believe me, his dukes were up. He was ready to fight again, but I was ducking and weaving, staying fast on my feet.

Living Well Is the Best Revenge

Some people are just contentious by nature. They argue with the image in the mirror. So smile and walk away, because there will never be a short supply of people looking to pick a fight or start an argument.

According to 2 Samuel 16:5–14, King David was walking down the street and a young man started making fun of him, calling him names, even throwing rocks. He followed him everywhere, just pestering him, trying to pick a fight, trying to aggravate him.

Finally, King David's friends said, "Do you want us to put a stop to him? Do you want us to shut him up? He is a real pain."

I love the way King David answered. He said, "No, let him keep talking. Maybe God will see that I am being wronged and bless me for it."

That's the attitude you need. It takes all the pressure off. You don't have to retaliate. In fact, your attacker has done you a favor because God will serve as your vindicator. What this person meant for your harm will be used by God to promote you, and blessings will come your way.

CHAPTER EIGHT

Silencing the Voice of the Accuser

Nine-year-old Sam was visiting his grandparents' big farm where he loved to walk in the woods with his slingshot. He practiced shooting rocks at trees and bottles and cans, but he didn't hit much. You see, Sam was still working on his accuracy.

One evening after a day in the woods, he heard the dinner bell calling him home. As Sam walked toward the house he spotted his grandmother's pet duck walking by the pond. He never dreamed in a million years he could hit the duck, but just for fun he pulled the slingshot back, and let it fly. Believe it or not, the rock hit the duck square in the head. The duck dropped dead without even one last quack!

Sam was shocked. He'd never hit anything he aimed at! He felt terrible.

In a panic, he ran to the dead duck and carried it behind the barn where he buried it in the woodpile. Sam was headed into the house, feeling terrible still, when he spotted his twelve-year-old sister, Julie, and realized she'd watched the whole sordid affair.

That night after dinner, their grandmother said, "Julie, I'd like you to stay and help me do the dishes if you don't mind."

"Grandmother," she replied, "I'd love to, but Sam said he wants to do the dishes tonight."

As she walked out past Sam, she whispered in his ear, "Remember the duck." Trapped, Sam went over and did the dishes.

The next morning their grandfather invited both Sam and Julie to go fishing, but his wife had another plan.

"I really need Julie to stay here and help me do some chores," Grandmother said.

Julie countered, "Grandmother, Sam said he'd like to stay with you and help you out today."

Once again, his sister walked by Sam and muttered, "Remember the duck." Sam did the chores. Julie went fishing.

After a couple days of hard labor, doing both Julie's chores and his own, Sam had had enough. He fessed up.

"Grandmother, I'm so sorry. I didn't mean to, but I killed your duck."

His kindly grandmother gave him a big hug.

"Sammie, I know what happened," she said. "I was standing at the window watching the whole thing take place. I saw how shocked you were and I've already forgiven you. I've just been waiting to see how long you would let Julie make a slave of you."

Sam's grandmother was not standing alone at that window. God was right beside her. He sees your every mistake, every failure, every weakness. The good news is that He, too, has forgiven you. He's not holding anything against you. He's just waiting to see how long you will allow the accuser to make a slave of you.

Seek Forgiveness and Move On

The Scripture says, "There is now no condemnation for those who are in Christ Jesus...who do not walk according to the flesh but *according to the Spirit*" (Romans 8:1, 4 NASB).

Those last four words are the key. When you make mistakes, if you are in the flesh, you beat yourself up. You feel guilty and unworthy. You live depressed and defeated. But choosing that response will leave you on a dead-end street.

Instead, embrace the Spirit and say, "Yes, I made mistakes. It was my fault. But I know the moment I ask for forgiveness, God will forgive me and forget my mistakes so I can move ahead."

Too many people go around feeling bad about themselves. When they make mistakes, instead of receiving God's mercy and moving forward, they listen to the voice of the accuser. That voice constantly rails at them about their mistakes, their blown diets, their temper tantrums, and their shortcomings. After so long, they are weighed down with guilt and self-condemnation.

A member of our congregation, Sheila, told me she felt guilty for giving her baby up for adoption as a teenage mother. It had been ten years, and she was still down on herself.

"I feel ashamed, like I'm a terrible mother," she said. "I don't know what was wrong with me."

Sheila is listening to the voice of the accuser because of something in her past. Now she is carrying a heavy load of guilt that could destroy her future even though she knows that she made the best decision for her baby at the time.

> *Guilt puts you on a treadmill; you're constantly working and struggling and sweating, but you don't move forward.*

Guilt puts you on a treadmill; you're constantly working and struggling and sweating, but you don't move forward.

Guilt Is a Dead-End Street

The burden of guilt drains your strength, your energy, and your enthusiasm. Guilt will prevent you from forming healthy relationships. It can affect you not only emotionally but even physically. I've known people who have suffered nervous breakdowns because of guilt. Year after year, they have carried the heaviness. They are worn down and can barely function.

You may have made mistakes and done things that you're not proud of, but the moment you asked for forgiveness, God forgave you. The Bible says in Isaiah that He remembers our sins no more.

If God doesn't remember your sins, then that accusing voice is not God's. That's the accuser trying to sour your future. You have two choices in response. You can believe those lies, dwell on them, and allow guilt to weigh you down. Or, a much better decision is to rise up in faith and say, "No, thanks. I'm not going there. If God doesn't condemn me, I'm not condemning myself!"

There is a difference between God's voice and the accusing voice. When we make mistakes, as believers, we feel a conviction on the inside. We feel guilty. Our conscience tells us, *That's not right.*

That's the Spirit of God convicting us. The right thing to do is repent; ask for forgiveness and go forward. The moment we do that, God doesn't remember the mistakes. He has no record of them.

Your mistakes and transgressions are not kept in a secret database somewhere. But as soon as God lets them go, the accuser begins working on you. Even though God has forgotten about your mistakes, the accuser tries to keep you feeling bad about yourself and your mistakes. He reminds you of everything you've done wrong and tries to force you to give up and sit on the sidelines.

The accuser's goal is to deceive you into living condemned, to make you feel inferior and unworthy of God's blessings. Be keen enough to recognize who is speaking to you. The accusing voice is not God's voice.

Tell yourself, *That's the accuser trying to dump another load of guilt on me, trying to keep me feeling bad. But I know better. I don't have to listen to his lies. I believe what God says about me. I'm forgiven. I'm redeemed. My past is erased and my future is bright.*

By not dwelling on those lies, you silence the voice of the accuser. The Scripture says, "You shall know the truth, and the truth shall make you free" (John 8:32 NKJV). The truth is that the price for your mistakes was paid two thousand years ago on the cross at Calvary. You don't have to pay again.

You have been redeemed. God's mercy is bigger than any of your mistakes. So press forward with your head held high, knowing your best days lie ahead of you.

Take the Sack Off Your Back

You can't do anything about your past, but you can do something about your future. Receiving God's mercy and moving forward is illustrated by a story of three men carrying two sacks each. A passerby asked the first man what was in the sacks.

"The sack on my back is filled with all the good things that have happened to me," he said. "The sack in the front is filled with all the bad."

He was constantly focused on the bad things in front of him so he couldn't even see the good on his back.

The stranger asked the second man the same question but received the opposite response.

"The sack in the back is filled with the bad things," he said. "The sack in the front is filled with the good things."

At least he could see the good and not focus on the negative. But both of the sacks being so full still weighed him down and made life a burden.

Finally, the stranger asked the third man the same question.

"The sack on my chest is filled with my accomplishments and victories," he said. "The sack on my back is empty."

"Why is it empty?" the stranger asked.

"I put all my mistakes, failures, guilt, and shame in that sack, and I cut a hole in the bottom to release them," he said. "That way, I'm weighted in the front more than the back so I keep moving forward. In fact, the empty sack in the back acts like a sail in the wind, moving me ahead."

Like that third man, you have to let go of the bad, hang on to the good, and keep moving forward toward your goals.

Focus on What's Right

One way you know that guilt and condemnation are not from God is that they don't help you improve. Guilt and condemnation don't make you do better. When you go around feeling bad about yourself, you are much more likely to make another mistake. I've seen people on diets despair so much they need a bowl of ice cream to recover. They give up on their goals because guilt doesn't make them do better; it makes them do worse.

Do not spend time thinking about what's wrong with you, but rather, think about what's right with you. I told that young lady who gave up her baby for adoption, "Look at you. You're beautiful. You're talented. You're successful. You've got a great job. Why are you still so down on yourself? That is over and done."

The correct way to handle guilt is to repent and ask for forgiveness. Move forward. The wrong way is to hold on to guilt for a week, a year, or a lifetime. There are some things you cannot undo. You can't unscramble eggs. You cannot relive yesterday, but you can live today. Don't let the accuser sour your future any longer. Start dwelling on what's right with you, not what's wrong with you.

Have you noticed how human nature is drawn toward the negative? I can have a hundred people tell me after a service, "That was a great message. I really needed to hear that." But then one person will say, "I don't know if I really understood the point. I'm not really sure I agree with you on that."

I used to go home depressed, discouraged, feeling like a failure. I've learned now to shake it off. If somebody doesn't like it, my attitude is, *I won't allow someone else's opinion make me feel bad about myself.*

I will not allow one bad report to cancel out a hundred good reports. In the same way, don't let one weakness or one mistake made cancel out all the other great things about you. You may have made a lot of wrong choices, but you've also made a lot of choices that were right.

Focus on your good qualities. Focus on your victories. Get off the treadmill of guilt. It's not taking you anywhere.

> *Guilt will steal your joy.*

Guilt will steal your joy. Don't live another moment in regret. The source of your guilt may have been your fault, but that's what mercy is all about. Rise up and say, "This is a new day. I'm unloading the baggage. I am done feeling wrong about myself. I'm done feeling condemned. I've focused long enough on what I've done wrong. I'm focusing on what I'm doing right."

Accept Forgiveness

It's very difficult for most people to accept the fact that God forgives us so easily. When we make mistakes, we think we have to pay for them. So we grow discouraged and get down on ourselves. Sure, we should be remorseful when we do wrong. We should be genuinely sorry and not flippant. But we don't have to spend month after month wallowing around in guilt and condemnation.

I know some people who made mistakes years ago and they are still asking God for forgiveness. They've probably asked a thousand times. They don't realize God granted it the very first time they asked. The problem is they have not accepted God's gift of forgiveness. They think they must show God how sorry they are by giving up their joy and paying some kind of penance. They live defeated and discouraged. And they beg and beg, "God, please forgive me. God, I'm so sorry. Please, God."

Don't be a beggar. Be a believer. Believe God forgave you the very first time. You don't have to keep asking.

I love the story of the prodigal son (see Luke 15:11–32). The young man took his inheritance and left home, went out partying, living wild, undisciplined, and making terrible choices. He blew his whole inheritance. He lost it all. Finally he had no money, no place to stay.

He ended up working on a farm feeding hogs. He was so desperate, so hungry. He had to eat the animals' food just to stay alive. But one day as he was sitting in the hog pen, guilty, condemned, ashamed, and depressed, something rose up on the inside.

He thought to himself, *Even the servants at my father's house live better than this. And here I am sitting in the hog pen, wallowing in defeat and mediocrity.* He made a statement that changed his future. Without this statement, we would have heard no more of this young man. He said, "I will arise and go to my father."

He was saying, "Yes, I've made mistakes. I brought the trouble on myself, but I won't allow one bad season of my life ruin the rest of my future. I will arise."

Maybe today you've made some poor choices. You're not where you want to be in life. The accusing voice keeps telling you, *It's your fault. Too bad. You've brought it on yourself.*

If you're to be restored, if you're to fulfill your destiny, it's not up to God. It's up to you. Do like this young man and say, "I may be down, but I'm not staying down. I've made mistakes. It's my fault. But I know the secret; I will arise and go to my Father."

I believe one reason this young man could arise was because deep down he knew who he was. He knew what family he belonged to. When you understand your position, you can change your condition. Understand that you are a child of the Most High God, who breathed His life into you. You were never created to live depressed, defeated, guilty, condemned, ashamed, or unworthy. You were created to rule, to reign, to be victorious.

Your condition may be down because of poor choices and mistakes you've made. You don't feel like you deserve it. You don't feel like you're worthy. But shake that off and say, "I understand my position. I know who I am; a child of almighty God. I may not feel like I deserve it. I may not feel like I'm worthy, but I know because of what Christ did He made me worthy. He took my guilt so that I can be free. So I will arise and go to my Father."

That's what this young man did. And when the father saw him coming way down the road, the father took off running toward him. He gave his son a big hug, put a ring on his finger, a robe on his back. He said to his servants, "Let's celebrate. My son has come back home."

God will do the same thing for you when you make that decision to shake off the guilt, shake off the condemnation, and say, "I'm moving forward with my life." When you make a move, God will make a move. He'll come running toward you with mercy, forgiveness, restoration, favor, increase. God can still get you to where you're supposed to be.

But so often when we make mistakes the accusing voices repeatedly tell us, *You can't ask God for help. It was your fault. You've been a hypocrite. You brought this trouble on yourself.*

No, this is when mercy comes in. When you do wrong, you ask for forgiveness, and God forgives you. But when you really understand who you are, you won't just ask for forgiveness. You'll take it one step further and ask God for His mercy.

Ask God for Mercy

One who expects mercy says, "God, I believe You will bless me in spite of these mistakes."

That's what Jacob did. He had lived his life as a cheater, a deceiver, doing people wrong. He grew tired of living that way. One day he decided he wanted to make things right. He went down to the brook so he could be alone.

Genesis 32 talks about how the angel of the Lord appeared to him in the form of a man. Jacob and the angel began to wrestle. Their struggle went on all night. Jacob said to the angel, "I know who you are, and I'm not letting you go until you bless me."

When the angel saw how determined Jacob was and how he would not give up, he reached over and gave God's blessing to Jacob. Jacob left there a different person. God even changed his name from Jacob to Israel, which means "prince with God."

But can you imagine the nerve of Jacob? Don't you know that took incredible boldness? Here he had practically lived his whole life making poor choices, deceiving, cheating, and lying. He should have felt overwhelmed with guilt, condemnation, all washed up. Somehow he had the confidence to not only ask for forgiveness but also to say, "God, I believe You will bless me in spite of the way I've lived."

Surely God would say, "Jacob, what are you talking about? Are you crazy? You don't deserve to be blessed, not even really forgiven. I'm not blessing you."

No, God said, in effect, "Jacob, I love the fact that you know who you are: My child, redeemed, forgiven, made worthy. You not only asked to be forgiven, but you also asked for My mercy. And Jacob, if you're bold enough to ask for it, I'm bold enough to grant it."

That kind of faith grabs God's attention, not when we drag around guilty, condemned, feeling wrong on the inside. No, it's time for us to arise and go to our Father. God is not the one condemning you. That is the accuser. Stop dwelling on those thoughts.

> *God is not the one condemning you. That is the accuser.*

You may have failed, but God's mercy never fails. The sad thing is, most people accept the condemnation quicker than they accept God's mercy. Don't let that be you. Shake off the guilt. Shake off the negative mistakes from the past. Don't go another minute in regret, feeling bad about yourself.

The moment you asked for forgiveness, God forgave you. Now do your part and unload the baggage. Leave the guilt right where you are. Don't take it with you. Leave the bag of regrets. Leave the bag of failures. Leave the bag of condemnation behind. If you learn to silence the voice of the accuser, guilt and condemnation cannot weigh you down. You will live a life of freedom, rising higher, overcoming obstacles, and accomplishing dreams!

CHAPTER NINE

A No-Excuses Life

I'm a sports fan. I love the classic and true story of a boy whose dream was to play professional baseball. He was extremely gifted. All through junior high and high school he was by far the most talented player in his league. Professional scouts were regularly at his games.

Then one day he had a farming accident. He lost the whole forefinger and most of the middle finger on his throwing hand. It looked like his baseball days were over. But this young man had a "no-excuses" mentality. He learned to throw the ball without those two fingers, even though they are usually the main fingers used to throw a baseball.

He had always been a third baseman, but one afternoon during practice the coach was standing behind this young man and noticed some interesting movement on the ball when he threw from third to first. The coach asked him to try pitching. Turns out that was a very good idea.

Mordecai "Three Finger" Brown went on to become one of the greatest pitchers in the early history of Major League Baseball. In fact, he played for six different teams including the St. Louis Cardinals and the Chicago Cubs, competing until the age of forty. He helped win two World Series and was inducted into the Baseball Hall of Fame in 1949.

What many thought would be a liability turned out to be a great asset. The spin Three Finger Brown could put on the ball made it very difficult to hit. God knows how to take what should be a disadvantage and turn it into an advantage.

It's often easy to come up with explanations as to why you can't do or be your best. Most people think they have a handicap of one kind or another, something that is holding them back. It may be a physical challenge, a personality issue, or maybe a divorce or a financial problem.

I've heard many explanations including "I'm just the wrong nationality." And "I was born on the wrong side of the tracks."

Each of us has challenges to overcome, but just because you think you have a "disadvantage" doesn't mean you should sit back and settle where you are. God still has something great for you to do. You may not look like everyone else. You may not be able to do what others can do. But if you will stay in faith and stay positive about your future, you can turn your liabilities into assets.

If you find yourself apologizing for being different, why not start looking at yourself as unique instead? You are not too tall or too short. You are just the right size. You have just the right personality, just the right looks, and just the right talents.

When God made you He wasn't having a bad day. He made you to be the way you are on purpose. He finished creating you and then He stepped back and said, "That was good. I like that; another masterpiece." There may be things about you that you don't like, but you can't allow those things to hold you back or keep you from pursuing your dreams.

You Are Made in God's Image

My mother had polio as a child. She wore braces on her legs. Today, one of her legs is much smaller than the other. When she buys shoes she has to pick up two pairs because her feet are two different sizes. But one thing I've always loved about my mother is that she never allows her "differences" to stop her from pressing forward.

She could have shrunk back and tried to hide her differences and felt insecure, but instead she has a "no-excuses" mentality. She knows she's been made in the image of almighty God. She wore shorts and dresses growing up, never trying to hide her legs. She still wears dresses today.

My mother is seventy-seven years old and still showing off her legs! Don't let her fool you. She loves it!

The effects of her polio never stopped her from working in the yard and around the house or wanting to help others. She could have thought, *I can't pray for others to heal. My legs are not well*, but she did not allow her own health issues to stop her from praying for others in need of healing.

You don't have to be perfect for God to use you. Take the hand you've been dealt and make the very most of it. Believe that God turns situations around. Believe that He'll bring healing. Even if it doesn't happen, you can still honor God by being the best you can be right where you are.

My sister Lisa was born with symptoms similar to cerebral palsy. The doctors told my parents that she'd never be able to walk, never be able to feed herself. They said, "You might as well prepare to take care of a disabled child." Of course, my parents were devastated. They prayed. They believed. They stood in faith, and little by little Lisa got better and better. Today she is perfectly normal. She's on staff with us here, and she often ministers for us.

I have another minister friend by the name of David Ring. Like Lisa, he was born with a form of cerebral palsy. But God's plan for his life was different. David Ring was not healed. When he talks it takes him three or four times as long to get the words out. When he walks, his legs and arms don't function normally.

David easily could have sat at home and thought, *Too bad for me. I have this disability. My speech is slow. I can't get around. God, I thought You wanted me to do something great. I thought You wanted me to be a minister. I must have been wrong. I have this handicap.*

Let me tell you about David Ring: Nothing slows him down. He travels the world speaking to thousands of people, telling them about the goodness of God and encouraging them to overcome obstacles. When he speaks, he is difficult to understand because he speaks very slowly. But I love the way he always starts. He says, "My name is David Ring. What's your excuse?"

Think about this. Lisa was healed from cerebral palsy, and she's honoring God with her life. David Ring is living with cerebral palsy, and he's honoring God with his life. What am I saying? You must take what God gives

> *You must take what God gives you and make the very most of it.*

you and make the very most of it. You cannot sit around thinking, *Why did this happen to me?*

Quit Focusing on the Whys

Faith is all about trusting God even when you don't understand His plan. God could have healed David just like He restored my sister Lisa. But God is sovereign. I don't claim to understand it all, but I do know this: God is good. He has a great plan for your life, a destiny for you to fulfill. No matter how many disadvantages or setbacks you must deal with, if you shake off the self-pity, stop blaming, and keep pressing forward, nothing will be able to keep you from becoming all that God created you to be.

Stop making excuses. Quit dwelling on disappointments, on the unfairness and hurt inflicted upon you. Know that God has something great coming your way. The worst handicaps are those you place on yourself. Too many people are waiting for God to make them perfect before they pursue their dreams and destinies. Go after yours right now.

Honor God with what you have. He wants to take your liabilities and turn them into assets. First, though, you have to accept that God may not remove your challenge, but He will use it to your advantage.

In the Scripture there is a story of a man who was born blind (see John 9). Some people were asking Jesus, "Why was he born this way?" and "Whose fault was it, his or his parents?"

They were trying to find someone to blame, a reason or an excuse. We tend to do the same things today. But I love the way Jesus answered. He said, "It's not anybody's fault, not his or his parents. The reason he was born this way was so that the goodness of God could be displayed."

Jesus was saying when you have a setback, or when life deals you a tough blow, don't be bitter. Don't settle there. Recognize that you are a prime candidate for God to show His favor and goodness through.

If you feel you are disadvantaged or disabled, instead of saying, "It's not fair, God," your attitude should be: *God, I'm ready. I know You have something great in store. I refuse to live defeated and depressed. I know this disadvantage is simply another opportunity for You to show up and show out.*

That's exactly what Tony Melendez did. He was born without any arms. As a little boy he had a desire to play the guitar. Something inside said, *You're supposed to sing and write music.* Tony didn't know any better. He could have said, "Too bad for me. I'd love to play the guitar, but I don't have any arms." Instead, his attitude was, *I may not have any arms, but I do have feet. I may not have any fingers, but I do have ten toes.*

Tony learned to play the guitar with his feet. He can play better with his feet than most people can play with their hands.

When God puts a dream in your heart, when He puts a promise on the inside, He deposits in you everything you need to accomplish that dream. God wouldn't have given Tony the desire without giving him the ability. It just wasn't the "normal" way. Tony had to be bold enough to say, "I am living a no-excuses life. Yes, this may look like a handicap. Yes, in the natural, I may have a disadvantage, but I know with God there are no handicaps. I know when God made me He wasn't having a bad day. He made me with a purpose, with a destiny to fulfill, and I will do my best to bring honor to Him."

Tony has a "can-do" attitude. Other people are hung up on what they can't do or what they don't have, but those "disadvantages" are really advantages just waiting to come to life.

Today, Tony has unprecedented favor. He has traveled to more than forty countries, singing and sharing his story of faith. God is using him to do great things.

Most people never have to deal with anything as challenging as Tony's missing limbs. Yet people often let more common problems like divorce, job loss, or financial challenges overwhelm them. They need to adopt Tony's no-excuses mentality, press forward, and give God time to turn their liabilities into assets.

Pray for God's Guidance

In my early days as pastor at Lakewood, I felt as though my laid-back personality was a disadvantage. My father was a fiery leader. I felt I needed a more dynamic, outgoing personality when I took charge.

I said, "God, You have to change me. I have a disadvantage. I'm soft-spoken. I'm more reserved."

My father could fire up a crowd. I've seen other ministers with powerful voices preach deep theological messages with great eloquence. They can move the whole congregation just with their delivery and enunciation. They are very dramatic. I have a Southern drawl. I talk softly, in a normal tone.

When my father went to be with the Lord I said, "God, I don't know if I can fill his shoes. I'll see what happens." But what I thought would be a liability turned out to be an asset. I realized that God made me like this on purpose.

I don't have the booming voice. I don't have the dynamic personality. I don't preach fancy sermons. But people tell me my messages are easy to understand, because my voice is calm and soothing. In fact, one lady said, "Joel, I listen to you before I go to bed every night. You put me right to sleep!"

She meant it as a compliment!

What is your handicap? What is keeping you from believing in yourself and from pursuing your divine destiny? God knew all the issues you would face, your struggles, your weaknesses and inadequacies. You are no surprise to God.

God Will Use Your "Handicap" to Deliver Your Divine Destiny

Luke 19:1–10 tells the story of a man named Zacchaeus. He had a disadvantage. He was too short. No doubt, growing up in school the other children teased him, calling him "Shorty" or "Peanut." I can imagine he wanted to be more like everyone else. But understand, God makes us like we are on purpose.

One day, Zacchaeus heard that Jesus was coming through his town. All the people were lined up on the streets trying to get a glimpse of Him. Zacchaeus didn't have a chance. He was standing at the back and could not see over anyone. He could have easily given up and felt sorry for himself. Instead, he climbed a tree and had a great view, maybe the best. His disadvantage turned into an advantage.

When Jesus came down the street He looked above the crowd and saw Zacchaeus in the tree. Jesus called out to Zacchaeus and asked to have dinner at his house.

If Zacchaeus had been "normal" size, he wouldn't have climbed the tree and caught the attention of Jesus in the crowd. But because of his "handicap," Zacchaeus climbed higher and reaped one of the highest possible rewards!

Take a higher perspective as Zacchaeus did. Look at your supposed liability and consider that it may be an advantage. I realize now my laid-back, easygoing, soft-spoken personality is an asset. For me to act like someone else would not work. I've accepted who I am and so has our congregation.

You, Too, Have What You Need to Succeed

I heard about another young athlete who was born without a right hand. One day he was at the doctor's office having a physical so he could play football. The doctor asked him what his disability was.

He said, "Sir, I don't have a handicap. I just don't have a right hand."

I love that attitude. "I don't have a handicap. I just play the guitar with my feet." "I don't have a handicap. I just speak a little slower." "I don't have a handicap. I'm just not as tall as somebody else."

I encourage you to live without excuses. Dwell on what you can do. Focus on your gifts. Refuse to feel sorry for yourself. Shake off self-pity. Concentrate on being everything God created you to be.

> *Live without excuses.*

If you'll live that way, in faith and unbowed, God will turn your handicaps and disabilities for your good. He will take every stumbling block and turn it into a stepping-stone. Something may look like a liability, but as with all the examples I've cited, God will transform it into an asset. There are no disadvantages with your God. You have everything you need to succeed!

CHAPTER TEN

You Can Have the Last Laugh

Many years ago my father received a letter from another minister that was very mean, critical, and hurtful. He accused my father of things that were totally false. My father was extremely hurt and a little angry. He wrote his attacker the meanest, ugliest letter he could come up with. He ripped his critic apart.

Then, he sealed the scathing letter in an envelope, walked to the end of the driveway, and put it in the mailbox for pickup.

As my father walked back to the house, an inner voice said, *You got even, didn't you?*

"Yeah, I got even," Daddy replied.

You feel better, don't you?

"Yeah, I feel better."

You paid him back, didn't you?

"Yeah, I paid him back."

Then the voice said, *You sure did. You paid him back evil for evil.*

My father gulped. He could feel that conviction. He knew God was speaking to him. He realized he had responded in the wrong way.

Daddy returned to the mailbox, retrieved the letter, and tore it up. He never sent it; never said another word about it to the man. He chose to let God be his avenger. He chose to let God make his wrongs right.

Sixteen years later my father received a phone call from the man who had attacked him. He was weeping. He said, "Pastor Osteen, that letter I sent you was so wrong. I feel so bad. Can you forgive me?"

God knows how to bring justice in your life. It may not happen overnight, but it will happen.

We all go through situations in which we are treated unfairly. Maybe somebody is gossiping about you, or picking on you, trying to make you look bad at school or work. The natural response is to defend yourself or to strike back. Human nature wants to get revenge. We like to get even. But the Lord says, "Vengeance is Mine" (Deuteronomy 32:35 NKJV). That means God will make your wrongs right. God wants to repay you for every unfairness. He is a God of justice.

The bottom line is this: God wants you to have the last laugh.

Here's how it can happen. Romans 12:19 says to never avenge yourselves, but to let God do it. Notice, you can avenge yourself, or you can let God be your avenger; but you cannot have it both ways.

If you take matters into your own hands, God will step back and say, "You go ahead. You don't need My help." But if you learn to stay on the high road, control your emotions, and let God be your avenger, He will show up and say, "All right. Let Me go to work."

God Knows Those Who Have Done You Wrong

He sees every time you are hurt. He keeps the records. If you learn to stay on the high road and don't waste time trying to pay back those who've hurt you, God promises to be your vindicator.

God will release favor and promotion in your life only when He knows your character can handle it. If you get upset every time somebody wrongs you and you try to vindicate yourself, you will not reach the place where God wants you to be.

David was anointed to be king many years before he took the throne. He had to go through a period of testing. During this time, King Saul was trying to kill him. It was very unfair. David had been good to Saul, but Saul turned it around. On two occasions, David had the opportunity to end Saul's life (see 1 Samuel 24; 26). He could have put an end to his frustration and misery. But David would not do it.

After the first incident where David had spared Saul's life, he told Saul, "May the LORD avenge the wrongs you have done to me, but my hand will not touch you" (1 Samuel 24:12 NIV).

No wonder David was a champion. No wonder he was promoted. He knew how to let God be his avenger.

I wonder how many people, just like David, have been anointed to do something great in life, to be in a position of leadership, a place of honor, and to fulfill their God-given dreams, but they never passed the test. They were too busy trying to pay back those who hurt them, the Sauls in their lives. They do not realize that those who do you wrong are simply distractions.

Use your time and energy to move toward your God-given destiny. Avoid the trap of the payback, and understand you cannot avenge yourself as God can avenge you. God's ways are bigger and better than your own. He can take those who try to hurt you and use them to promote you.

Your attitude should be: *I'll let God be my avenger. I know when God vindicates me I'll come out smelling like a rose. You may look down on me now, but one day you'll look up to me. I may not have much today, but one day you'll wish you had what I have.*

Your Table Is Set

I love the way David put it in Psalm 23, verse 5: "You prepare a table before me in the presence of my enemies" (NKJV). God will not only avenge you and make your wrongs right, but He will also bless you in front of your enemies. He could promote you anywhere, but He'll promote you in front of

> *God will not only avenge you and make your wrongs right, but He will also bless you in front of your enemies.*

those trying to make you look bad. He'll give you favor, honor, and recognition. One day those who stabbed you in the back will watch you receive the credit you deserve.

Knowing that God prepares the table for us in the presence of our enemies keeps me from being discouraged when people talk unfavorably of me. You see, I know God just sent the angels to the grocery store. If somebody lies about you, no big deal. You can see Gabriel setting the table.

Your critics can see the meal on God's table, but they aren't invited to the party. They'll have to watch you enjoy what God has prepared for you. They will watch as you are promoted.

Be ready. If you've done the right thing and overlooked offenses and negative words and blessed your enemies, then know God's table is set. Your dinner is ready. It's just a matter of time before you're seated at the table.

Your enemies may try to spoil the party by stealing your joy. They'll plant doubts, but shake them off. The dinner bell will ring for you at any moment. Those hindering you, trying to bring you down, will see you stepping to a new level. They will see God's favor and goodness enter your life in a greater way.

A mechanic at a big diesel shop told me that for many years he was treated unfairly at work. It was a very negative environment. His co-workers constantly made fun of him. They thought he was a stiff because he wouldn't party with them after work. Year after year he had to endure this ridicule.

He was one of the best mechanics at that company, but in seven years he had never had a promotion, not a raise, or a bonus—nothing—because his supervisor didn't like him. He could have worked with a chip on his shoulder, but he took the high road, knowing God was his vindicator.

Then, one day, the owner of the company called him. They had never met because the owner wasn't involved in the day-to-day operations. But for some reason he called the mechanic and said he was retiring. He offered to sell his business to the mechanic.

"I don't have money to buy your company," the mechanic said.

"You don't need money," the owner said. "I will loan it to you."

Today, the mechanic owns the company free and clear. God set the table, and he was served. Now those who had called him names must call him Boss instead. They used to look down on him. Now they look up to him. They used to blow him off and not give him the time of day. Now they have to make an appointment if they want to see him!

God Knows How to Avenge You

Don't take matters into your own hands. If you'll let God be your vindicator, He will bring justice and He will promote you right in front of those trying to make you look bad.

Proverbs 16:7 says, "When GOD approves of your life, even your enemies will end up shaking your hand" (The Message).

I met a man in our church lobby who said, "I was your biggest critic. I was always talking about you, blogging against you. And I came to one of your services to find something else to criticize. But I liked it so much I came back the next week. It's been six months. I haven't missed a service yet. Now I'm your biggest supporter." He reached out and shook my hand.

God will cause your enemies to shake your hand, too. You may have people you're at odds with. You may have a co-worker or family member who holds a grudge against you. Maybe you've done your best to be kind and respectful and acted toward them just the opposite of what they've shown you. Maybe the kinder you are, the more hateful they are.

It would be easy for you to be bitter toward them, but don't sink to their level. Keep doing the right thing. God is a God of justice. He knows how to change people's hearts. It may take a week. It may take a year or twenty-five years. But God promises that one day those who would hurt you now will reach out and shake your hand.

You Will Receive the Respect You Deserve

A friend of mine, Larry, is in the real-estate business. He is a hard worker who has always given his job 100 percent and maintained a great attitude. However, the owner of the firm where he started out, Charles, treated him poorly. He refused to listen to any of my friend's suggestions and made things difficult. Larry continued to do his best, but inevitably the owner fired him.

To his credit, Larry didn't become bitter. Instead, he started his own real-estate company and became extremely successful. He forgot all about Charles, but God is a God of justice. He never forgets what you are owed.

You may let it go, but God doesn't let it go. He makes sure you get everything you deserve.

Several years later, Charles had to downsize his business. He needed a new building, and the one he found was owned by Larry. The former boss nearly passed out when he walked in and realized that he was about to rent a building owned by the man he had fired.

You can believe that this time, Charles listened to everything Larry had to say. He treated his former employee with respect and honor. He listened carefully. He valued his opinion. Today, Charles pays rent, a very steep rent, to Larry. That's God causing your enemies to shake your hand. That's God giving you the last laugh.

God wants to promote you in front of your opponents. Part of His justice is vindicating you so those who said you would fail see you succeeding and accomplishing your dreams.

A minister I know spent more than fifty years traveling the world and doing good. He was beloved everywhere he went. But the newspaper in his hometown was always finding something wrong with his church. He could do a hundred things right. They wouldn't report on that. They would find the one thing he did wrong and make a big deal about it. This went on year after year.

My minister friend had an interesting perspective. He said, "If it had not been for that newspaper, I would not have accomplished so much. They not only kept me on my knees, they also gave me fuel to prove them wrong. Their critical spirit, that injustice, put me in a position to receive God's favor in a greater way."

He went on to build a big university in that town. Thousands of young people have attended. It seemed the least likely place for him to be blessed, the least likely place for him to accomplish his dreams. But God says, "That's where I prepare the table. That's where I want to increase you. That's where I want to show you unusual favor."

Stay at the Table for the Blessing

According to Genesis 26:1, there was once a great famine in the land of Israel. For many months there was a drought that turned the region into a wasteland. A young man named Isaac was about to pack up and move to another place. But God said, "No, Isaac. I don't want you to leave there. I'm blessing you right where you are."

Isaac obeyed God's command and planted his fields. The Philistines who lived there didn't like Isaac and were already jealous of him. This added fuel to their fire and their ridicule of him. But Isaac, whose name means "laughter," just stayed in peace.

Several months later, all those who had mocked and criticized Isaac were amazed to see his fields. They couldn't believe it.

The Scripture says that Isaac "reaped in the same year a hundredfold" (Genesis 26:12) more than he planted right there in the midst of the famine.

Isaac's critics were dumbfounded, but he knew God had set the table and blessed him.

At some point, you may be tempted to run from a bad situation, but I want you to have a new perspective. You do not have to leave in order to be blessed. God wants to bless you right where you are.

> *God wants to bless you right where you are.*

Part of His vindication is promoting you so the opposition can see it. Your attitude should be: *They may be laughing now, but I know this challenge is preparing the way for God to promote me. They meant it to hold me down, but God will use it to thrust me forward!*

You may be dealing with critics, naysayers, backbiters, backstabbers, those who are jealous and who say you'll never make it. Let me assure you that God will give them a clear view of your table. He'll make sure they see you promoted, honored, and accomplished.

Let God be your avenger. Let God right your wrongs. If you let Him do the avenging, you will always come out better. He will even cause your enemies to end up shaking your hand. They may be laughing now, but know this: God is faithful. In the end, you will have the last laugh. He will bring justice into your life.

PART
III

Live Without Crutches

CHAPTER ELEVEN

Living Without Crutches

When I returned from college to begin Lakewood's television outreach, I was nineteen years old. I didn't know a lot about television production, so we hired an experienced producer from California. He was in his sixties and had produced major-league sports and network morning shows in a long career.

He was knowledgeable, talented, and had a great personality. He was fun to be around. We hit it off from the very start. I would come in early, stay late, go to dinner with him, and hang out. I watched very carefully how he put the programs together and how he chose certain camera shots.

I was learning so much from him. I used to think, *I could never do what he does. He is so creative. He can write. He can direct. I'm just not that talented.*

The veteran producer had been mentoring me for about a year when he came in one day and announced that he was leaving in a month.

"No way," I said. "You cannot leave me with this job. I don't know what to do."

He assured me that I'd do just fine.

"You've watched me for a year, and I've watched you, too," he said. "You can handle the job by yourself now."

I wasn't convinced. I pleaded with him to stay, offered him a raise and more time off, but he insisted that it was time to move on.

The first couple of weeks after his departure, I was so nervous. I didn't know what I was doing. I called him every other hour with questions. But in a month I started to feel more comfortable. In six months I thought, *I'm pretty good at this.* A year later I said, "What did I ever need *him* for?"

I realize now that my mentor did me a favor by leaving. He forced me to stretch and to use my God-given talents. If he had not departed, I never would have stepped into my divine destiny.

Moving Ahead

A crutch is a temporary tool we use for walking following an injury to a leg or foot. Once the injury is healed, we put the crutch away and walk on our own. The word *crutch* is also used to describe something or someone we may rely on short-term to help us get through a period of challenge. The term takes on a bad connotation, though, when used to describe something that we've become unnecessarily dependent upon, usually to the detriment of our physical, mental, or emotional progress.

A crutch is supposed to be temporary, just until we heal, or until we can get by on our own. It's not supposed to be permanent, even when our crutch is someone important to us. One of the hardest things to accept is that not everyone is meant to be in our lives forever. Some people are meant to be with you for the long-term, of course—your spouse, your children, your siblings, your parents, and your closest friends. But then there are those God brings across your path for a season, maybe a mentor, a teacher, or a guide of some sort to help you through a certain stage of life or a difficult time.

If God didn't move them away, we would become too dependent. Instead of helping us, they would hinder us. Their presence might limit our growth.

You have to be big enough to recognize when someone's part in your life story is over. It doesn't mean the person is bad. You still can be friends. You still can love and respect each other. But you must accept that everything changes. To move forward, you have to let go.

> *Just as God supernaturally brings people into our lives, He will supernaturally move some out.*

Just as God supernaturally brings people into our lives, He will supernaturally move some out. When a person walks away and you think you can't live without them, that's God saying, "It's time for you to go to a new level."

You don't need someone to constantly think for you, drive you, believe in you, and encourage you. You can do that for yourself. If you are to keep growing, eliminate your dependency on crutches.

Don't try to talk people into loving you. Don't try to persuade them to stay beyond their usefulness. *Let them go.*

Your destiny is not tied to your mentor's. His or her leaving will launch you ahead. It's not a step back, it's a step up. When someone walks away, it's not an accident. God will open new doors. You will discover greater strength and new talents. God may be preparing to bring in someone even *better* for the future.

The Gift of Good-Bye

When my mentor from our television broadcasts left, I had a choice. I could either mope around in self-pity or move toward my destiny. I came to realize that there's something called "the gift of good-bye."

You may not realize it at first, but losing your crutch is a gift from God. Don't be sad. Rejoice.

I saw this principle in action during my father's ministry whenever someone announced he or she was leaving the congregation. They expected my father to be down and discouraged that they were leaving. So the person was often shocked when he seemed happy at their departure.

He never tried to talk them into staying, or to convince them they were making a mistake. My father was always very gracious. He always thanked them, prayed over them, and then he walked them to the door. He didn't say it, but I know what he was thinking: *The sooner you go, the better for both of us.*

You want people in your life who are supposed to be there. When God wants them present in your life, they don't find fault in everything you do, and you don't have to manipulate them to stay. That's what I love about our church members at Lakewood. There are so many, I can't know most of them by name. I can't call them personally. But I know they don't come to church because they need me. They come because God led them to our church. They don't need me to touch them. They need God to touch them.

When God sends people your way, you don't have to play up to them and do everything perfectly to keep them happy. You don't have to walk on eggshells trying not to offend them. You don't need friends who are hard to please. If someone tries to manipulate you like that, let go and walk away. You don't need anyone else to fulfill your destiny.

I love this Scripture verse: "They went out from us, but they were not of us; for if they had been of us, they would have continued with us" (1 John 2:19 NKJV). When people leave your life, they are no longer a part of your destiny. Their time is over. If you stay open, God will give you people who are not just *with* you, but *for* you.

That's a big difference. When you're only *with* me, you're there as long as I perform perfectly, as long as I give you everything you need, as long as I don't make any mistakes. But when you're not just with me but you're *for* me, you believe the best in me.

You don't try to control me. You give me room to make mistakes. You don't need my attention all the time. You give more to the relationship than you take away. That's the kind of people God wants to bring into your life. You don't have to *try* to make this happen. Just be your best each day, and God will bring you divine connections. And then when the season for that relationship is over, you don't have to be upset. You can let the other person leave with your blessing, continuing to love and respect him or her.

I've learned this: God will always bring the right people into your life, but you have to let the wrong people walk away. The right people will never show up if you don't clear out the wrong people.

Driving Dependence

Be wary of people who play up to your weaknesses as a way to convince you that you need them in your life. They'll try to make you think you're not smart enough on your own. You're not talented enough, and you need them to make up for what you're lacking. Don't believe those lies.

Years ago there was a bright young lady who moved from a small town to work for our ministry. (I'll call her Diana here, but that's not her real name.) I noticed she always had a young man drop her off for work. One day, I asked her if she didn't have a car.

"Oh, I have a car," she said. "I drove everywhere in my small town. But when I moved here, my friend told me the city is so big and so complicated to drive in and since I'm not used to driving on the freeways, he would have to bring me to work every day."

I asked Diana if she ever planned to get behind the wheel herself, and she said probably not because her friend told her traffic is just so congested and difficult.

She was using this man as a crutch, and it appeared he might be manipulating her, controlling her for some reason, so I felt I had to say something.

"Diana, you are extremely talented," I said. "Do not allow anyone to convince you that you cannot drive on our freeways. I know eighteen-year-olds who drive every day in this city."

Diana shared with her friend what I'd said, and he still insisted that the streets were too dangerous for her and that she would get lost.

I told Diana that it seemed this young man was trying to make her dependent on him and that if he was a true friend, he would teach her how to get around so she could build up confidence enough to drive alone.

About a month later Diana told me that she'd driven to work on her own for the first time.

"That's great. I knew you could do it!" I said.

Then I asked how it had been to drive on the freeways.

"Oh, I don't drive on them," she said. "I take the side streets."

It should have taken Diana a half hour to drive to work. Instead it took her an hour. I encouraged her to keep driving and to work her way up to the freeways.

A month later she did it. Now Diana drives all over the city, and, isn't it interesting that the young man she was leaning on is no longer around?

He was interested in Diana only if he could keep her dependent on him and feeling that she owed him something. People like that are not true friends.

> *You don't need people in your life who try to limit you.*

They are not helping you. They are hindering you. You don't need people in your life who try to limit you. Let them go, and God will bring you the right people.

Be a Do-It-Yourself Person

God told Moses to tell Pharaoh, "Let my people go."

Moses said, "God, I can't do that. I stutter. I'm not a good speaker. Please send someone else" (see Exodus 4:10, 13). God decided that Moses' brother, Aaron, who was a good communicator, should accompany him. God told Moses: "You'll speak to [Aaron] and tell him what to say.... He'll act as your mouth, but you'll decide what comes out of it" (Exodus 4:15–16 The Message). Moses fully intended to use his brother as a crutch. He took Aaron with him. But I love what happened. When they stood before Pharaoh, just as Aaron stepped up to speak, something rose up inside Moses. He felt it was his time.

Moses put his shoulders back and held his head high and, together, they said: "Thus says the Lord God of Israel: 'Let My people go'" (Exodus 5:1 NKJV).

Moses wanted his voice to be heard, too. You don't need your friend to speak for you. You don't need your neighbor to drive for you. You don't need anyone to tell you what to do. You are equipped. God wouldn't have presented you with opportunities if He had not already given you everything you need.

God has equipped you. You are anointed. You are empowered. You are well able. Don't let anyone play upon your supposed "weaknesses." Yes, there may be times when you need help, and that's fine. But don't let someone do for you what you can do for yourself. Don't become too dependent on others. Don't use crutches when you are able to walk on your own.

God would never have told Moses to go speak in front of Pharaoh unless He knew Moses could do it. You may have some limitations, but you don't need a crutch. You have been equipped with everything you need to fulfill your destiny. You can make your own decisions. God has given you wisdom to run your own life. You don't need somebody constantly telling you what to do and what not to do.

It's good to hear other people's opinions. It's good to listen to advice. But understand, you can also receive input from God. You can hear that *still, small voice* from God's Holy Spirit. You have a direct line to the throne of God. And if somebody is always trying to tell you what to do, just say, "Thanks, but no thanks. God and I are on speaking terms."

You Have a Direct Connection to God

A congregation member once said to my father, "My friend prayed for me. He said God wants me to go to Africa and be a missionary. What do you think?"

My father said, "It's your decision, but if you go to Africa based on his advice, make sure you take that friend so he can tell you when to come back home!"

You don't need someone else to tell you what God wants *you* to do! Walk with God on your own. I was reminded of this when a young lady asked my advice on a relationship issue.

"This man that I hardly even know is saying God told him that I was supposed to marry him."

I had to laugh because she is a beautiful young lady. Then I told her not to take this guy too seriously, because every single guy who sees her will think the same thing. "He's just the only one bold enough to tell you," I said.

You can hear from God for yourself. You don't need a crutch. Listen to the *still, small voice* inside you. God sometimes speaks to us through an impression that is always consistent with His written Word, the Bible.

Judges 6–7 tells the story of a man named Gideon who faced three armies marching against him and his men. As Gideon prepared for the battle, God said, "You have too many people with you. If you win with this many, you'll be tempted to think you did it on your own strength and I won't get the credit I deserve."

To trim the numbers, God told him to let everybody who was afraid go home.

I can imagine Gideon was depressed and fearful he'd lose the battle because he didn't have enough warriors.

But God wasn't done trimming down his army.

"Gideon, you still have too many people," God said.

His army dropped from 32,000 to just 300 by the time God was done. I'm sure Gideon thought his depleted forces would be wiped out.

But it's not important how many you have on your side. What is important is having the right people on your side. Gideon and his three hundred men defeated tens of thousands of enemy troops.

Quality, Not Quantity, Counts

If you're not willing to let people walk away, you'll miss out on God's best. Don't be surprised if God streamlines your own army. If that happens, know that He is not trying to take you backward. He's getting you prepared for a new level. When you quit depending on others, you will experience victories that had seemed impossible before, and you will step into a greater anointing

Years ago, I didn't think public speaking was a possibility for me. I'm too shy. But today, almost every week, I speak to thousands. That tells me God doesn't give us half the talent we need. He gives us *all* we need.

God did not create you to be dependent on anyone else as an adult. Do not rely on another person to pray for you, to speak for you, to believe for you, to encourage you. Throw down the crutches and walk on your own. Do not depend on anyone to do for you what you can do for yourself.

Look inside and tap into the power God put in you. Like Moses, you will rise up with a new confidence. Yes, it may stretch you. But you will discover new gifts and talents. God will bring the right people at the right time. I believe and declare you will become everything He's created you to be.

CHAPTER TWELVE

Don't Live for the Approval of Others

When I announced plans to move our church to the former Compaq Center, 99 percent of the congregation supported the move. Most were very excited. But there was one very vocal opponent. He made sure I heard about his opposition. Every week after the service, he would come find me in the visitors' reception area. He would say, "You know, your father said he would never move the church. You're making a big mistake. And I just want to let you know if you move it, I'm not following."

I thought, *Is that a promise?*

Everyone has a right to an opinion. But he didn't know what I was feeling on the inside. He didn't know what God was speaking to me. I could not allow him to stop the move. The easy thing is to play it safe. But be strong and follow what God has put in your heart.

The easy thing is to play it safe. But be strong and follow what God has put in your heart.

I've learned I may have to displease a few people so I don't displease God. I never like to see anyone leave the church, but if I'll stay true to my heart, I believe for every one who leaves the church, God will send me two dozen more in return.

Now when somebody threatens to leave, I just smile and say, "Can I show you the door? The sooner the better." (Okay, I may not say it, but that's what I think!)

Too many people base their worth and value on what other people think of them. They worry if others like them, approve of them, or think of them as important. Because of such insecurities, they are constantly playing up to others, trying to win their favor and to meet others' every expectation.

When you do that, you set yourself up to be controlled and manipulated. You allow others to put you in a box. Some people do not follow their dreams because they are so concerned about falling from the good graces of others. You may lose the approval of others if you follow your own dreams. But if your friends approve of you only when you meet their expectations, they aren't true friends. They are manipulators. They are controllers.

There is a real freedom when you realize you don't need the approval of others. You have almighty God's approval. Don't try to keep everyone around you happy. Some people don't even want to be happy. You've got to be secure enough to say, "I love you, but I won't allow you to control me. You may not give me your blessing, but that's okay. I have God's blessing. And I'm not a people pleaser; I'm a God pleaser."

Take charge of your life. If you're being manipulated and pressured into being someone you are not, it's not the other person's fault, it's your own fault. You control your destiny. You can be nice. You can be respectful. But do not allow anyone to make you feel guilty for being your own person.

Life is too short to spend it trying to keep others happy. You cannot please everyone. To fulfill your destiny, stay true to your heart. Do not let anyone squeeze you into a mold.

Seek God's Approval

When my father went to be with the Lord and I stepped up to pastor the church, an older gentleman I had known my whole life took me aside and said, "If this is to work, here's what you have to do."

He told me how to run the church, how to minister, how to lead the staff, how to move forward. I listened to his advice. I was very open. But nothing he said matched what I felt on the inside.

I prayed. I searched my own heart about what he'd told me, but nothing bore witness. I risked falling out of his good graces by following my own heart. The decision was difficult, but I went for God's approval, not this man's.

I stepped out and followed my heart, and God blessed my decision. The church thrived. I did fall out of the man's good graces, however. He wasn't happy that I did not take his advice.

Those who become upset if you don't do things their way are not really *for* you. They don't have your best interests at heart. If they were for you, they would be mature enough to say, "Even if you don't do it my way, even if you don't take my suggestions, I'll support you. I'll be behind you because I'm your friend and I want to see you succeed."

That's a true friend.

When I didn't take this man's advice, he was no longer on my side. It wasn't something big and obvious, just subtle things. I'd walk into a room and I could feel his sense of disapproval.

Thank God I didn't need his approval. He wasn't God. He wasn't sitting on the throne. He didn't write the plan for my life.

I looked to God instead and said, "He may not be for me, but I know You are for me. God, I may not have his approval, but I know I have Your approval. That's all that really matters."

I pressed forward doing what God put in my heart to do. God not only brought our church through that transition, but He brought us through bigger and better and greater than we ever had been. God knows what He is doing.

Be Secure in Who God Made You to Be

Before you were born, God stamped His approval on you. You don't need to buy the friendship of anyone else. If you start a friendship off by buying it, you'll have to continue paying to keep it going. When you grow tired of doing what your new friend wants you to do, the friendship will end. They'll cut you loose. You are better off trusting God to bring you divine connections.

God will always give you direction for your life. Other people may have suggestions. They may have ideas. But God speaks directly to you. The Holy Spirit lives inside you. He leads you. He guides you.

Yes, be open and listen to your parents and mentors and friends, but follow your own heart. There is a still, small voice; a knowing inside you—that is God talking to you.

Be careful, though, about those who always have a word from the Lord to share with you. I grew up in church. I've heard a lot of words from the Lord, some of them right on, some of them way off. But anytime someone gives you a "word from the Lord," it should simply confirm what you already know on the inside.

When that older man told me how to run the church, his words didn't agree with anything that I was feeling. They were totally foreign. I've learned that God will not tell others what He wants for my life without telling me Himself. God and I are on speaking terms. We talk every single day.

If I would have been a people pleaser and run the church like that man wanted and ministered like he told me, I wouldn't be where I am today. I would have his approval, but what good would that do me?

I would rather have the approval of the Creator of the universe. I would rather have the God who spoke the worlds into existence smiling down on me.

To Please God, You May Have to Displease People

This was a difficult concept for me because I want to please everybody. I want to be liked. When you follow what's in your heart, though, some may be unhappy with you. They may not understand. You may fall out of their favor. You may even lose friends.

When my mother was twenty-six years old, my father decided to leave the church that he had been pastoring for many years. The old congregation wasn't really behind his new doctrine of faith and healing and miracles. My mother had longtime friends in that church. Instead of celebrating my mother's new beginning, those friends wouldn't have anything to do with her.

Lifelong friends walked away, all because my father decided to launch out on his own. I love what Jesus said in Luke 18:29–30: "Everyone who has given up house or wife or brothers or parents or children, for the sake of the Kingdom of God, will be repaid many times over in this life" (NLT). Notice it doesn't say when you get to heaven God will bless you. It says, right here on the earth, if you give up anything for God's sake, He will reward you more than you can even imagine.

> *If you give up anything for God's sake, He will reward you more than you can even imagine.*

My mother lost all of her friends. They wouldn't give her their approval anymore. But can I tell you God is a faithful God? My mom found many more new friends, even more than she could ever have imagined.

My parents could have played it safe, stayed in that church, and held on to the approval of those friends. They could have stayed aboard that boat, but God asked them to board another.

At some point God will ask you to get out of the boat. It wouldn't be as difficult if all of your friends and family members encouraged you to do that, too. But most of the time, your friends will advise you to stay put.

Some gave my parents an ultimatum: "Stay here and we'll support you. But if you leave, you're on your own."

That's when my parents followed the words of the apostle Paul: "I'm not trying to win the approval of people, but of God" (Galatians 1:10 NLT).

God Will Not Forsake You

Don't be held back by the fear that people will abandon you. If they leave you, you don't need them. God said He would never leave us or forsake us. So if they walk away when you truly need them, they aren't of God. We know God can't lie. So you can draw the conclusion: *If they left me, they weren't a part of my destiny. If they don't want to be my friends, I don't need them. If they don't give me their approval, it's no big deal. I have God's approval.*

Sometimes a well-meaning person may try to hold you back. Jesus told Peter that He was going to Jerusalem "and suffer many things" (Matthew 16:21 NKJV). Peter said, "Far be it from You, Lord; this shall not happen to You!" (v. 22 NKJV).

Peter loved Jesus. He was concerned about Him, but he didn't understand Jesus' destiny. Others may not understand what God has put in your heart. You don't have to write them off, but you do have to be strong and follow your destiny, with or without their approval.

That's what Jesus did. He looked at Peter and said, "Get behind Me, Satan! You are an offense to Me, for you are not mindful of the things of God, but the things of men" (v. 23 NKJV). He was strong. He was firm. But He wasn't disrespectful.

He didn't say, "I'm never speaking to you again because you don't agree with Me."

Jesus simply spoke the truth in love and went on to fulfill His destiny without Peter's approval.

In the same way, you will not become everything God has created you to be if you must have the approval of everyone around you. I would love to tell you that all of your family and friends will be there to cheer you on and encourage you and support you. Most of the time, though, somebody will be jealous. Someone won't understand. Some will try to belittle or discredit you.

You can't please everyone, so let those who disapprove know you love them and that the only approval you need is God's. Tell them, "I have almighty God's approval, and He has promised if I give up anything for His sake, He will reward me greatly."

That's a powerful attitude. When you are secure enough in who you are, you will be confident in the destiny in front of you. Keep being your best. Do that, and nothing will stop you.

The Creator of the universe will break down every barrier and take you to where you're supposed to be. Keep a good attitude. Shake off the negative voices. Don't pay any attention to the naysayers trying to discredit you and make you look bad. If you stay in faith, the more they talk negatively of you, the higher God will take you.

Focus on Winning the Favor of God

The Scripture says promotion doesn't come from people but from God. You may not have the approval of someone "important," but focus on winning the favor of God instead.

How do you do that? By being a person of excellence, by having an attitude of faith, by blessing your enemies, by being good to people. When you do that, you curry favor with the Creator. He will fight your battles. God will bring you those divine connections: people who celebrate you and cheer you on.

I love loyal people. I love faithful people. I have friends, family, and staff in my life right now who I know will give me their approval until the day I die.

God has put people in my life who celebrate me and give me the freedom to become who He created me to be. He has put the same type of people in your life—the right people. So don't waste your time trying to win the approval of those who would manipulate you and put you into a box of their design. Your destiny is too great for that. You don't need their approval. You have the approval of almighty God!

CHAPTER THIRTEEN

Freedom from Competition

I was out jogging one day and I noticed a person in front of me about a quarter of a mile. I could tell he was running a little slower than me and I thought, *Good. I'll try to catch him.*

I had about a mile to go on my path before I needed to turn off. So I started running faster and faster. Every block, I was gaining on him just a little bit. After just a few minutes I was only about one hundred yards behind him, so I really picked up the pace and pushed myself. You would have thought I was running in the last leg of an Olympic competition. I was determined to catch him.

Finally, I did it. I caught and passed him by. On the inside I felt so good. *I beat him!* Of course, he didn't even know we were racing. After I passed him I realized I'd been so focused on competing against him that I'd missed my turn.

I had gone nearly six blocks past it. I had to turn around and go all the way back.

Isn't that what happens in life when we focus on competing with our co-workers, or our neighbors, trying to outdo them or trying to prove that we are more successful or more important? We spend our time and energy running after them, and we miss out on our own paths to our God-given destinies.

Many of us would see our lives reach higher levels if we would quit competing with everyone around us and focus on our own races to be the best at what God made us to be. It takes a lot of energy, physical and emotional, to constantly be in competition with our neighbors, co-workers, or family members.

When you let go of that need to compete, it's very freeing. Tell yourself, *I don't have to impress anybody today. I have nothing to prove. I'm secure in who I am. I don't have to keep up with anyone. I'm not in that race.*

The problem with unhealthy competition is that it's a never-ending cycle. There will always be somebody ahead of you; someone with a better job, a bigger circle of friends, a nicer car, or more money in the bank. It's a very freeing thing when you realize you are not in a competition with your neighbors, friends, or co-workers. The only person you are competing with is yourself.

Be the Best You Can Be

Know that the "Best Possible You" may not be as successful as your neighbor, but that's okay. The best you may not be as thin as your sister, but that's fine. The best you may not be as talented, as dynamic, or as outgoing as your co-worker, but that's all right, too.

Be comfortable with the person God made you to be. You can't get distracted and lose your focus by comparing yourself to others. Run your own race.

I realize I may not be the best minister in the world. I'm okay with that. But I'm dedicated to being the best minister I can be. I may not be as good a father as some other men, but that's okay. I'm not competing with anyone. I'm trying to be the best father I can be. I may not be the ideal husband. (Don't say, "Amen," Victoria.) But I'm working to be the best husband I can be.

I have a friend who puts me to shame in the way he is so romantic with his wife. He plans big weekend getaways with her. He writes beautiful poetry to her. He'll go on for hours about how beautiful she is in their conversations.

I want to tell him, "Would you quit doing that? You're making me look bad." But I've learned I'm not Romeo. I'm Joel-*eo*. God made us different on purpose. You can be inspired by others. You can be challenged to rise higher. But don't condemn yourself if someone else does better at one thing or another.

Some people are stronger in certain areas, but we all have our strengths. My romantic friend writes beautiful poems to his wife, but I've written some pretty good books!

God Did Not Create Us to Compare and Compete

Some people are insecure because they pay too much attention to what others are doing, where they are going, what they are wearing or driving. Instead, they should stay focused on their own goals. You're not anointed to compete with others. God gave you the grace to be who He has called you to be.

When you have unhealthy competitive feelings, life is a constant struggle. You will never be good enough because as soon as you catch up to one person you'll find another ahead of you. That's not the way to find happiness in your everyday life, is it?

Ladies may have friends who wear a much smaller dress size, but their attitude should be, *I'm not feeling inferior because I can't measure up to those standards. No, I'm wearing this size 14 like nobody has ever worn a 14 before. I'll dress it up. Accessorize it and strut around like it's the hottest thing going!*

I've known ladies who normally wouldn't stand out because of their looks, but they make themselves attractive because they carry themselves with confidence and seem so secure in who God made them to be. You meet a woman like that and you can't help but think, *She's got it going on.*

Confident, happy, and secure people stand out because what's on the inside shows on the outside. They are so comfortable in their own skins they're not easily intimidated. They don't feel inferior if they don't wear the best fashions or have the perfect physiques. They understand they're not in a competition. They're focused on being the best they can be.

> *Confident, happy, and secure people stand out because what's on the inside shows on the outside.*

Take what God has given you—the height, the weight, the personality—and make the most of it. Dress it up and wear it proudly. I see too many people constantly frustrated and down about their looks, their height, or their weight. They're always fighting to fix what they don't like about themselves instead of accepting themselves.

Don't misunderstand me, I'm all for people improving their health by staying in shape, working out, and eating right. I'm not saying we should be sloppy. But we have to realize that genetics plays a role.

Our parents, grandparents, and God determine our genes. Those genes, for the most part, determine our ideal size, weight, and height, as well as how much hair we have and whether we have strong, athletic, muscular physiques or one like my brother, Paul!

Most of our features are predetermined by our genetic makeup. We may be able to adjust that weight 15 or 20 percent. Still, if your genes are set for a weight of 150 pounds, no matter what you do, you can't maintain your weight for long at 100 pounds. That's not who God made you to be.

If you feel you have to compete with someone who is naturally fifty pounds lighter, you are setting yourself up for frustration and feelings of inferiority. You're competing with someone who is not even in your race.

Stay in Your Own Race

Your race to be the best is yours alone, and it is yours to win. God will not measure you against others. He won't judge you according to what a co-worker accomplishes, what your neighbor drives, or whether you are as thin as your best friend.

God will judge you by what you've done with the gifts He gave you. He'll be interested in how confident and secure you are. Or did you feel insecure and beat yourself up while comparing yourself to others?

I was watching the Indianapolis 500 on television and admiring the sleek race cars. They're low to the ground, extremely aerodynamic. They are equipped with huge engines that power them at 200 miles per hour down a straightaway. They can take curves at 100 miles an hour. They're quick. They're fast. They're precise.

But in spite of all these strengths, the Indy cars also have weaknesses. They only have room for the driver. They're not that comfortable. The inside is all metal and equipment. No A/C. No stereo. No luxury. Why is that? The Indy cars are designed for a specific purpose, to be the best in their particular race.

Victoria and I have a Suburban SUV that can easily hold eight people comfortably. The trunk area is so big we can put all of our bicycles and luggage back there. The SUV has air-conditioning and a nice stereo system and sits so high you feel like the king of the road.

But if you took our Suburban out on the Indianapolis 500 track, the race cars would run circles around us. The SUV would be lapped again and again. If you tried to take a turn at 100 miles an hour, you would hear the angels say, "Welcome to heaven." The Suburban couldn't handle the Indy track. The big, comfortable vehicle would be competing in a race it was never designed to run.

On the other hand, if Victoria and I traded our SUV for an Indy race car and tried to use it every day, we might draw a lot of attention—those cars have a lot of sizzle—but I don't know where we'd put the kids or the groceries. If you hit a pothole in one of those things, you'd feel like you were in an earthquake. In a few days we'd be asking for our SUV back.

Each type of car is designed for a specific purpose. The Suburban won't be winning any races on the track at the Indianapolis 500, and the Indy race cars aren't any soccer mom's choice for an everyday vehicle. Still, both types of cars have incredible strengths. The key is to make sure you run each of them in the right race.

Today, you may be the human version of that Indy car with the speed, the agility, and the looks. If that's you, go for it. Be the best you can be. Run your race.

If you're not an Indy-model person, don't feel bad about it. There is nothing wrong with saying, "Those are not my strengths. I'll never be that fast. I'll never be that agile. I don't look that sporty, but I'm okay with that." After all, the SUV may not have as much sizzle, but there are far more of them on the road than Indy cars.

Know What You Are and What You Are Not

In the New Testament, John was baptizing hundreds of people and making a name for himself when someone asked him: "Who are you?" (John 1:19 NKJV).

John knew what they were really asking, and without missing a beat, he said, "I am not the Christ" (v. 20 NKJV).

John knew what he was, and he also knew what he was not. It's just as important to know what you're not because if you don't realize your limitations, you may be drawn away from what God anointed you to do. Then you will be in a constant struggle.

Pride and competition can make it hard sometimes to admit what you are not. It takes a secure person to say, "I'm not gifted in that area, but I have my own talents."

When I hear our Spanish pastor, Marcos Witt, preach and then burst into song at the end of his sermon, I'm in awe of him. Of course, he is a musical person. He's won several Grammys, but he makes it seem effortless when he sings. I heard him the other day, and his singing gave me chill bumps up and down my arms.

My first thought was, *God, that's not fair. How come he's got two good gifts? He can minister and sing.*

Then I realized, I've got two good gifts, too. I can minister, plus I'm good at picking Spanish-speaking ministers with many talents!

You see, there is always a way for us to feel good about ourselves without comparing or competing. You can feel good about yourself right where you are. You have an anointing to be you. The good news is, nobody can be a better you than you.

Be the Best You!

I read about a seven-year-old boy, Joey, who was never content with himself. He always was much more impressed with Billy. He walked like Billy and talked like Billy.

Well, Billy didn't like who he was either. He admired Corey. So Billy walked like Corey and talked like Corey. So, Joey was copying Billy, who was copying Corey.

It turned out that Corey had an inferiority complex, too. He was much more impressed with Frankie. So he walked like Frankie and talked like Frankie.

Thus, Joey was copying Billy, who was copying Corey, who was copying Frankie.

You'll never guess what happened next. Frankie wasn't happy with himself either. He admired Joey. So he was walking like Joey, talking like Joey.

All right, let me see if I've got this straight: Joey was copying Billy, who was copying Corey, who was copying Frankie, who was copying Joey! Joey was copying himself!

This story points out the truth that the people you want to be like, very often, want to be like you. They may admire you just as much as you admire them. So there is nothing wrong with looking up to people. It's good to show respect and admiration. But don't give up your identity for theirs. Run your own race. You have something great to offer.

> *Run your own race. You have something great to offer.*

You Are Anointed in Your Own Way

The first time Victoria and I went to Billy Graham's home to visit him and Ruth, we were so honored. When we walked into the living room and saw Billy Graham sitting in a chair, it was like seeing Moses. He is one of the heroes of our faith. I've always had the utmost respect and admiration for him. I have looked up to him and held him in awe. It was an honor to meet this giant of our faith.

As I shook his hand, he said, "I love watching you on television, and I just so admire how you can take that message of hope around the world."

That is so amazing, I thought. *I've admired him my whole life, and somehow he's found something in me to appreciate.*

Billy has a very gracious personality, but we all need to believe that we are special. You are anointed in your own unique way. You are gifted. You have accomplishments.

You may tend to see how great everybody else is, but let me tell you, there is something great about you. Somebody thinks you're amazing. Someone else is inspired by your life. Some even wish they could be you. You are a person to be celebrated. So put your shoulders back. Hold your head up high. You don't have to compete with anyone else. Just be the best you can be.

Accept the Gift God Has Given You

This is one of the things that threw King Saul off-track. He was doing fine. Samuel had anointed him to be king. His future looked very bright. But he didn't understand this principle.

One day he and David were in a battle. They defeated the Philistines. Everything was great until some of the women said, "Saul has slain his thousands, and David his tens of thousands" (1 Samuel 18:7 NIV).

First Samuel 18:9–10 says Saul was very angry and jealous; he never again looked at David the same way. Saul was so insecure that David's success made him feel inferior. (Saul wasn't comfortable being an SUV. He had to be that Indy race car.)

You'd think King Saul would be thrilled to have someone as skilled as David on his team. But it takes a secure person to say, "Even though I'm ahead of you, I will let you shine. I'll let you rise higher."

One of life's tests requires learning to celebrate the successes of others. You may be tempted to be jealous or critical when someone rises higher, passing you up, whether it's in the office, on a team, or in an organization. The Scripture says, "Having then gifts differing according to the grace that is given to us, let us use them" (Romans 12:6 NKJV).

The real test as to whether God continues to promote you is how well you handle the successes of others. Can you celebrate what God is doing in their lives and not be jealous and critical, or feel you are in competition with them?

Saul lost the kingdom, in part, because he could not tolerate anyone being celebrated more than him. A spirit of competition, pride, or jealousy will cause us to do things we never dreamed we would do.

Prior to that jealousy, Saul loved David. He treated him like a son. He took him into the palace. David ate dinner with Saul and his family every night. Saul never dreamed that one day he would throw a javelin at David and try to kill him. He never imagined that one day he would hunt him down in the wilderness.

What was his problem? Saul couldn't handle being number two. He couldn't stand the fact that David's reputation as a warrior had grown greater than his. Saul should have been like John the Baptist and said, "Hey, this is what I am, and this is what I'm not, and I'm okay with that."

If Saul had just been satisfied with his gift and run his race, he could have fulfilled his God-given destiny. But instead, he grew distracted. He wasted his time and energy competing with someone who was not even in his race. God had already ordained David to go further.

You have to be big enough to recognize your limits and be the best you can be. Run your race. Understand, there is nothing wrong with being who you are. Quit thinking that you have to measure up to somebody else to feel good about yourself.

My brother completed twelve years of college and became a skilled surgeon. I finished my first year of college and returned to work in our father's church. Paul and I aren't in competition with each other. We respect each other because we know who we are and we focus on being God's best.

You are in a class all by yourself. When God made you He threw away the mold. So don't compare yourself. Celebrate yourself. You have everything you need to fulfill your God-given destiny. Be comfortable in your own skin.

> *Don't compare yourself.*
> *Celebrate yourself.*

Remember, you don't have to impress anybody. You don't have to prove who you are. You are a child of the Most High God, anointed, equipped, empowered. Keep your shoulders back. Keep your head held high. Be secure in who God made you to be. If you will stay free from a spirit of competition and just run your race, you'll not only enjoy your life more, but you'll also see your gifts and talents come out to the full. Because when you celebrate others, God will celebrate you.

CHAPTER FOURTEEN

Connecting with the Right People

Your destiny is too great to reach on your own. God has already arranged supporters to speak faith into you. He has placed others in your path to inspire you, to challenge you, to help you grow and accomplish your dreams. But some people never reach their highest potential because they never get away from the wrong people.

Not everyone can go where God is taking you. Connect with those who understand your destiny, friends who appreciate your uniqueness, encouragers who can call forth your seeds of greatness. You do not need those who push you down, tell you what you can't become, and never give their approval even when you do well.

God Will Replace the Negative with the Positive

If you remove the negative people from your life, God will bring positive people into it. Is your inner circle of friends holding you back? Are those closest to you with you but not for you? If you find that it takes constant effort to win their support and encouragement, they likely don't understand your destiny.

The Scripture says, "Do not throw your pearls before swine" (Matthew 7:6 NASB). You could say your pearl is your gift, your personality. It's who you are. When you get around true friends, people who really believe in you, they won't be jealous of your gifts. They won't constantly question who you are. They won't try to talk you out of your dreams. It will be just the opposite. They'll help you polish your pearl. They'll give you ideas. They'll connect you with people they know. They'll help push you further along.

Do not waste time with people who don't value your gifts or appreciate what you have to offer. That's casting your pearl before swine. Those closest to you should celebrate who you are and be happy when you succeed. They should believe in the very best of you.

If that doesn't describe those in your inner circle, move them out. You can be nice. You can still be friends from a distance. But your time is too valuable to spend with people who are not 100 percent for you. It's not the quantity of friends that's important; it's the quality of friends. I would rather have two good friends who I know are for me 100 percent than have fifty friends who are only for me 80 percent.

Scripture shares the story (see Mark 5:22–24, 35–43) of a man named Jairus who pleaded with Jesus to come to his house where his daughter lay dying and heal her. Jesus and the man were on their way when word came by messenger: "You don't need to come. She has already died."

But Jesus replied, "Don't worry about it. She'll be okay. We're coming anyway."

Jesus would not let anyone go with Him except Peter, James, and John. They were members of His inner circle. Now, the others with Him were good people, too. They loved the Lord. But Jesus said, "I only want these three to go."

Why was that? Jesus knew when He entered the room where the little girl was dead, He needed to be surrounded by true believers who would not question who He was or what He intended to do. Jesus did not need doubters or skeptics asking, "Are You sure You're the Son of God? Have You ever done this before? What if it doesn't work? Do You have a backup plan?"

When you are in the heat of the battle and need God's favor, you can't afford to have naysayers and doubters in your inner circle. Jesus did not need to hear things like, "Do You really think she'll get well? My grandmother died of that same thing."

> *When you are in the heat of the battle and need God's favor, you can't afford to have naysayers and doubters in your inner circle.*

We all need people who are joined in spirit with us and say, "If you're bold enough to believe, count me in. I'm bold enough to agree with you."

You need supporters who will come into agreement with you and release their faith, not doubters who tell you what you can't do.

When Jesus entered the child's room, all those gathered were distraught and weeping.

"Don't be upset. She's not dead," Jesus said. "She's only asleep."

Some mourners turned on Jesus, mocking Him.

His response is one of the keys to living a life of victory. Mark 5:40 says, "They laughed and jeered at Him. But [Jesus] put them all out" (AMP).

Jesus showed them the door. His attitude was, "I don't need your doubt."

If you find yourself surrounded by people who mock and doubt you, show them the door just as Jesus did.

He didn't allow anyone into the room except the girl's parents and His inner circle. He then spoke to the child and she came back to life. Jesus could have healed her in front of the laughing and mocking crowd. He's the Son of God. He could do anything.

But I believe Jesus wanted to make the point that your inner circle is extremely important. If Jesus took the time to weed out the doubters, surely you and I should be that concerned about our own inner circles.

Evaluate Your Team

Who's speaking into your life? Who are you giving your time and energy to? Who are you meeting for lunch every day? Who are you texting?

Are those in your inner circle building you up or tearing you down? Are they inspiring you to go further, or are they telling you what you can't do? Are they modeling excellence, integrity, generosity, and godliness?

Or are they lazy compromisers, going nowhere? Don't waste your time with anyone who drags you down instead of making you better.

I once worked with a man who just wore down the entire office. He spoiled every fresh idea that came along. He was a "fun sponge," soaking up all the enthusiasm and laughter and draining us dry. When he announced after many years that he was leaving, we held a farewell party, but I have to admit I was celebrating something different than he was. His departure lifted a burden off our entire staff. I did my best to act sad, but on the inside I was jumping up and down. Once he was gone, it was like night turned to day. We didn't realize how much one negative person in our inner circle could affect the rest of the team.

You may not be aware of the draining effect a negative person is having on you. How much more could you accomplish, grow, and enjoy if you moved out those who are with you but not for you? Make sure the people in your inner circle believe in you. They should celebrate your gifts and push you ahead, not hold you back.

I can't think of anything worse than to come to the end of life and realize that someone you trusted kept you from becoming the person God created you to be. You may be fearful of losing a friend and being lonely, but you never give up something for God that He doesn't make up for by giving you something better in return.

If you'll make the change, God will not only give you new friends, He will give you better friends. Friends about whom you don't have to wonder, *Are they for me or against me?* Friends who don't try to manipulate you into who they want you to be, but rather they celebrate you and help you become who God has created you to be.

Beware the Negative and Needy

As a minister, I expect that people in need will come to me. I welcome them and try to help any way I can. That said, there are some people who just keep coming back for more. These negative, needy people constantly dump their problems on your doorstep and expect you to clean them up. They know only one song, and it's sad. After crying with them through eight or nine verses, you realize they don't want to be helped or encouraged. They just want to unload on you. They bask in the attention. They suck the energy right out of you. Spend an hour with them, and you'll feel like you've run a marathon.

Needy people can abuse your kindness. Sometimes, you have to put up with their difficulties and love them back to wholeness, but you can't spend your whole life knee-deep in their troubles. You have a God-given destiny to fulfill. I've found that in some cases the best help you can give negative, needy people is to not help them at all. Otherwise, you are just enabling their dysfunction.

Iron Sharpens Iron

Proverbs 27:17 says, "As iron sharpens iron, so one person sharpens another" (NIV). Are your friends making you stronger? Are they challenging you to become a better parent, a better spouse, a better co-worker, a better member of your community?

You cannot soar with the eagles as long as you're hanging out with the turkeys. So rid yourself of relationships that drain you, drag you down, or leave you feeling the worse for wear.

When I was in my early twenties, just a couple of months ago (Don't laugh!), I regularly went to a very nice, good-hearted young lady for my haircuts. Unfortunately, every snip of the scissors brought another tale of woe. She unloaded on me even as she trimmed me up. Month after month, year after year, she poured into my ears her stories of being mistreated by her bosses, her relatives, and her girlfriends, and on and on.

Every time I left her shop I had less hair, but my head felt heavier. I was depressed. She was a very good sad storyteller. She reminded me of the guy who was about to jump off a bridge and end his life. A good Samaritan ran over to save him, saying, "Don't jump! Don't jump! Tell your troubles to me instead!"

Two hours later, they both jumped.

That's the way this young lady was. I did my best to encourage her. I would pray with her. I gave her money. I sent her customers. It was never enough. One day I realized what I'm telling you: I could not go where God was taking me with her in my life. I love her. I pray for her. I miss her good haircuts, but I couldn't fulfill my God-given destiny with her putting poison in my ears month after month.

So, I made a change.

You, too, may have to change where you do business, where you play ball, where you work, where you shop. Your time on this earth is brief and valuable. You have a destiny to fulfill, and you can't make it happen if you are carrying needy and negative people on your back. The solution is found in Mark 5:40. Show them the door. Be kind. Be polite. But pull away.

Make a Leap Toward Your Destiny

In the Scripture, you'll find the story of Elizabeth, who was struggling to have a baby. In those days a lady was despised if she couldn't produce a child. Finally, late in life, Elizabeth conceived. She was so excited about being able to have this baby.

For the first few weeks Elizabeth was just on cloud nine. Her dream was coming to pass. Then, as the delivery date approached, she began to worry. She'd never had a baby before. She was hoping and praying that everything was okay, but three months, four months, five months passed and she hadn't felt any movement.

The longer it went, the more concerned she became. Then one day there was a knock on her door; an unexpected guest. It was her younger cousin Mary, a teenager. Elizabeth opened the door. Mary gave her a great big hug and said, "Elizabeth! Congratulations! I've heard the great news that you're having a baby."

The Scripture says in Luke 1:41, "When Elizabeth heard Mary's greeting, the baby leaped in her womb" (AMP).

At that moment Elizabeth knew the child was alive. She knew the promise would come to pass!

God has designated people to come into your life to make your baby, your dream or promise, leap. These are positive, faith-filled people who will help bring your dreams to life and your promises to pass.

Mary, of course, was a divine connection. She was ordained by the Creator of the universe to bring hope, faith, and vision into Elizabeth's life. She didn't even have to say anything profound. She just said hello, and the promise within Elizabeth came to life.

God has already lined up your Mary. When you meet the right people, they can simply say "Good morning," and your dreams will leap. That's a supernatural connection.

But here's a key: If you keep answering the door and your dreams never leap, you're answering the door for the wrong people. Don't answer the door for a gossiper, a complainer, or a user. Answer the door only for those who inspire you, encourage you, and challenge you to fulfill your God-given destiny.

> *If you keep answering the door and your dreams never leap, you're answering the door for the wrong people.*

Mary was pregnant with Jesus, the Son of God. Elizabeth was pregnant with John the Baptist. When the promise in Mary connected with the promise in Elizabeth, there was an explosion of faith. When you meet and mix with the right people, when you connect with big dreamers and big doers, then the promise in you will connect with the promises in them. You will see God show up and do something supernatural in your lives.

Like Elizabeth, you are carrying a promise. You know God has spoken to you, but maybe it's been a long time. Maybe you haven't felt any movement on the inside. Now you're thinking, *Did I hear God right? Is the promise still in me? Am I still giving birth to this promise?*

I believe God sent me today to be one of your Marys. Concerning that dream or hope of yours you're about to give up on, God is saying, "It will come to pass." The promise is in you. It's alive and well. You may not see anything happening. You may feel that you didn't hear God correctly. But God is still on the throne.

Right now He is arranging things in your favor. What He promised you, He will bring to pass. If you will receive those words by faith, you'll feel something down in your spirit; a kick, a push, a shove. What is that? That's your promise coming alive.

You are a child of the Most High God. You have seeds of greatness on the inside. There is no mistake you've made that is too large for the mercy of God. There is no obstacle too high, no sickness too great, and no dream too big. You and God are a majority.

When you hear words like that, let them take root and you will feel faith springing up. That's your baby, your promise, starting to leap. Before long you'll be convinced that you can achieve all that you desire through

God's plan. But if you are to become all He created you to be, you must fill your inner circle with people of vision, faith, and encouragement.

It's not too late. You're not too old. You haven't made too many mistakes. The promise is still alive. Now it's up to you to eliminate those who are holding you back and replace them with those who lift you up. God has already sent them to your door! Let them in, then as iron sharpens iron, you will cut through your challenges and rise higher. I believe and declare that just like with Elizabeth, you will give birth to every promise God put in your heart, and you will become everything God created you to be!

PART
IV

Travel Light

CHAPTER FIFTEEN

Forgive So You Can Be Free

We all have unfair things happen to us. We can choose to cling to that hurt and let it destroy our day-to-day happiness and poison our futures, or we can choose to release the hurt and trust God to make it up to us. You may think you can't forgive those who've hurt you, whether friends, a spouse, or co-workers. But you don't have to forgive them for their sakes; you forgive for your own sake.

When we forgive others, we take away their power to hurt us. The mistake we make so often is to hold on to hurt. We go around bitter and angry, but all we're doing is allowing those who hurt us to control our lives. The abuser, bully, or critic isn't hurt by our anger and bitterness. We're just poisoning our own lives with it.

I know people who are still mad at others who are long dead and gone. They're still bitter at their parents or a former boss or an ex-spouse who is no longer living. It's bad enough that someone hurt you once; don't let them continue to hurt you by staying angry. When you forgive someone, you set a prisoner free. That prisoner isn't the person who hurt you; the prisoner is you.

Someone may have lied about you, betrayed you, or mistreated you, but what they did was not enough to keep you from your destiny. You cannot let one divorce, one betrayal, or one bad childhood experience keep you from the awesome future God has in store for you.

Joseph's brothers betrayed him. They sold him into slavery. He could have been angry and let that one bad break, that one injustice, steal his destiny, but he let it go and moved forward to claim his rewards. There is no telling how many people in Joseph's time were kept from God's best because they went for revenge instead.

Don't let that be you. Your destiny is too great to let what someone did to you keep you from moving forward. Forgiveness is not about being nice and kind; it's about letting go so you can claim the amazing future that awaits you.

> *Forgiveness is not about being nice and kind; it's about letting go so you can claim the amazing future that awaits you.*

I know there are valid reasons to be angry. Maybe you were mistreated at a young age. It wasn't your fault. You had no control over it, and what was done to you was wrong. Forgiving doesn't mean you're excusing anything or anyone. It doesn't mean you're lessening the offense. I'm not saying you have to go be friends with someone who hurt you. I'm simply saying to let it go for your own sake. Quit dwelling on the offense. Quit replaying it in your memory. Quit giving it time and energy.

You have a destiny to fulfill. You have a joyful life to claim. Every time you let past hurts consume your thoughts, you are just reopening an old wound.

Let Your Bruises Heal

When you hold on to a hurt, you never let it heal. It's like a bruise that won't go away. If you've ever hit your arm and bruised it and then had someone bump it, you know how it hurts. You pull back because the bruised area is very sensitive. You become overly protective and you make sure no one gets close. In the same way, when you've been bruised emotionally, you tend to be overly sensitive. If your hurt isn't allowed to heal, the smallest bump will cause you to be defensive. You can't develop healthy relationships while your emotional bruises remain unhealed.

I know women who don't trust any men because one man hurt them. One messed-up male did them wrong, and they've never let it go. What's the problem? They're still bruised. They're defensive and distrustful and they think every man is out to hurt them, so they can't have healthy relationships.

It's not just women, of course. I had a man tell me a few months ago that he liked listening to me speak, but he didn't really trust me. I asked him why and he said twenty years earlier he was on the committee for his church and the pastor wronged him. He was hurt and he left the church. He's been holding on to that hurt year after year. Now he thinks all ministers are bad.

He is still bruised. The Scripture says that Jesus was sent "to announce release to the captives . . . to send forth as delivered those who are oppressed [who are downtrodden, bruised, crushed, and broken down by calamity]" (Luke 4:18 AMP). This indicates that when we're bruised, we're not free. Unfair things happen to all of us. If you want to see that bruise go away and walk into the freedom God has in store for you, you have to forgive the wrongs. You have to let go of what somebody did and move forward with your life.

There's nothing the enemy would love any more than for you to let one bad thing that happened—one messed-up person who did you wrong, or one injustice—ruin the rest of your life. Put your foot down and say, "My destiny is too great, my future is too bright, and my God is too big to let an old hurt cause me to be sour and bitter and stuck where I am. No, I'll shake it off and press forward into the bright future God has in store for me."

A woman recently told me that when she was a child, she was abused by her father. It was very unfair. She grew up confused and ashamed. She thought it was her fault. She didn't trust men. But she would do anything to try to win their approval. That's all she had known. On the inside she was bitter and angry. She had a chip on her shoulder.

For twenty-six years, she did not speak to her father. She hated him. Every time she thought about him, she became angry and bitter. But one day she heard me talking about forgiveness. She took it to heart when I said no hurt or offense should keep us from our destinies because when we forgive, it frees us to move forward.

At thirty-six years of age, she traveled to another city and found her father. When he answered the door and saw her, he didn't know what to do. She said, "Dad, I've hated you every day of my life, but I can't live with that poison in me anymore. I'm not allowing you to mess up my life. I'm forgiving you for everything you've done."

She told me that when she walked away from her father that day, it was like she'd been released from prison. Up to that point she had floundered in life, jumped in and out of relationships, and failed at several jobs. But today, ten years later, she is happily married with three beautiful children. She owns her own business and she is very successful. She says life could not be any better. Her recovery began when she let her hurt go.

God Will Settle the Account

Forgive so you can be free. Don't let the person who hurt you keep you in prison. If you let the wrong go, then God will do for you what He did for the woman mentioned above and what He did for Joseph. He'll take what was meant for your harm and He will use it for your advantage. What happened to you may have been painful, but don't waste your pain. God will use that pain to promote you.

Hebrews 10:30 says God will settle the cases of His people.

You may need some of your accounts settled. Maybe somebody stole your childhood, or somebody walked out and left you with a bunch of children to raise, or somebody cheated you in a business deal and you lost a lot of money. You could easily live angry and upset with a chip on your shoulder. Instead, be encouraged. God is a God of justice. He knows every person who hurt you and left you lonely and afraid. Nobody else may have seen it, but He saw it and He knew it wasn't right and He's saying today, "I'm settling your accounts. I'm making your wrongs right. I'm paying you back not just what you deserve but double."

God said in Isaiah, "Instead of your shame you shall have double honor, and instead of confusion they shall rejoice in their portion. Therefore in their land they shall possess double; everlasting joy shall be theirs" (61:7 NKJV). If someone lied about you and tried to make you look bad, let it go and double will come your way. Those who hurt you? Forgive them and double is on its way. The business partner who cheated you out of money? Get over the resentment and double is coming. The spouse who was unfaithful? Forgive and you will see double the joy, double the peace, and double the fulfillment.

God Never Brings You Out the Same

You may feel guilty about something that wasn't your fault. Maybe someone mistreated you and you blamed yourself. But if someone abused or took advantage of you, there is no reason to feel ashamed. Don't feel guilty. Hold your head up high. You're a child of the Most High God.

Your value doesn't go down because someone mistreated you. You are still the apple of God's eye. You are still His most prized possession. That situation may have been unfair, but if you shake off the shame and the blame and

> *Your value doesn't go down because someone mistreated you.*

do not let bitterness take root, God will make the rest of your life better than it would have been if the bad things had not happened. He will pay you back with more.

God will not allow one of His children to be constantly taken advantage of. If you're in a situation where somebody is doing you wrong or has done you wrong, don't be depressed, don't give up and think life is over. Keep believing because your payday is coming.

If your husband packed up and ran off with another woman, you don't have to be ashamed. Don't believe those voices telling you that you're not good enough or you're not attractive enough. Those are all lies. There's nothing wrong with you, there's something wrong with him. You don't have a problem, he does.

If he hurt you, he will hurt the next woman, too. Keep your head held high, knowing that God will bring justice into your life. He will settle that case.

Ours Is a God of Justice

It will help you to forgive if you'll realize that the people who hurt you have problems. Hurting people hurt others. When somebody lashes out at you or treats you unfairly, they've got unresolved issues of their own. There's no excuse for hurting you, but they are part of a chain that needs to be broken. Somebody hurt them, so in turn they hurt you. Take a merciful approach and say, "God, I know what they did was wrong. They hurt me and it was not fair, but God, I'm not looking for revenge. I ask you, God, to heal them and give them what they need."

When you can pray for your enemies and even bless those who do you wrong, as the Scripture says, God will settle your accounts (Matthew 5:44; 18:21–35). Les was raised in a very abusive environment. His father was an alcoholic and he would come home in these violent rages. Les was afraid his dad would hurt his mom or him. He was afraid for his life.

There was no peace in his home. He lived constantly on edge. One night his dad came home drunk and started abusing his mother, not only verbally but also physically. Les was fourteen years old. He stepped up and told his dad to leave his mom alone. They fought and in the end his dad threw him out of the house.

"I don't want to ever see your face again," his father told him. "If you ever set foot in this house again, it will be the last time you ever do it."

Les was devastated, so despondent he considered ending his life. He was standing on a bridge in the middle of the night about to jump when something unexpected stopped him. Les had never been to church. Religion was not part of his life. But suddenly he heard a voice say, "Don't do it. I'll be your Father. I'll be your Protector. I'll take care of you."

At that moment he felt as though warm oil was pouring all over him. It was like something he had never felt before. That was his heavenly Father showing up to bring about justice. The psalmist said, "Although my father and my mother have forsaken me, yet the Lord will take me up [adopt me as His child]" (Psalm 27:10 AMP).

Les was on his own from that day forward. He was filled with all these hurts and pain, so much rejection. But he made a decision at the very beginning that he would no longer hate his father. He forgave him and went on with his life.

He became a minister. Les had reached out to his father through the years, but the father wouldn't have anything to do with him. Then, one Sunday morning twenty-two years later, Les was standing in the pulpit and out of the blue in walked his father. It was the first time Les had seen his dad since that night when he was fourteen years old.

At the end of the service, his dad walked down to the altar with tears running down his face. He asked his son for forgiveness and also gave his life to the Lord.

God is a God of justice. I don't know how long it will take, but God has promised He'll make the wrongs right. He'll restore what the enemy has stolen. It doesn't matter how badly someone has hurt you. It doesn't matter how wrong they were. If you'll let it go, God will settle your accounts. God will pay you back.

At the end of that service, this dad and son sat down and talked. The father told his son things Les had never known before. The father said his own father was an alcoholic. He'd fought with his own mother growing up. The father's childhood home was so unstable that by the time his dad was six years old, he had already lived with four families.

There was no excuse for his father's behavior, but what I want you to see is that hurting people hurt others. Les's father had all that anger and abuse on the inside, and he made the mistake of carrying it around. He didn't realize he was passing it on to the next generation.

Forgiveness Will Free You

When Jesus rose from the dead and came back to talk with His disciples, He said, "If you forgive the sins of any, they are forgiven them; if you retain the sins of any, they are retained" (John 20:23 NKJV). When you retain a sin, you hold on to it. God was saying that when you hold on to the wrongs people have done to you, then the poison contaminates *you*. When you don't forgive, it's easy to become what you hate.

Sharon hated her father because he ran around on her mother. Sharon didn't have a good childhood. She always resented the fact that her father wasn't faithful and he wasn't there for her growing up. She couldn't stand to be around him.

But do you know that when Sharon grew up she ran around on her husband and broke up her own home? She was not there for her own children. She became exactly what she hated in her father.

That's why it's so important to forgive and let things go. The bitterness, the sin you retain, can produce the same results that hurt you. If you were raised in an abusive environment, if you come from a family filled with anger and dysfunction, instead of becoming bitter and angry, why don't you be the one to put an end to the negative cycle?

You can be the one to make a difference. Are you holding on to anger and unforgiveness and passing poison down to the next generation? Or are you willing to let it go so your family can rise to a new level?

I realize it can be very hard to forgive, especially when someone has hurt you, but God will never ask you to do something without giving you the ability to do it.

Forgiveness is a process. It doesn't happen overnight. You don't snap your fingers and make a hurt go away. That's not realistic. But if you'll continue to have the desire to forgive and ask God to help you, then little by little those negative feelings will fade. One day they won't affect you at all.

> *Forgiveness is a process. It doesn't happen overnight.*

God Will Compensate You

The Lord's Prayer is found in Matthew 6. In verse 12 Jesus says, "Forgive us our debts, as we forgive our debtors" (NKJV). When God talks about debts, He's not just talking about monetary debts. He's talking about the times when people hurt you, the times when people do you wrong. God refers to that as a debt because when you are mistreated, you may feel you are owed something.

Human nature says, "I was wronged. Now I want justice. You mistreated me. Now you've got to pay me back." But the mistake many people make is in trying to collect a debt that only God can pay. The father can't give his daughter's innocence back to her. Your parents can't pay you back for not having a loving childhood. Your spouse can't pay you back for the pain he caused by being unfaithful. Only God can truly pay you back.

If you want to be restored and whole, get on God's payroll. He knows how to make things right. He knows how to bring justice. He'll give you what you deserve. Leave it up to Him. Quit expecting people to make it up to you. They can't give you what they don't have.

Jesus told a parable about a man who owed ten thousand talents (see

Matthew 18:23–35). And the Scripture says, "He could not pay" (18:25 AMP). It doesn't say that he didn't want to, but that he could not. He didn't have the means to pay. If you're always looking for people to pay you back for the wrongs they've done, you will lead a life of frustration.

I've seen more than one person go through a bitter divorce, start a new relationship, and then make the mistake of trying to make the new person pay for what the previous spouse did. They're always trying to collect a debt, and it ends up ruining the relationship. Don't punish the person you're married to now for something that happened years ago in another relationship. They can't pay you back. Get on God's payroll.

I spoke with a man who was wronged and lost his business. It happened years ago, but he's still mad at the world. He's been with three different companies. He can't keep a job. He is bitter, and he thinks he's owed something. He's waiting to be paid back.

What's the problem? He's on the wrong payroll.

Your attitude should be, *God, You know what I've been through; You've seen every wrong, every hurt, every tear; and God, I will not be bitter, trying to get people to give me what they don't have. God, I'm leaving it up to You. I know You promised You would settle my cases. You said You would pay me back double for every injustice. So I'm letting all my family, my friends, my co-workers, my neighbors off the hook, and I'm putting my trust, my confidence, my hope in You.*

When you get on God's payroll, He'll make sure you are well compensated. If you would let people off the hook and stop thinking they owe you something, your life would go to a new level. They may have done wrong, and it may have been their fault, but it's not their fault that they can't pay you back.

If you spend your life trying to get from them what only God can give, it will ruin that relationship, and the sad thing is, you'll take that same problem into the next and the next and the next.

Mark It Paid in Full

Sometimes when I'm looking over the bills I'll see these big red letters that read "Paid in Full." Somebody has stamped it with one of those big rubber stamps. See your accounts, your hurts, as paid in full. Instead of trying to collect from those who hurt you and thinking they owe you, get that big red stamp out and mark the account as paid in full.

When you see the person who did you wrong, stamp the account paid in full in your imagination. It's very freeing to say, "Nobody owes me anything. They may have hurt me, they may have done me wrong, they may have stolen my childhood, they may have cheated me out of money, but I'm not looking for people to pay me back. I'm on God's payroll. The good news is, God never misses a payment."

Mark your accounts paid in full. Let it go. God will settle your cases. Forgive so you can be free. Forgive so God can pay you back double.

Many airlines now charge you for baggage. It's the same way in life. You can carry around baggage, but it will cost you. You can carry unforgiveness, but it will cost you the day-to-day happiness and joy you desire. You can carry bitterness, but it will cost you peace. You can haul that bag of "They Owe Me Something" around with you, but it's not free. If you do it long enough, there will be a very heavy price. It will keep you from your destiny.

You may say those who have hurt you don't deserve to be forgiven. Maybe not, but you do. If you don't forgive them, your Father in heaven can't forgive you. Why don't you let go of the baggage? Why don't you mark some accounts paid in full?

You have to forgive so that you can be free to live each day with happiness in your heart. If you will let go of the hurts and pains and get on God's payroll, God will settle your case. He will make your wrongs right. He will bring justice into your life. You will get what you deserve, and God will pay you back with double the joy, double the peace, double the favor, and double the victory.

CHAPTER SIXTEEN

Overcoming Discouragement

The people of Israel were headed toward the Promised Land, but they "became very discouraged on the way" (Numbers 21:4 NKJV). What's interesting is God was leading them, so it's not like they were actually lost. Yet, since they were so easily discouraged, they felt lost.

Little by little, they were worn down. They were good people who loved the Lord. They had seen great victories in the past. Deep down they knew they were headed toward the Promised Land, but over time they lost their passion for life.

Finally they said, "Forget it. Let's just go back to Egypt. It will not work."

What happened? They didn't pass the discouragement test. No matter how successful you are or how many victories you've had in the past, sooner or later there will be an opportunity to give up your happiness and become discouraged.

I see too many people who've allowed life to wear them down. They once were joyful. They walked with a spring in their steps. They greeted each day with excitement. But over time, they've allowed their happiness to give way to heaviness. Just like a dark cloud, it follows them everywhere they go. Unless they learn how to pass the discouragement test, it will keep them from God's best.

You may face problems and setbacks, but remember, God is still leading the way. He has given us the strength to be where we are with a good attitude. When that discouraging spirit comes knocking on the door, you don't have to answer. Just say, "No, thanks. I'm keeping my joy. I

> *You may face problems and setbacks, but remember, God is still leading the way.*

know God is in control of my life. He will allow me to go where I'm supposed to be."

There will be opposition on the way to your destiny. It may take longer than you had hoped. It may be more difficult than you'd thought. You can easily feel discouraged and think it will never work out, whatever the challenge might be. But you have to realize, on the other side of that discouragement awaits a new level of your destiny. When you pass the test, there will always be promotion.

If you are to become everything God has created you to be, you must be willing to say, "I have come too far to stop now. It may be tough. It may be taking a long time. I may not understand it, but I do know this: My God is still on the throne, and what He promised, He will bring to pass."

Have a made-up mind, and resolve that no matter what comes your way, no matter how long it takes or how impossible it looks, you are in it for the long haul. You will not lose your passion. You will pass these discouragement tests. Your victory is already on the way.

Galatians 6:9 puts it like this: "Let's not get tired of doing what is good. At just the right time we will reap a harvest of blessing if we don't give up" (NLT).

God Will Lift Your Head

Like the people of Israel, you are right next door to your promised land. Your due season is right around the corner; that breakthrough, that dream coming to pass, meeting the right person, and overcoming that obstacle.

God has already put it on His schedule. He has already set the time and the date to make it happen. So now is not the time to be discouraged. Now more than ever is the time to be a believer. It's the time to stay in faith.

The Scripture says, "Lift up your heads...and the King of Glory shall come in" (Psalm 24:9 NKJV). If you want God to come in and show you His favor, you've got to lift up your head. That's where your help comes from. The psalmist said, "I look up to the mountains; does my strength come from mountains? No, my strength comes from GOD, who made heaven, and earth, and mountains" (Psalm 121:1 The Message). We cannot go through life looking down, thinking about our problems, and dwelling on how bad it is, reliving every negative thing that's happened and expect to have God's best. Lift your head. Create a fresh new vision for your life. There are greater victories in your future than you have experienced in your past. But as long as you are looking down wondering why it's not working and why it's taking so long, you will not rise higher.

David says in Psalm 3:3, "You, O Lord, are a shield for me, my glory, and the lifter of my head" (AMP). Sometimes circumstances may convince you to keep your head down. You may feel you have too many problems, but God is the Glory and the lifter of your head.

The word *glory* means "favor." The enemy tries to weigh you down with heavy burdens and convince you to stay focused on your difficulties. Before long that discouragement is like a heavy weight you are dragging around. But if you will allow God to be the Glory and the lifter of your head, and work with Him to shake off that discouragement, the only thing that will weigh on you is the favor of God.

Instead of being heavy with discouragement and depression and burdens, you'll be heavy with joy, heavy with favor, heavy with blessings, heavy with victory. He is the Glory and the lifter of our heads. When you can't lift your head on your own strength or when circumstances have overwhelmed you, that's when God will show up as the Glory and the lifter of your head.

David experienced this lifting power. He said in Psalm 40:1–3, "[God] brought me up out of a horrible pit, out of the miry clay, and set my feet upon a rock. . . . He has put a new song in my mouth" (NKJV).

There is some lifting going on today in your life. The Creator of the universe is saying, "If you put your trust in Me and shake off the discouragement, I will lift you to places that you could not reach on your own. I will lift you out of trouble into victory. I will lift you out of sickness into health. I will lift you out of lack into abundance." God will lift you out of unfair situations and give you beauty for ashes.

In those times when you begin to feel discouraged, it's good to just look up and say, "Father, I want to thank You that You are the Glory and the lifter of my head."

Psalm 30:5 reads, "Weeping may endure for a night, but joy comes in the morning" (NKJV). Morning starts at 12:01 a.m. What's interesting is, even though it's a new morning, at midnight it's still dark. At 1:00 a.m., 2:00 a.m., 3:00 a.m., 4:00 a.m., it's still dark. It doesn't look like anything is happening. But as dark as it remains, the light is coming. You've entered a new day.

Usually between 6:00 a.m. and 7:00 a.m., you will see the sun break forth over the horizon. Things will start to brighten up. In other words, business will increase. Health will be restored. Dreams will come to pass. In these discouraging seasons you've got to remind yourself that the One who lifts your head, the Most High God, has promised that joy is coming. Just because it's dark doesn't mean joy is not on its way. You've entered a new day. It's just a matter of time before you see the sun break forth.

Stretch Out Your Hand

I see too many people become discouraged along the way. They start out fine, but then they hit a setback. Instead of shaking it off and creating a new vision, they let life wear them down and they lose their passion. They end up settling for less than God's best.

In the Scripture there is a man who did this. We are never given his name, but he was one of the many sick people at the pool of Bethesda. He'd been sick for thirty-eight years. When Jesus saw him, he realized he had been ill for a long time and asked him, "Would you like to get well?"

The man said he couldn't get well because there was no one to put him into the healing waters of the pool and he was too weak to make it on his own. Jesus told him to "Stand up, pick up your mat, and walk!" (John 5:1–15 NLT).

The man had to make a decision right then and there. Could he do what he had never done before? I'm sure there was a battle going on in his mind. There were strongholds that had been there for years that had convinced him he would never be better. He could have made plenty of excuses, but he did not offer any.

He dared to take a step of faith and he was instantly healed.

Life may have weakened and discouraged you over time, but God is saying to you what He said to this man. If you want to be healed, stand up. Believe you can go places you've never been before. Stretch into a new way of thinking. Stretch into a greater vision for the possibilities in your life.

> *Stretch into a greater vision for the possibilities in your life.*

Where you are is not where God wants you to stay. Just because your dream hasn't happened in the past doesn't mean that it cannot happen in the future. If you join in agreement with God and stand up, so to speak, God will have new seasons of promotion and increase coming your way.

I was in my backyard talking to Manny, who helps with our landscaping. This was the middle of winter and the grass was very brown. It looked dead. I told Manny that I feared the lawn was dead and he said, "It doesn't look very good, but the truth is the grass is not really dead. It's just not in season. In the spring, this same grass will be lush and green."

That's the way it is in life. Sometimes our dreams appear to be dead or dying. But you have to realize, they are not really dead. They are just not in season. They are coming back. New seasons of growth are coming. New health. New relationships. New opportunities. Just because something looks dead, don't write it off.

Our God is a God of new beginnings. When you go through these disappointments and setbacks, instead of being down and discouraged and giving up, have the attitude of *It may not look good, but I know the truth. It's not really dead. It's just not in season. I'm in wintertime, but I know springtime is coming. So I'm lifting up my head to get ready for the new things God is about to do.*

Nothing Remains the Same

If you want to overcome discouragement, learn how to transition into the different seasons of life. The Scripture tells us of a lady named Naomi who didn't do this very well. She failed to realize that just because a season was over, it didn't mean her life was over.

Often we want a certain season to last forever, but that may not be how

God has it planned. You have to be open and willing to adapt and adjust when changes come. Do not be bitter when something happens that you don't like or don't understand.

Of course, no one likes to go through traumatic changes or loss or disappointment, but it's all a part of life. In those difficult seasons, you have to remind yourself that God is still on the throne, and the fact that the grass looks dead doesn't mean it will never be green again.

Naomi was going along just great. Life was good. But over time she went through a series of losses. Her husband died. Later, her two sons died. It's difficult to go through a loss. There is a proper time for grieving. But you have to make sure you don't let a season of mourning turn into a lifetime of mourning.

Naomi made the mistake of letting the bitterness and the discouragement remain inside her. She despaired and lost all happiness. She didn't think the grass would ever be green again. She actually changed her name to Mara, which means "sorrow," because she wanted to be reminded of her pain and misery every time someone called her name.

Naomi's attitude was, "All my dreams have been shattered. I'll never be happy again. Just leave me in my trouble and heartache."

Obviously, I do not recommend you follow the path taken by Naomi. When you suffer a loss, a disappointment, an unfair situation, you have to make sure that you don't let your circumstances rob you of happiness for the rest of your life.

Remember, God is good. If you refuse to live in discouragement, if you lift your head and rise from your despair, you will discover, as Naomi did, that just because one season is over, it does not mean your entire life is over.

After suffering so much, Naomi moved back to her hometown with her daughter-in-law Ruth. There, Ruth met a man, fell in love, and was married. Eventually, Ruth had a son. By then Naomi was an old woman. But when she saw that little baby boy, something lit up on the inside. She felt a new sense of purpose, a new sense of destiny. As she was holding the baby, something amazing happened. Milk began to be produced in her body. The Scripture says this older woman, way up in her senior years, was able to nurse the little baby. Naomi was just as happy and fulfilled as could be.

She discovered that spring always comes after winter. Bad times do not last forever. (You can read Naomi's story in the book of Ruth.)

God Prepares You for His Tests

You wouldn't be alive if God didn't have a purpose for you. You may have been through a disappointment, a good season may be over, but if you'll shake it off and keep moving forward, you will come into another good season. God will reveal to you a new purpose, with new friends, with new opportunities. It doesn't matter if you're thirty, or fifty, or ninety-five. God still has something for you to do.

A young lady named June lost both her legs in an accident. She was naturally distraught and depressed. For a time, she didn't think she had any reason to be alive. She didn't see anything good in her future. But I love what she did. She would refer to Jeremiah 29:11, and say, "God, even though I don't have any plans and I'm too overwhelmed to see anything good, I know You have plans and they are good to give me a future and a hope." If you ever find yourself overwhelmed and you don't see anything good in your future, I would encourage you to do like June and just get in agreement with God and say, "God, I know You've got a good plan. You've got a purpose for me. You've got brighter days in store for me up ahead."

Sometimes when we're being tested by discouragement, it seems God is silent. We pray and we don't hear anything. We read the Scripture and still come away feeling like God is a million miles away. But remember, this is a test. When you're in school, teachers never talk during tests. They stand up at the front of the room very quietly just watching all of the students taking the exam.

The teachers have been preparing you in the days and weeks prior to the test. Often, they've put in extra hours making sure everyone has the opportunity to succeed. On test day, they want to see if you've learned the lessons. They know that you have the information you need. They know you're prepared. You're ready. Now all you've got to do is put into practice what you've learned.

God works the same way as your teachers here on earth. When He is silent, don't assume He has left you. He is right there with you during the test. The silence means only that God has prepared you, and now He is watching to see if you have learned. He would not give you the test unless He knew you were ready.

God is not mad at you when He is silent. He has not forsaken you. His silence is a sign that He has great confidence in you. He knows you have what it takes. He knows you will come through the test victoriously or He would not have permitted you to be tested.

The key is to remain upbeat and not be discouraged or bitter. Put into practice what you've learned. Stay in faith. Hang on to your happiness. Treat others kindly. Be a blessing. If you do that, you will pass the test and flourish in a new season. God will bring things out of you that you didn't even know were in you. Understand, if you don't allow the enemy to discourage you, one of his greatest weapons has been lost.

> *If you don't allow the enemy to discourage you, one of his greatest weapons has been lost.*

Today is a new day. God is breathing new hope into your heart and new vision into your spirit. He is the Glory and the lifter of our heads. Look up with a fresh vision, and God will do for you what He promised David. He will lift you out of the pit. He will set your feet on a rock. He will put a new song in your heart. You won't drag through life defeated and depressed. You will soar through life full of joy, full of faith, full of victory.

If you have struggled with discouragement, depression, and heaviness, I declare right now, in the name of Jesus, that the spirit of discouragement is broken in your life. I declare that the spirit of heaviness and depression is broken off you, off your family, off your future. It will no longer have any effect on you. Happiness will be yours to claim each and every day of the week. I declare this so and I believe it.

CHAPTER SEVENTEEN

Dealing with Unexpected Difficulties

I was on a flight to India with my father years ago when the friendly skies turned mean. We had been flying for about thirteen hours. We had another couple of hours to go. Up to that point the flight had been very smooth and comfortable. But at one point we hit some turbulence like nothing I had ever experienced.

This was worse than the worst roller coaster. The plane was going every which way. Food and bags went flying, hitting the ceiling, passengers, and the floor. For ten minutes it was the wildest ride of my life. People were hollering. Babies were crying. That plane was shaking so violently, we were sure the whole thing was breaking apart.

Being the great man of faith that I am, I thought, *This is it. It's over. There is no way we will survive.*

Yes, I surrendered my happiness and joy to sheer, unadulterated panic.

The turbulence seemed to last an eternity, but sure enough, in about ten minutes we were through it and returned to a calm and smooth ride. Two hours later we landed safely at our destination.

That's the way it is in life. One minute you are happy and filled with contentment, doing just fine. You have a good job, healthy children, and you are feeling blessed. Then you hit some turbulence. Your routine medical tests turn up a problem. Your relationship becomes rocky. A lawsuit is filed.

The challenge is to keep looking ahead, knowing that the turbulence will not last forever, that one day soon, happiness will be possible. At the time, you may feel the good life is over, but take it from me, this, too, shall pass.

God is still on the throne. He has brought you this far. Your life may have taken a plunge, and you may feel like you've been put in a giant mixer. Others around you may be panicked. But sooner or later, calm will be restored.

My theory is that every person has at least ten minutes of turbulence in life. Usually, the scary moments don't come all at once. You may experience a minute here, five minutes there, a couple of minutes down the road. In those tough times when you feel like the plane is breaking apart and panic overwhelms you, go to your faith. Trust that the Creator of the universe is piloting your plane. The Most High God is directing your steps. Remember that He said no weapon formed against you will prosper. God said not to be surprised by these fiery trials. Do not panic. Go to that place of peace even in the midst of turbulence.

I've heard that "trouble is inevitable, but misery is optional." Trouble descends on all of us from time to time, but we can decide whether to fall apart or to pull it together. We have that power even when we are blindsided.

God Has the Solution

It's one thing to know that you are entering a challenging season and facing a test of discouragement. You can mentally prepare for those trials. But what about the difficulties you do not see coming? What about life's earthquakes, tsunamis, and tornadoes; the unexpected illnesses, sudden deaths, divorces, and other tragedies and crises that catch us totally unprepared and off-guard? They can be overwhelming, even devastating. They come out of nowhere and suddenly our lives are turned upside down.

Our family has had its share of unexpected hits, but probably the most shocking was the mail bomb that exploded and injured my sister Lisa in January 1990. The package contained a pipe bomb packed with seven-inch nails. Lisa opened it in her church office, holding it in her lap. Miraculously, she was not seriously injured. She had minor burns and cuts. To this day, we don't know who sent the package addressed to our father.

Lisa was just opening the morning's mail, a daily routine. Her life was spared. She did not suffer long-term injuries. Yet, you can imagine how it turned her life upside down. We were all affected to some degree, but she dealt with both the physical and, even more, the emotional impact for many, many years. In the end, the power of her faith pulled her through.

We all have to deal with unexpected tragedies and trauma. Being a believer doesn't exempt you from life's turbulent times.

The Scripture says rain falls on the just and on the unjust. When you find yourself facing a crisis, it's easy to give up your happiness, panic, and fall apart. But you have to realize that crisis is not a surprise to God. It may be unexpected to us, but God knows the end from the beginning. God has solutions to problems that we haven't even had. And God would not have allowed the difficulty unless He had a divine purpose for it.

God Will Turn Your Test into a Testimony

You have to remember, you are in a controlled environment. It may seem that your circumstances are out of control, but the Creator of the universe is in complete control. He has you in the palm of His hand. Nothing can happen to you without God's permission.

In fact, God is even in control of our enemies. The Scripture talks about how God caused Pharaoh to harden his heart and not let the people go. Notice that God *caused* him to be difficult. Why was that? So God could show His power in extraordinary ways.

When something unexpected happens and catches you off-guard, instead of falling apart and blaming God and panicking, your attitude should be: *God, I know You are still on the throne. This is not a surprise to You. I know You wouldn't have allowed this unless You had a purpose. The surprise may look like a setback, but I know the truth. It's a setup for You to show Your power in a greater way. It's a setup for You to show my unbelieving co-workers Your greatness.*

God's purpose in crises is to show not just us His power but to show other people what He can do. If you will view that adversity as an opportunity for God to display His greatness, God will use you as an example. He wants your neighbors to say, "How in the world did she make it? The medical report said 'impossible,' but look at her today. She's as strong and healthy as can be." Or, "He was laid off at the worst possible time, but look at him now. He has an even better job than before."

God wants to turn your test into a testimony. That's why God will allow you to face adversity. Being a believer doesn't make you immune to difficulty. But God promises if you will stay in faith, He will take what was meant for your harm and use it not only to your advantage but to display His greatness to other people.

> *God wants to turn your test into a testimony.*

When something unexpected happens, instead of falling apart and panicking, expect God to show up and turn the situation around. Expect God's favor. Expect His supernatural power.

It is true that the rain falls on the just and the unjust. But here is the difference. For the just, for the believers—that's you and me—the Scripture says no weapon formed against us will ever prosper. It doesn't say that challenges will never take form. Instead, it says you may face difficulties, but because you're a child of the Most High God, they will not prosper against you. They will not get the best of you. You will get the best of them. God will bring you out better off than you were before.

You Are Advancing the Kingdom

When you face an unexpected challenge, it's easy to get down on yourself and think, *I'm trying to do my best, trying to honor God. I must be doing something wrong. I must just not be doing good enough.*

Often, you have difficulties not because you're doing something wrong but because you're doing something right. It's because you are making a difference. It's because you are taking new ground for your family. It's because you are a threat to the enemy. He would leave you alone if you weren't advancing the kingdom. He wouldn't bother you if he didn't know God had something amazing planned for you in your future. That's why he is trying to make you discouraged and bitter and blaming God, to keep you from the new levels that God has in store for you.

Darkness never likes the light, but don't worry about it. Light will always overtake the darkness. Just keep shining. Keep smiling. Hold on to your happiness and your joy. Keep treating people well even though they mistreat you. Do the right thing even though the wrong things happen to you again and again. Your troubles are a sure sign that God has something amazing planned in your future. Your happiness will be restored, in abundance.

The enemy will not roll out the red carpet and allow you to fulfill your destiny unopposed. He will throw out unexpected challenges, unexpected trouble, and unexpected difficulties. But know this: The God we serve has unexpected favor, unexpected healing, unexpected breakthroughs, and unexpected turnarounds.

Your Weeds Will Become Wheat

In Matthew 13:24–30, Jesus tells a story about a man who planted wheat. He sowed good seed, doing the right thing, honoring God, being good to others. But while he slept an enemy came and planted weeds in his soil. He was expecting to have a great harvest of wheat. He had sown good seed, but when it came time for harvest, weeds sprang up among his wheat.

Don't be surprised if things turn bad on you even as you do the right things, honor God, and work to be your best every day. It may not seem fair, but the enemy is spreading weeds among your wheat, just as was done to this farmer.

The workers said to the farmer, "Where did these weeds come from? We saw you. We know you sowed good seeds."

The farmer said, "An enemy has come in and sown these destructive seeds."

The good news is, those weeds do not have to keep you from your God-given destiny. Scripture says when the wheat was ready for harvest, the weeds sprang up unexpectedly. The message is that when you are close to victory, when you are on the verge of your greatest accomplishment and your greatest breakthrough, when you're about to go into the harvest season, that's when the unexpected challenges will pop up as the enemy tries to keep you from moving forward.

The parable of the weeds and the wheat ends with the workers asking the farmer, "Should we go out and pull up the weeds?"

"No. Just wait, and at the right time the weeds will be destroyed," the farmer said.

That's what God is saying to us. You don't have to spend your life constantly trying to pull the weeds that pop up. If you do that, you will destroy the harvest, too.

Just Wait and Let God Take Care of It for You

A dog bit a man on his walk one day. He went to the doctor and discovered the dog had rabies. When he learned he would have to have a series of painful antirabies shots, the man went into a rage.

The doctor left him to prepare the shots. When he came back, he found the man writing out a list. He thought his patient was writing a will.

"Sir, it's not that bad," the doctor said. "You won't die from this."

"This is not my will," his patient said. "This is a list of all the people I'm planning to bite."

I know people like that. They encounter some turbulence, and they become mad at the world. They spread poison everywhere they go. Don't let that be you. When unexpected challenges appear, your attitude should be: *This, too, shall pass. God will help me handle this. It's just another step on the way to my divine destiny.*

Joseph had to have this attitude in the Bible. He was constantly dealing with unexpected difficulties. He never expected his own brothers to throw him into a pit and sell him into slavery. He could have said, "God, that's not fair. I thought You put a dream in my heart."

Instead, Joseph understood this principle. He knew God would take care of the weeds, so he just kept being his best. He never expected Potiphar's wife to lie about him and have him thrown into prison. He never expected the cellmate he had helped to turn his back on him.

Joseph was hit with one bad break after another. He could have turned bitter and angry. Instead, he kept being his best, and he ended up second in command of a whole nation.

"What was meant for my harm, God used to my advantage," he said (see Matthew 50:20).

You may be in one of your ten minutes of turbulence right now. Your situation may look very difficult, but I'm here to tell you, "This, too, shall pass."

God did not bring you this far to fail you now. It may be rocky. But

God is saying, "I still have a way. I am Jehovah-Jireh, the Lord Your Provider. I'm Jehovah-Rapha, the Lord Your Healer. I am El Shaddai, the God Who Is More Than Enough."

If that unexpected crisis you are facing could stop you, be assured God would have never allowed it to happen. If that sudden challenge could have kept you from your destiny, the Most High God would not have permitted it.

> *If you're alive and breathing, you can still become everything God has created you to be.*

If you're alive and breathing, you can still become everything God has created you to be. Don't allow a crisis to steal your joy or keep you from pressing forward.

Remember Romans 8:28: "All things work together for good to those who love God" (NKJV). The key word is *together*. A difficulty on its own may not make sense, but when it all comes together one day, it will make sense.

Nothing in life is wasted. God will use even your ten minutes of turbulence to your advantage. You've heard the saying "Bad things happen to good people." That is true. But it's also true that good people overcome bad things and come out better off than they were before. God will turn your test into a testimony. Your unexpected troubles are a sure sign that God has something amazing planned in your future. Remember, our God has unexpected favor, unexpected breakthroughs, and unexpected promotion!

CHAPTER EIGHTEEN

Don't Have a Critical Spirit

A couple moved into a new neighborhood, and one morning while they were eating breakfast the wife looked out the window and saw her neighbor hanging wash on the line to dry. She noticed the wash was dingy and dirty. She said to her husband, "That neighbor lady doesn't know how to wash. Her clothes aren't clean. I wonder if she's even using any detergent."

Day after day went by and she would make the same comments: "I can't believe the neighbor doesn't know how to wash. I can't believe they wear those dingy-looking clothes."

A few weeks later the woman looked out the window and the clothes were as clean and bright as could be. She was so surprised. She called her husband in and said, "Look, honey, I can't believe it. She finally learned how to wash. I wonder what happened."

The husband smiled and said, "Honey, I got up early this morning and cleaned our window."

How dirty the neighbor's clothes appear depends on how clean your window is. The Scripture says, "To the pure, all things are pure" (Titus 1:15 NIV). If you can't see anything in a positive light, if you drive up and down the freeway and see only the potholes, if you see only the scratch in the floor and never the amazing house, if you see only what your boss does wrong and never what he does right, then my advice is to clean your window.

The problem is not with everyone else; you have an internal problem.

It's like the man who had an accident driving to work. He got out and said, "Lady, why don't you learn how to drive? You're the fourth person who has hit me today."

At some point look in the mirror and say, "Maybe I'm the one who needs to change. If I'm always critical, maybe I've developed a habit of seeing the bad rather than seeing the good. If I'm always skeptical, maybe I've trained myself to be cynical and sarcastic rather than believing the best. If I'm always finding fault, maybe my filter is dirty. Maybe I've become judgmental and condemning instead of giving people the benefit of the doubt."

This is especially important in relationships. You can train yourself to see people's strengths or you can train yourself to see their weaknesses. You can focus on the things you like about your spouse and magnify the good qualities, or you can focus on the things you don't like and magnify the less-desirable characteristics that annoy you.

This is why some relationships are in such trouble. People have developed a habit of being critical. They can't see anything good. I heard about a man who asked his wife to make him two eggs, one fried and one scrambled. She made them and put them on a plate. When he saw the meal, he shook his head.

"What did I do wrong now?" she asked. "That's exactly what you asked for."

"I knew this would happen," he said. "You fried the wrong egg."

Some people have become so critical-minded that no matter what is done for them, it's not right. They never see the good their spouses are doing. They've forgotten the reasons they fell in love. It's because they're magnifying the wrong things.

If you struggle in this area, make a list of the qualities you like about your spouse. Write down the good things your spouse does. He may not be a great communicator, but he's a hard worker. Write it down. She may have some weaknesses, but she's a great mother. She's smart. She's fun. Put that on your list and go over it every day.

Start focusing on those good qualities. Your entire outlook is poisoned when you operate out of a critical spirit. You won't communicate properly. You won't want to do things together. It will affect you in every area. You have to make a shift. Start appreciating that person's strengths and learn to downplay the weaknesses.

Everyone has faults and habits that can get on your nerves. The key is to recognize what you are magnifying. You are magnifying the wrong thing when you let the critical spirit take over. That's when you'll start complaining that the wrong egg was fried. There are relationships today where two good people are married. They have great potential, but a critical spirit is driving them apart. When you are critical you start nagging: "You never take out the trash. You never talk to me. You're always late."

People respond to praise more than they respond to criticism. The next time you want your husband to mow the lawn, instead of nagging, "Why don't you ever mow the lawn, you lazy thing?" say instead, "Did I ever tell you that when you mow the lawn you look really good out there, and when your muscles bulge out of your shirt and that sweat drips down your face you look so handsome and so attractive?"

> *People respond to praise more than they respond to criticism.*

You praise him like that, and he'll mow the lawn every day! People respond to praise.

A Critical Spirit Taints Everything

Here's what I've learned: A critical spirit follows you everywhere you go. You can't get away from it. You can leave one job bitter, angry, and upset, saying, "They didn't treat me right." But if you don't deal with the root of the issue, you'll have the same problem at the next job. Because your window is tainted, you'll think everybody is against you and they can't do anything right and your boss doesn't know what he's doing.

I grew up with a woman who has been critical as long as I've known her. Even as a teenager she complained about things at school that I didn't even think about. I never knew I had it so bad until she told me. I heard just the other day (and this is thirty years since high school) that she just left another job upset, saying the people didn't treat her right. The sad thing is, she will go through the rest of her life bitter and frustrated if she doesn't clean that window.

She's looking through a filter that's been clouded by years and years of criticism and judgment. Parents, it's important that we deal with these issues ourselves and break any critical, faultfinding spirit so we don't pass it down to our children. That's what happened with this young lady. I remember going over to her house when we were kids. Her parents were the same way. They were always critical about something; critical of the city, critical of their neighbors. The father was critical of his employer. The mother was always complaining about the place where she worked.

A critical spirit taints everything. What's the solution? Number one, recognize when your window is dirty. Number two, just as you've developed a habit of seeing the worst, retrain yourself to see the good. Don't go to work focused on all the things you don't like about your employer. Focus on the fact that you have a job. Be grateful that you're not unemployed.

Don't drive up and down the freeway and see only the potholes and construction and traffic. Train yourself to see the things that are good. Be grateful that you have a freeway to drive on. Be grateful that you live in a place where there's law and order and you don't have to fear for your safety. Look out at the beautiful trees, look up at the sky. Breathe in the goodness of God.

Give the Benefit of the Doubt

When the temptation comes to be critical, catch yourself. You have to deal with negative thoughts one at a time. If you see something or someone you don't understand or you don't agree with, don't be quick to judge. Don't allow that critical spirit to come out.

Switch over and say, "You know, I may not understand them, and I may not agree, but I will not be a faultfinder. I'm giving this person the benefit of the doubt."

A few months ago I met a young man with his girlfriend after a service. They had more piercings and tattoos than any two people I've ever seen. The man had tattoos up and down his arms, all over his neck, and even on his face. The young lady must have had a hundred piercings.

They definitely did not look like our usual visitors. When you see people whose appearance is out of the ordinary, that critical spirit tries to rise up and make you think, *Why do they look like that? They must have some real issues.*

But instead of seeing them through my critical eyes, I looked at them through God's eyes. When I did that I had a different perspective. I was glad they felt comfortable coming to our church. I was glad they took time to honor God.

When I talked to them, I realized they weren't anything like I'd expected. They were the kindest, most respectful people you could ever meet. On the outside you could find a thousand reasons to be judgmental or critical. A religious attitude wants to point out all the faults and ask: *Who do they think they are, and what's their problem?*

But what better place for them to be than in church? Come to find out, this young man was the leader of a very successful heavy-metal band. They'd had a big concert at the arena the night before. He looked to be about thirty years old. He said, "I've never been to church in my life. This is my first time to ever set foot in a place of worship."

He gave me one of his CDs and told me to listen to track seven.

"That's a song I wrote from listening to you," he said.

Don't judge people by their outside appearance. When you're tempted to be critical and find fault, remember that the enemy is called "the accuser of our brethren" (Revelation 12:10 NKJV). Recognize the source of your criticism. That's who's giving you the desire. I don't know about you, but I'm not getting on the side of the accuser; I'm staying on God's side. I'm believing the best.

There may be a thousand things wrong, but I will search until I find the one thing that's right. I've been forgiven much, so I try to love even more. If I err, I'm not erring on the side of judgment; I'm erring on the side of mercy.

I've learned that somebody may look rough on the outside, but you can't judge a book by its cover. Give people the benefit of the doubt. After all, if it were not for the mercy of God, how do you know you wouldn't be just like that person?

If I hadn't been brought up in church by good parents, who knows where I would be? I'm not judging. I'm not finding fault. I'm keeping the Windex handy. I'm keeping my window clean.

But people today are quick to criticize, quick to condemn, quick to judge. If somebody is not just like them, if they're a little different, some don't understand. Instead of giving a person the benefit of the doubt, instead of believing the best, they look him or her up and down and pick out all the faults they can find.

I would never dress like that. I don't know why they drive that kind of car. If I were them, I wouldn't take a vacation in this economy. If I were them, I wouldn't send my kids to that school. If I were her, I wouldn't wear that much jewelry.

A visitor told me last week that his pastor had taken six weeks off to go on an around-the-world cruise. He just couldn't understand that. He was complaining and going on and on, telling me how that just wasn't right. The whole time he complained I was thinking the reason his pastor went on the cruise was to get away from people like him.

How someone spends money, what they drive, how they raise their children, where they go on vacation, what neighborhood they live in—that is all none of my business.

Mind Your Own Business

I don't know about you, but I have a hard enough time trying to run my own life without trying to run somebody else's. One of the best ways I can keep my windows clean is to mind my own business. If a neighbor takes four vacations a year, it's none of my business. If a friend wears a ring on every finger and two on every toe, it's none of my business. If a Lakewood member drives around in a limousine or comes to church in a boat, it's none of my business.

Don't be nosey. Nosey people are critical people. They want to know all the details and all the latest scoops, not so they can pray about it, not so they can help the person, but because they know there

> *Nosey people are critical people.*

might be something in there that's juicy. It will feed their judgmental nature.

They'll go to work and say, "Did you hear what I heard? Did you hear what they said? Did you hear the latest?"

Your answer should be, "No, and I don't want to hear. I don't want to be poisoned. My ears are not trash cans to fill with garbage."

Don't sit there and be passive; a gossip *wants* to tell you something bad about another person. "I couldn't help it. They wanted to tell me," the gossip says.

Before they tell you anything bad, just say, "You know what? I just remembered I have an important appointment to go to."

If you can't leave, just be bold enough to say, "You know, instead of talking about this person, let's pray for him."

Be on the Offensive

Don't let people poison you. If your friends are critics, faultfinders, and busybodies, find some new friends. That critical spirit can poison you. Don't go to lunch with co-workers who sit around and criticize the boss and talk about the company and gossip and complain.

"But I'm lonely," you might say.

Yes, but I would rather you be lonely than poisoned. I would rather you be lonely than allow people who are not going anywhere to keep you from your destiny.

"Well, if I don't go to lunch with them, they might start talking about me."

Let me tell you a secret: Most likely they're already talking about you. If they'll talk about other people when they're not there, they'll talk about you when you're not there.

I have a friend who worked for a well-known ministry years ago. He was very young when he started there. They were on the road in another city holding a conference. One night after the meeting, the two main staff members for this large ministry invited the young man to stop by their hotel room and have some snacks. He went and was just hanging out, watching a ball game, and these two men began to talk about their boss, a well-known minister.

They were so critical and so negative toward the minister, the young man was shocked. He was right out of college. These men had been with the minister more than twenty years. When they started talking poorly of the minister, the young man felt something deep down inside saying, *Get out of here. This is not right.*

He very politely excused himself. He never said a word about it, but the next week the minister called those two staff members in and said, "I was praying today, and I feel in my spirit that you are not on board with me and so it's time for you to leave."

Today this young man is an extremely successful minister. He preaches all over the world. He said, "I know if I had not left that night, if I had allowed them to poison me and become critical and judgmental, I wouldn't be where I am today."

Those two men were just as gifted. They had all kinds of potential, but they just floundered around. Because of their critical spirits, they never walked in the fullness of what God had in store for them.

When people are stirring up trouble around you and talking negatively about their leaders, their family members, or their friends, don't sit there and be part of it. Their critical spirits can keep you from your destiny.

God will not promote a critical spirit, a backbiter, a gossip, or someone sowing discord. If you have a problem with someone, talk to the person face-to-face, not behind his or her back. You may not agree with everything. You may have things you don't understand, but don't be a gossip.

Bad Words Can Boomerang

Matthew 7:1 tells us to not pick on people, jump on their failures, and criticize their faults, unless, of course, we want the same treatment. A critical spirit has a way of boomeranging back to us.

Moses' sister, Miriam, criticized him because she didn't like the woman he married (see Numbers 12). The bride wasn't from the same nationality, so Miriam criticized and stirred up trouble and gossip. All the while, Moses was just as happy as could be. It didn't bother him. He rose above it. But his sister the critic came down with leprosy. Her skin was totally covered with disease.

I don't know about you, but I'm not talking badly about people. I may not understand someone. I may not agree. I may not choose to associate with that person, but I'm not bad-mouthing anyone, trying to ruin anyone's reputation or make anyone look bad. I need God's protection. I want to stay under His covering.

Make a decision with me that you won't have a critical spirit. Train yourself to see the best. There is good in every situation if you'll look for it. Start with your relationships. Make a list of the qualities you like in your spouse and in your children. Start focusing on the good. Magnify the good. Give people the benefit of the doubt. Don't be a faultfinder. Being critical can keep you from your destiny.

I believe your windows are getting cleaner. You are wiping away judgment, no longer criticizing or finding fault. Habits like that may have held you back for years, but today is a new day. I declare a critical filter will no longer cloud your vision.

You are viewing the world with clean windows, believing the best, seeing the good, minding your own business. If you do that, God will fight your battles for you. He will defeat your enemies, make wrongs right, and you will live the life of victory He has in store for you.

CHAPTER NINETEEN

Seeing Through Eyes of Love

Too often we judge people without knowing their stories. We haven't walked in their shoes. We don't know the struggles they've been through. We don't know how they were raised. We don't know the challenges they face. All we know is, "He sure is unfriendly." Or, "She wears strange clothing." Or, "He has some hang-ups."

The truth is, people are the way they are for a reason. If we took time to know their stories, we would be much more forgiving. If we understood the battles they've fought, the pain they've endured, the people who've done them wrong, we would give them a lot more mercy.

We shouldn't be critical because they went through a divorce or they have an addiction or they were unfriendly and didn't speak. You and I don't know what's going on behind the scenes. We don't know the stress someone else is under.

For too long, we've seen people through eyes of judgment. My challenge is to start seeing people through eyes of love. Instead of being critical and writing others off, take time to get to know them. Find out what they are all about.

> Instead of being critical and writing others off, take time to get to know them.

I remember in high school a young man moved to our city and joined the basketball team. He was a very good athlete, but he was extremely quiet. He had a different personality. We all thought he was odd. He never laughed with us. He just stayed over in the corner and did his own thing, never really joining in.

One day it was just him and me in the locker room. I had never really spoken to him before. Just to be friendly I said, "Hey! Where did you come from? Where did you grow up?"

I'll never forget how sincere he was. He opened up and told me how he had come from a very dysfunctional home. He had been passed from family to family, six different foster homes in three years. He had all this hurt, pain, and insecurity. Once I understood where he was coming from, I saw him in a whole new light. After that, my friends and I made sure to include him in activities. We went the extra mile to make him feel loved, accepted, welcomed, and part of our team. Over the years, I watched him come out of his shell, become more confident and more secure. By the time we graduated, he was just like the rest of us, as happy and friendly as could be.

When you understand people's stories, it's very easy to understand their outward demeanor. When I found out why my new teammate was the way he was, it changed my perspective. I realized how easy it was for me to be secure and happy. I was raised in a good environment. It was easy for me to be confident and expect good things. I'd been surrounded by loving people all my life. But if I hadn't had that loving family, I don't know how I would have responded.

Too often we judge people based on our own backgrounds and on the experiences we've been through. If we are strong in an area where somebody is weak it's easy to think, *I would never do that. I would never be as unfriendly as that young man. I would never have been divorced. I would never have married that person in the first place.*

You don't know what you would have done in their situation. You haven't walked in their shoes. You weren't raised in their environment. You haven't been through the experiences they've been through.

Believe the Best

All of us have strengths, and we all have weaknesses. We are strong in certain areas not because we're great and we just decided to be strong, but because of the grace of God in our lives. I am secure and confident because

God blessed me with great parents. I cannot judge the actions of someone who was not blessed in that way. If my situation and the new teammate's situation had been reversed, I don't know if I could have handled the situation even as well as he did.

Instead of being holier than thou and judging people, our attitudes should be *But for the grace of God, that could be me.* If not for God's goodness, I could be struggling with an addiction. I could be insecure, angry, and dealing with all kinds of issues. I'm not judging. I'm showing mercy. I won't be critical. I'll be understanding. After all, we don't know what people are going through. We should give people room.

A good friend told me that his boss jumped down his throat for no reason. He said he hadn't done anything wrong and his boss just let him have it in front of the whole sales staff, embarrassing him. He was understandably upset about it.

I told him what I'm telling you: Just give the boss the benefit of the doubt. Something else is going on. He found out two weeks later that his boss was going through a divorce. It gave him a whole new perspective. Now he understands why he was so uptight, why he was on edge. Instead of taking his boss's criticism personally, he is making allowances. He is showing him mercy. He is doing what he can to help lighten the load.

Give the Benefit of the Doubt

Most of the time if someone is not up to par, there is a very good reason. We don't know what's going on behind closed doors. We don't know the heartache or the pain the person may be pushing down. Maybe they are doing the best they can to just keep it together. The last thing they need is for someone to dump another load on them. God puts people like that in our lives not to be judged, condemned, or criticized. God puts them there so we can help love them back into wholeness.

Where are the healers? Where are the sensitive people who recognize when someone is hurting? Who will step up and say, "I can tell you're stressed out. I can tell you're not feeling up to par. Is there anything I can do to help? Can I pray for you? Can I buy you dinner? Can I come over and encourage you?"

Let's stop judging people and start healing people.

I was in a long grocery store checkout line of about nine people, and the young woman running the cash register seemed to be stressed out. She was very short with people and some of them were short with her in return. She made no bones that she did not want to be working.

The mood was tense and only worsened when she had a problem with her register. She had to call the manager, causing further delays. Then she needed a price check on someone's groceries. It was taking so long my bananas were no longer green!

Customers in line were grumbling about her bad attitude, which seemed to only make her more rude. The checkout clerk was wrong. She should not have been rude to the customers, but her actions were so out of line I knew something else was bothering her.

I'd been put off at first by her rudeness, but there was obviously a deeper problem than work stress. I decided to be part of the solution rather than part of the problem.

When my turn finally came to check out, I smiled and encouraged her.

"Hey, I can tell you're stressed out about something and people are aggravating you, but I'm here to tell you that whatever the problem is, it will work out. Everything will be all right. God has you in the palm of His hand. He knows what you are going through. He has the solution."

Big tears streamed down her cheeks. At first she struggled to say anything, biting her lip, but then the words poured out.

"My baby is in St. Joseph's, the hospital, and I've been so worried," she said. "Then yesterday, my husband was laid off. I don't know how we'll make it."

I've been known to offer a prayer in all sorts of situations, but this was my first time in the grocery checkout line.

"Let me pray for you," I said to her.

Right there in Express Lane #2, we prayed. When we finished, the lady in line behind me walked around and gave the checkout clerk a big hug.

A man back in the line said, "My good friend is the head nurse at that hospital. I will call her and ask her to go check on your baby."

The whole atmosphere changed because once we heard her story, we understood. Instead of looking at her with a critical view, we looked at her with the eyes of love. Instead of responding to her rudeness, we responded to her sadness and concern. We understood and we empathized after realizing why she was so uptight.

Before I left she said, "You'll never know what this has meant to me."

A Few Kind Words Work Wonders

Proverbs 15:4 says a gentle tongue brings healing. It's amazing what a few kind words can do. It's amazing the impact you can have when you tell somebody, "Hey, everything will be all right. I'm praying for you. I believe in you. You've got good days up ahead."

> *It's amazing what a few kind words can do.*

Those words have healing power. But when somebody is rude to you, it's easy to respond the same way. Instead of judging that person, if you first step into his or her shoes, it will help you put on the right set of eyes: eyes of love and not of judgment.

This doesn't mean you are excusing the person's behavior. What they are doing may be wrong. It may be their fault. They may have brought the trouble on themselves. But I've learned I'm not the judge. God is the Judge. I'm not here to straighten everybody out. I'm here to help bring healing.

Our job is to pour the healing oil on the wounds. Our job is to lift the fallen, to be a friend to the lonely, to encourage the discouraged. When you take this merciful approach, instead of giving them what they deserve, you start the healing process. You say, "I understand. They're not having a good day. I understand they're under a lot of stress. I understand life is not treating them fairly."

There was an older farmer who had puppies for sale so he put a sign on his fence. A boy about eight years old from across the road came over and said he wanted to buy a puppy. He then pulled out a pocketful of change and said, "I've got thirty-nine cents; is that enough?"

The farmer laughed. "I don't know," he said. "Let me count it."

He counted coin by coin. "That's exactly the right amount," he told the boy.

He called to his farmhand and told him to let out the puppies. Four of the cutest little fur balls you could imagine came scurrying toward the little boy. He reached down and played with them, trying to figure out which one he wanted to buy.

Then he looked up and saw that a smaller pup was just coming down the ramp from the puppy cage in the barn. There was something wrong with this puppy's back legs. It tried to run, but the best it could do was hobble along.

The little boy was immediately drawn to it. Without hesitation he said to the farmer, "That's the puppy I want."

The farmer was puzzled. He said, "No, son. You don't want this puppy. It will never be able to run and play like the rest of the litter. There is something wrong with its back legs."

The little boy reached down and rolled up the legs of his jeans to reveal steel braces on his legs. For the first time, the farmer noticed he wore specially made shoes.

He said to the farmer, "You see, I don't run well either. This puppy needs someone who understands it."

Take Time to Know Their Stories

This world is full of people who need to be understood. We don't know what others are going through. We don't know the hurt or the pain they have endured. They may be different and have hang-ups and do things we wouldn't do, but that's okay. Give them a little room.

If you took time to know their stories, you wouldn't be critical. If you would first attempt to walk in their shoes, you would find out why they are the way they are.

The puppy story reminds me of the dancing man who attended my father's church when I was growing up. This member of the congregation was in his thirties, and he was always dancing during the service. As soon as the music began, he'd be up on his feet, hands in the air, dancing without inhibition.

I was ten years old or so and I'd sit with my friends making fun of the dancing man. We just thought he was so odd. We would even look for him before the service so we'd know where to get a good view of him dancing. We'd do a play-by-play when the music started. "There go his hands! There go his legs!"

We just couldn't understand why he was always so excited, why he was dancing. My father, being the man he was, called the dancing man up on the platform one Sunday and asked him to tell his story.

You can believe our young ears were tuned in. Finally, we were to find out what made him so strange, why he danced all the time in church. Our attitudes, and our perspectives, changed as he spoke.

He explained that he'd never known his father and that his mother committed suicide at an early age. He'd grown up angry and bitter, with no direction and no purpose.

He'd always felt lost and alone until he'd found Lakewood Church, he said. In our church, he'd felt a sense of belonging for the first time. He felt loved and supported. That encouragement helped him turn his life around. He found a good job and married a woman who loved him. My father's church gave him the foundation that his life had lacked, something he could build upon and draw strength from.

"When I think about all God has done for me, I just can't be still. My arms go up in the air," he said. "When the music starts, my legs just go to dancing. I'm so happy I've just got to give God praise."

When my friends and I heard his story we felt about two inches tall. We never made fun of him again. We learned that when you imagine walking in somebody's shoes, when you hear their entire story, you gain a new and deeper perspective.

Help the Hurting

Could it be the person you've been judgmental toward has a good reason for the way he is? Maybe he has an addiction. You're tempted to write him off, to be critical, but have you imagined walking in his shoes? Do you know how he was raised? Do you know what battles he has fought?

Most of the time we don't know all the facts about the people we judge and criticize. Even if they are in the wrong, God did not put us here to condemn them. They need our mercy, our forgiveness, and our understanding to get back on the right track. Being hard and critical doesn't bring healing. We aren't lifting people up. We just push them further down.

In dealing with thousands of people over the years, one thing I can tell you is that 99.9 percent are not bad people. They may make poor choices, but deep down they have good hearts. Most want to do what's right. If you will just see them through eyes of love, you could be one of those to help them come up higher and still fulfill their God-given destinies.

The longer I live, the less judgmental I become. I had a man tell me after the service awhile back, "Joel, that was a hell of a sermon today."

Do you know that didn't offend me? I thought the sermon was good, too! His choice of words just told me he wasn't raised the way I was. The way I grew up, if you said "hell," that meant you were going there. But I found out that his parents owned bars. So when I grew up as a little boy hanging out in the church, he was hanging out in the bars.

I'm not holier than thou. I know if it were not for the grace of God, I wouldn't be where I am today.

Give People Room to Grow

If a girl with a bad reputation walks into my church, my feeling is that I would rather her come to Lakewood than be out on the street or in a club somewhere. Jesus said, "It is not the healthy who need a doctor, but the sick" (Luke 5:31 NIV). Our churches should not be museums to display perfect people. They should be hospitals to help the hurting and the lonely.

> *Our churches should not be museums to display perfect people. They should be hospitals to help the hurting and the lonely.*

Before you judge that young lady or anyone else, let me ask, "Have you walked in her shoes? Do you know her story? Did she have good parents who gave her wisdom and guidance? Did they make her feel valuable and loved, or was she taken advantage of? Have you tried to see life from her perspective?"

Give people a little room while they're in the process of changing. Maybe the girl who walks into my church is trying to turn her life around.

Maybe God put that co-worker next to you not so you could judge him, but so you could help love him back into wholeness.

Your attitude should be, *God, how can I help this person come up higher? What can I do to inspire them to become better? How can I make them feel more loved, more accepted, more valuable, more secure?*

The closest thing to the heart of God is helping hurting people. The amount of love, mercy, understanding, and compassion you give to others will be given back to you by God.

Romans 15:1 says, "We who are strong ought to bear with the failings of the weak" (NIV). You will have to put up with flaws and overlook faults. You have to make allowances for the weaknesses of others. Bottom line is this: Be generous with your mercy. Show acceptance to everyone, not just those who are like you.

Bill was a college student known for his wild hair and sloppy dress. Every day he wore the same T-shirt with holes, blue jeans, and sandals. He didn't care to dress well, but he was a very sharp young man, a straight-A student. He was just a little different.

One day he went to a campus ministry event. His heart was touched, and Bill gave his life to Christ. The campus ministry encouraged him to get into a good church. There just happened to be one across the street from the university campus. This was a small and very formal church, very conservative, and members of the congregation dressed up for services.

You can imagine what they thought when Bill walked in late for a service the first time. The little church was packed and he couldn't find a seat. He walked down the center aisle toward the platform. He was wearing his usual tattered old T-shirt, blue jeans, and sandals. He went row by row and couldn't find a seat.

Finally Bill reached the front row, and found there still was no place to sit, so he plopped down right on the floor in the center of the altar area. He wasn't trying to be disrespectful. He just didn't know any better. He was acting as if the church were a college classroom with no seats.

About that time the head deacon came up from the back of the church and walked down toward Bill. This deacon was in his eighties, a very distinguished gentleman, silver hair, glasses, wearing a very expensive suit.

He walked slowly down the aisle with his cane. There was such a commotion that the minister had to stop his sermon and wait for the head deacon to reach the front.

Everyone was thinking that he was planning to ask the strange young man to find another seat or leave the church. The expectation was that the disciplined eighty-year-old man would have little understanding of the ways of an undisciplined young college student.

Imagine their surprise when the head deacon stopped next to wild Bill, laid his cane down beside him, and with great difficulty lowered himself to the floor and sat next to him so he wouldn't have to sit there all alone.

At the sight of the two of them sitting side by side on the altar, the whole church erupted in applause. The minister said, "The sermon you hear me speak today is one you'll remember maybe for a week or two, but the sermon you just saw will be remembered for the rest of your lives!"

When you see people through eyes of love, eyes of compassion, and eyes of understanding, you won't be nearly as critical. Instead of being quick to judge, you will be quick to give people the benefit of the doubt. That deacon realized, *Bill wasn't raised like me. He doesn't come from my same background. He didn't come out of my same value system.* Once he imagined stepping into Bill's shoes, he understood where he was coming from.

Be the One to Lighten the Load

Teddy was a fifth grader struggling in school. He wouldn't participate. He was moody and hard to deal with. His teacher, Ms. Thompson, always said that she loved all of her students, but later she would admit that she hadn't cared for Teddy at first. She couldn't understand why he was so unmotivated and unwilling to learn.

At Christmas the students brought Ms. Thompson presents that she would open in front of the class. Most were wrapped in fancy holiday paper with sparkling bows, but Teddy's present was wrapped in brown paper from a grocery bag. When she opened it up, out fell a very plain-looking bracelet that had half the rhinestones missing, plus a bottle of cheap perfume, half of which was gone.

Some of the students giggled at Teddy's present, but Ms. Thompson hushed them and acted pleased, dabbing on some of the perfume and placing the bracelet around her wrist. She then held it up and said, "Oh, it's so beautiful."

After class Teddy came up to the teacher and said very quietly, "Ms. Thompson, that bracelet looks as beautiful on you as it did on my mother. And with that perfume you smell just like she did."

After Teddy left, Ms. Thompson rushed to the files to find out more about his family. She found the paperwork. It read: "First grade: Teddy shows promise but has very poor home situation. Second grade: Teddy could do better but mother is seriously ill. Third grade: Teddy is a good boy but distracted. Mother died this year. Fourth grade: Teddy is a slow learner. Father shows no sign of interest in him."

After reading the reports, Ms. Thompson wiped away the tears and said, "God, please forgive me."

The next morning when the students went to class they had a new teacher. You see, Ms. Thompson had become a new person. She exchanged her critical eyes for the eyes of love. She'd come to understand why Teddy was so distracted and unmotivated.

She made the boy her personal project, showing him love and encouragement, tutoring and mentoring him. The empathy and acceptance of Ms. Thompson changed the course of Teddy's life. Years after he'd moved on to high school, the teacher received a letter from her former student Teddy.

"Ms. Thompson, thank you for all you did for me in grade school. I'm about to graduate from high school second in my class."

Four years later, another letter: "Ms. Thompson, thanks again for all of your encouragement years ago. I'm about to graduate from college first in my class."

Then came one final letter: "Ms. Thompson, thank you. I am now Dr. Teddy. I just graduated from medical school. Also, I'm about to be married and I wanted to see if you would come to the wedding. I'd like to seat you where my mother would have been if she were still alive."

What a difference it makes in your happiness and the joy of others when you take time to hear the stories of others. It's easy to be critical. It's easy to write people off. But I'm convinced, like Ms. Thompson, if you will make an effort to find out what they're all about, it will be a lot easier to show mercy.

Make sure you see people through eyes of love, not eyes of judgment. Don't be critical, and don't write people off. Give them the benefit of the doubt. Go the extra mile. Consider that they might be going through incredible difficulties and they are doing the best they can. Be a person who helps lighten the load.

> *Make sure you see people through eyes of love, not eyes of judgment.*

All it takes for some is just one person stepping up or lending a hand. You can be the Ms. Thompson in someone's life. You can be the difference-maker. Take an interest in that co-worker who is so discouraged. Find out what's going on with that relative who has lost his passion.

You can be the catalyst for change. If you see people through eyes of love and do not judge them, you will live as a healer, lifting the fallen, restoring the broken. Let me assure you, when you help others come up higher, God will make sure you come up higher. He will pour out His blessings and His favor.

PART
V

Laugh Often

CHAPTER TWENTY

The Healing Power of Laughter

When my father was seventy-five years old, he still laughed and kidded just like he did when he was twenty. He was a responsible and serious man, but he knew how to have fun. One time we were in Mexico, walking down the main street of a little town, when an American couple approached my father.

They asked him, "Do you know where the post office is?"

My dad looked at them real strange and said, "No comprende. No comprende. Español, amigo."

They thought, *Oh, no. He only speaks Spanish, too.*

So they said it real dramatically: "*Post office.*"

Daddy shook his head. "No comprende."

Frustrated, the tourist said it even more dramatically: "*Post office. Mail a letter.*"

Daddy brightened up and said, "Post off*eece*?"

They got real excited. "Yes! Yes! Post off*eece*!"

Then Daddy said, "If you're looking for the post office, it's right around the corner."

That man said, "Boy, I ought to whoop you."

We all had a good laugh at that.

My father believed that the world would be a healthier place if we stressed less and laughed more. He never lost that youthful spirit.

He knew that when people are uptight and on edge, headaches, digestive problems, and lack of energy are just some of the results. They don't sleep well. Much of this would go away if they would just learn how to properly deal with stress.

One of the greatest stress relievers God has given us is laughter. It's like medicine. Laughing makes us feel better and releases healing throughout our systems. When we laugh, the pressures of life fade and we feel restored and rejuvenated.

When was the last time you had a good hearty laugh? If it's been awhile, maybe your laugher is rusted and needs to be overhauled! You don't know how much better you would feel and the energy you'd pick up if you'd just lighten up and learn to laugh more often—not once a month, not once a week, but every single day.

Many people are too stressed to have fun. They need to restore balance. All work and no play is not healthy. Developing a sense of humor and looking for opportunities to laugh can make a big difference in the quality of your life. You may not be a jovial person by nature. God made us all unique. But I recommend training yourself to laugh as often as possible.

Hospital Humor Is No Joke

Medical science is catching on to the benefits of laughter as therapy for patients and to improve patient-caregiver relationships. There is even a "humor-in-hospitals movement" that includes using "clown care units" to entertain patients and improve their moods. Some hospitals now have "humor carts" that are wheeled into patients' rooms with funny-movie DVDs, cartoon books, games, and funny props to provide comic relief from stress and pain.

St. Joseph's Medical Center in Houston, where I live, had one of the first "humor rooms" in the country. These are special rooms set aside where patients and their families can laugh and have fun without disturbing others. The St. Joseph's staff found that visits to the humor room led to many patients leaving the hospital sooner because it helped relieve pain and other symptoms.

Another hospital had a humor program in its pediatrics ward. When there was a shortage of beds, a depressed seventy-year-old man with cancer was put in the pediatric ward temporarily. He felt so much better after staying there he asked to be with the kids the next time he was admitted.

I heard about another hospital that takes some of its long-term patients to a park several hours a week so they can watch children playing. The original purpose was to get them out of the hospital and into a more relaxing environment. But doctors discovered that watching the children play and hearing them laugh stimulated the body's natural healing process.

Just watching and listening to children at play helped change the patients' outlooks and they recovered more quickly. If just watching children laugh and play helps bring healing and joy and a better attitude, imagine what laughing and playing yourself can do for you.

Laugh Like a Child

I read that the average child laughs more than two hundred times a day, but the average adult laughs fourteen to seventeen times daily. The pressures of life, stress, and more responsibilities steal our joy little by little as we grow older. Just because we are no longer children doesn't mean we're supposed to be solemn and never have any fun. Most adults are borderline grumpy a good part of the time. But every healthy adult should hold on to that child inside. Know how to work, but also know how to play.

> *Know how to work, but also know how to play.*

A study said that one of the traits shared by those who live into their nineties is that they take joy in everyday life. Laughter is their best medicine. A friend of mine had a good-humored grandmother who lived to be 103 years old. When she went into the hospital at the age of one hundred, my friend called and asked her what was wrong.

"Well, so far they've ruled out pregnancy," she said.

I met someone just like her in our church visitors' line a few years ago. She was a very healthy and sharp ninety-six-year-old lady. Her skin was beautiful. Her eyes were bright. But what struck me most was how happy she was.

It appeared she'd never met a stranger. Everyone around her was her best friend. She was hugging all the people in the line. She was wearing a bright, colorful dress and was a breath of fresh air. After we talked, I hugged her. As I was leaving, I just said in passing, "I believe when I'm ninety-six years old I hope to look just like you."

She leaned over and whispered in my ear, "Just don't wear the dress."

I thought, *No wonder she's so healthy. She still has a sense of humor. She still knows how to laugh.*

Her good humor was like a healing light flowing through her body. I want to follow her example as I grow older. I've made up my mind that I'll never be a grumpy old man. I will not let myself grow more and more sour the older I become. I'm staying full of joy. When it's my time to go, I'm leaving with a smile on my face, a laugh in my heart, and a joke in my pocket.

Laughter Keeps You Young

Every time you laugh, you reduce the stress hormone and increase production of the human growth hormone, also known as the "youth hormone," by as much as 87 percent, according to some sources. That's the hormone that slows down the aging process and keeps you looking younger and fresher. I laugh all the time, and I don't look seventy-seven years old, do I?

I heard a story about Joey Grimaldi, a comedian in the early 1800s who kept people laughing during his forty-year career. Joey was known to turn angry mobs into applauding audiences, but he wasn't such a happy man himself. He was a workaholic. He felt pressured to always be funnier and funnier. He was a perfectionist, never satisfied with his routines or his success.

Later in his life he became ill, but he kept performing. He went to a doctor he'd never seen before. Joey had aged because of overwork and self-imposed stress. This doctor didn't recognize Joey as the famed comedian. After examining him, the physician told his new patient that there was no medical reason for his illness, other than stress from overwork and possible depression.

"I don't know what you do for a living, but I suggest you just take some time off from work and relax. Go see that great comedian Joey Grimaldi who's in town this week. I hear he's hilarious and laughter will do you some good."

Joey looked at the doctor and sadly replied, "But Doctor, I *am* Joey Grimaldi." A few weeks later, in March 1823, Joey collapsed and died from exhaustion. Sadly, he could make others laugh, but he never took the time to laugh himself. Don't let that be you.

I'm sure you've known stressed-out people like Joey Grimaldi who seem to age rapidly because of their challenges. When we're stressed and serious and grumpy, the chemicals that God designed to keep us young, to relieve stress, to reduce blood pressure, to make our immune systems stronger, sit unused. God has given us everything we need to live healthy and whole, but it's up to us to tap into those things through laughter and seeing the humor in life.

Playfulness Is as Important as Sleep

Dr. Stuart Brown, a psychiatrist, is the founder of the National Institute of Play. He became interested in the effects of laughter and play in our lives when the governor of Texas asked him to investigate the tower shootings on the University of Texas campus in 1966. As he studied the life of the troubled young man who had killed sixteen people and wounded thirty-two others, one thing that stuck out was that this young man had never played normally as a child.

He grew up in such a dysfunctional, high-stress family that his "play life" was very limited as a child. This so interested Dr. Brown that he went on to interview other death-row inmates. He discovered that a high percentage of them also had not played normally or freely as children. Dr. Brown concludes today that the opposite of play isn't work. It's depression. He believes we need play as much as we need sleep if we want to be physically and emotionally healthy.

Proverbs 17:22 supports this as it says, "A happy heart is good medicine and a cheerful mind works healing" (AMP). When you're in a good mood and full of joy, taking time to laugh and play, it's like taking vitamins or good medicine. In fact, medical science tells us that laughing boosts our immune systems. Laughter reduces blood pressure. People who laugh regularly are 40 percent less likely to have a heart attack than those who don't, some sources say.

Don't Take a Pill, Take a Joke

Laughter also triggers the right side of the brain, which helps creativity and decision making. When you have a good laugh, you activate the body's natural tranquilizers that calm you and help you sleep better. Many people today suffer from insomnia, but maybe laughing more would help them relax and rest.

> *When you have a good laugh, you activate the body's natural tranquilizers that calm you and help you sleep better.*

One poor lady, Virginia, was constantly taking tranquilizers because she hadn't been able to sleep well for so long. But she took the tranquilizers so often they hardly helped. Virginia tried different diets, doctors, and herbs, too, but nothing seemed to work.

Then a doctor gave her a very unusual prescription. He said, "Every night before you go to bed, watch something funny—a funny movie, a funny video, a funny sitcom—something that makes you laugh."

Virginia followed his advice night after night. She slept better and better. Finally, she was totally off her sleep medications and snoozing every night like a baby.

What happened? Virginia needed man-made tranquilizers because she wasn't releasing God's natural tranquilizers. Maybe you, too, would feel better if you lightened up and laughed more often. It could be that your headaches, backaches, migraines, chronic pain, or fatigue might ease if you played, laughed, and enjoyed life more.

When my mother was diagnosed with terminal cancer in 1981, she made sure she kept taking healthy doses of laughter. She was in pain and worried, but instead of staying in bed feeling sorry for herself, she watched cartoons on television. She would sit there and laugh and laugh.

My wise mother was releasing the healing God put on the inside. If she couldn't find something funny to watch, she'd just go look at my brother, Paul. That always made her laugh.

In case you missed it, my mother is still laughing today. Doctors had given her only a few months to live, but more than thirty years later she is cancer-free. That's the miracle of faith with a healthy dose of laughter.

Natural-Born Healer

Our immune systems are made up of millions of cells. The only purpose for some of these cells is to attack and kill anything foreign to the body. They're called "NK" or "natural killer" cells. They're responsible for searching out certain harmful bacteria and viruses and destroying them. One of their main functions is to attack the cells that commonly cause cancer. Researchers have found that every person develops these abnormal cancerous cells on a regular basis. Our natural killer cells usually go to work and make sure they are destroyed. But negative emotions like stress, worry, fear, anxiety, and depression weaken the natural killer cells.

Studies have shown that those who are happy and laugh regularly not only develop more of these natural killer cells than the average person, but the cells' activity is increased. So when you're good-natured, see the humor in life, and aren't stressed out, these beneficial cells function at their highest level.

With so much sickness and sadness in the world today, I don't know why people don't tap into the healing power of laughter more. It's a free cure with no side effects. You can take it as often as you'd like. I'm no doctor, but I'll write you a prescription today.

Here it is: At least three times a day, every day, take a strong dose of humor. Find something funny that makes you laugh out loud. No chuckling. No laughing on the inside. Release that joy into the atmosphere so everyone can hear it. Trigger those endorphins, your natural tranquilizers.

A doctor friend told me about a woman with a severe case of fibromyalgia. This disorder of unknown origins causes widespread and chronic pain throughout the body. This woman spent many hours in bed suffering. She also had chronic fatigue and was very depressed.

Her doctor treated the pain with medications, but he felt the pills were treating only the symptoms and not the cause. In talking to her, the doctor realized how depressed she was. Then he asked her an interesting question: "How long has it been since you've had a good, hearty laugh?"

The lady had to think about it a moment.

"Doctor," she said, "I haven't laughed that way in more than thirty years, since I was a child."

"Well, here's your prescription," he said. " Go watch every funny movie you can find. Go read every humorous book you can get your hands on, and laugh as much as you possibly can."

She followed his prescription and little by little, her joy returned. The pain subsided. Her energy was restored. Three months later she returned to the doctor for a checkup. The moment she walked in, he could see the difference. There was a sparkle in her eye, a spring in her step, a smile on her face.

"Doctor," she said, "I've never felt so good in all my life."

In the months that followed, she continued to laugh more and more. Her laughter cleansed her body of whatever was causing her pain.

Let me ask you what the doctor asked her: How long has it been since you've had a good, hearty laugh? A day? A week? A month? A year? Ten years? Make sure you're taking your medicine.

I know when I've had a hard, pressure-filled day: I have a backache down the center of my spine. I know it's from tension. To relieve that pain, I do just what I'm asking you to do. I'll go play with my children. They always make me laugh. Or, I'll watch something funny on television.

Invariably, after a few minutes of laughing, that pain is totally gone. It's just like I had a good massage but cheaper. The medicine of laughter will save you money. No more buying sleeping pills, tranquilizers, and antidepressants!

God Has Fixed the Fight for Your Health

Psalm 2:4 says that God sits in the heavens and laughs. Can you envision that? Right now God is on the throne. He's not mad. He's not worried about the economy. He's not upset with you and me. God is on the throne, full of joy.

Psalm 37:13 explains why He's laughing: "The Lord laughs at [the wicked], for He sees that their own day [of defeat] is coming" (AMP). In other words, the reason God laughs is because He knows the end of the story. He knows the final outcome. The good news is, you and I win. God always causes us to triumph!

It's just like we are in a fixed fight. The outcome is predetermined by God. Imagine you knew who'd win the Super Bowl before the kickoff. No matter how far behind the eventual winner fell, no matter how bad it looked for them, you wouldn't worry. You had inside information. You knew the final outcome.

That's what God is saying: When it gets tough and things don't look like they'll work out, you can laugh by faith, knowing that God has already written the final chapter. God has already recorded the victory in your favor.

> *When it gets tough and things don't look like they'll work out, you can laugh by faith, knowing that God has already written the final chapter.*

He's saying: In famine, when it gets tough, look that trouble in the face and say, "Ha, ha, ha! I know the outcome. God has destined me to win. He's already put my name on the trophy. He's already seen me standing on the podium as a winner."

God gave Abraham a promise that he would father a child. In the natural it was impossible. He was much too old. But the first thing Abraham did when he heard God's promise was to laugh (see Genesis 17:17). His was the laugh of faith. He said, in effect, "Ha, ha! God, I know You can bring this to pass. I know You are a supernatural God."

And so often when God puts a promise in our hearts it looks impossible. Maybe you're sick and God has assured you you'll be healthy again. Or maybe you are struggling financially, but God is saying you're coming into overflow. He will prosper you. Perhaps your family is pulled apart. God promises to heal the bonds.

Your mind may have doubts. But remember to laugh in faith like Abraham, because it's just a matter of time before those promises come to pass. You are in a fixed fight.

I'm asking you today to get in the habit of taking your medicine on a regular basis. Every day, find some reason to laugh. Look for opportunities. If you don't think you have a reason, then just know you can laugh by faith. Keep a happy heart and a cheerful mind, and you will enjoy life more; even better, you will feel God's natural tranquilizers flow through you.

CHAPTER TWENTY-ONE

Smile, and the World Smiles with You

I knew a steep charge was coming when I went to the airline counter to change the dates on four round-trip tickets. After I handed the tickets to the agent, she confirmed my fear.

"That will be fifty dollars extra per ticket," she said.

I laughed and smiled. "Yeah, I figured there would be a charge," I said.

My reaction seemed to surprise the ticket agent. "Why are you laughing?" she said. "Most people would be upset."

"I don't know," I replied. "I guess I'm just a happy person."

She shook her head and went to work on her computer. A few seconds later she handed me my new tickets and said, "I'm not charging you anything extra. We need more happy people around here."

The rest of that day I went around smiling and laughing at everybody who crossed my path! I'd always heard that being happy paid off, but this was the first time I'd actually pocketed some cash.

My guess is that the airline ticket agent had dealt with all sorts of cranky and stressed-out people before I walked up to her counter. I wasn't happy about the thought of paying extra for changing my tickets, but I'd decided that the ticket agent didn't make the rules, so why should she have to deal with my unhappiness? I made the decision to treat her with good humor instead.

The old saying claims you attract more flies with honey than vinegar. I never knew why anyone would want to attract flies, but I get the point: Being nice will take you further than being a grouch.

Is there always a payoff for wearing a smile instead of a frown? I think so. As I mentioned earlier, you'll enjoy better health with a positive approach to life, and also you will attract more friends, supporters, encouragers, and well-wishers.

When faced with unpleasant situations and challenging times, we need one another more than ever. Yet, too often, stressed-out people circle the wagons and isolate themselves. They become uptight and cranky, driving people off even though they need support more than ever at that point. The more pressure you feel and the more isolated you become, the more you should look for opportunities to smile and share a laugh to draw people to you.

Shine Your Joy in the Darkness

These days you hear constant reports of doom and gloom. More trouble in the economy. Higher taxes. A soaring deficit. Home foreclosures. A tight job market.

If you are not careful, you can fall into a trap of thinking, *This is no time to enjoy my life. This is certainly no time to laugh, no time to have a sense of humor.*

But in hard times, more than ever, activate your joy. In fact, Job 5:22 says, "You shall laugh at destruction and famine" (NKJV). At first that may not seem to make sense. We're supposed to laugh at famine? We're supposed to laugh at destruction?

Yes, that's exactly right, because in tough times you run a greater risk of losing your joy, so consciously keep your good humor and optimism up in the worst of times. If you become depressed, your brain shuts down, you lose your creativity, and you isolate yourself from friends and family. But the darkest days are when you need all of those assets the most.

Being joyful by laughing and enjoying even the small things reduces the effects of stress, increases brain activity, and heightens creativity, all of which can help you overcome your challenges in difficult times. We use the left side of the brain in most situations, but when we laugh we light up the right side. Research shows that people who've been struggling with a problem and feel stuck tend to do much better if they take a break and enjoy a good laugh. The experts say that without laughter, our thought processes can become stuck, our focus narrows, and our ability to solve problems is limited.

The bottom line is this: If you have a sense of humor and you laugh regularly, your mind lights up. You come up with fresh ideas and make better decisions. As a result, your problem-solving abilities are increased.

Sometimes, especially as leaders and as parents, we think being serious and solemn shows our maturity. We want to set a good example at home and at the office. We want to be responsible role models, but being serious all the time isn't good for us or for those who look up to us. Sure, there are times that call for being serious and focused, but there are also times when we need to lighten up, to demonstrate that we can handle pressure and stay in good humor so that creative solutions can be found.

> *Being serious all the time isn't good for us or for those who look up to us.*

Laughter and good humor offer a common denominator and a shared language. They build bonds that hold social networks together. A friendly smile draws people to you. Personal warmth melts away social barriers and eases natural reserve. How many times have you shared a laugh with a total stranger? How many times has that laugh sparked a conversation or led to a friendship? A romance? A working relationship?

Laughter Builds Bonds

A smile brings down the walls. Humor attracts people and bonds them to one another. That's one reason I start every sermon with a joke. It makes people more receptive. When I was growing up, my father's church held an annual Christmas banquet in the ballroom of a Houston hotel at the Galleria Mall. A thousand people attended those banquets.

Each year, the highlight of our Christmas banquet would be a fifteen-minute blooper film of funny things that had happened in church. We'd show clips of people sleeping and yawning through my dad's sermons. We might have other clips of kids acting up that we'd show in slow motion. Then we'd edit together various clips from my father's sermons, but we'd make him say funny things, or we'd speed him up and make him repeat the same phrase again and again so he sounded like a rap artist.

The audience would laugh for fifteen minutes nonstop. They'd still be laughing when the show ended and the lights came on. I'll never forget how all the serving crew from the hotel would come out to watch this video. The waiters, the cooks, and the busboys would line up along the walls around the ballroom to laugh with us.

Since the hotel was part of a mall, shoppers would hear the laughter, too. Within a few minutes, there would be a couple hundred people gathered at the doors, looking in and enjoying the fun.

Every now and then, I'd hear about a new member of the congregation who went shopping at the mall and found a place of worship with us, thanks to our ability to laugh and have fun while being strong in our faith. I guess it's no surprise that blooper shows and specials are so popular on television. Year after year, while other more polished and more sophisticated shows fade away, people still watch the bloopers because they are so funny.

According to Psalm 126:2, "Our mouth was filled with laughter, and our tongue with singing. Then they said among the nations, 'The LORD has done great things for them'" (NKJV). When you're filled with laughter, others notice. You bring honor to God when you live a joy-filled, faith-filled happy life.

There is too much sadness in our world. Many people have lost the joy of living. They're burdened down by problems, heartache, and disappointments. Make it your business to bring joy wherever you go.

There are already enough sour people. You and your smile should stand out in the crowd. One of the best examples you can set is to smile so brightly and laugh so warmly that others just want to share in your joy. They'll want to leave the dark bondage of sadness, depression, and no hope to stand in the light of your optimism and upbeat attitude.

God Favors Those of Good Humor

I've also found that when you are positive and friendly, you attract more of God's favor. When you are a blessing to others, God brings blessings your way. He rewards those who reflect His goodness and make the world a more welcoming place.

I recently met an older man who appeared to be in his seventies. I was surprised when he told me he was 106 years old. It wasn't just his unlined face or healthy appearance that threw me off. He was just so happy, so mentally sharp, and so engaged with everyone around him. He stood in the line nearly forty minutes waiting to visit with me. I told him we could have pulled up a chair for him so he would not have had to stand.

"I don't need to sit down," he said. "When I grow old, I'll sit down."

He was a good-natured, handsome African American fellow.

"I can't believe you're 106. You don't have a wrinkle on your face," I said.

"Joel," he replied, "black don't crack."

Then he ran off two or three more jokes. We laughed and laughed. I normally don't like it when someone in my church has better jokes than me, but I forgave him.

When he walked away, he turned around and said to everyone, "I'll see you next year."

I had no doubt that God would reward him with another year because he was spreading so much joy everywhere he went. I thought to myself that it was no wonder he seemed so healthy; he was so full of joy. He had a great sense of humor. He loved to laugh. Think about all of God's natural healing that had been released and flowing in him all those years.

Sometimes we think the older we are, the more somber we should be and the less fun we should have. But I don't believe that's God's plan. The Scripture says, "If only I may finish my course with joy" (Acts 20:24 AMP). If you don't have joy, laugh regularly, and take the time to play, you will not finish life the way God wants you to finish.

Laugh at Yourself

One of the things about the 106-year-old man that struck me was that he enjoyed poking fun at himself and his advanced age. He saw the humor in growing old, and he laughed at the same things that might frustrate others in their later years. Being willing to laugh at yourself and at life's ups and downs may be one of the greatest gifts you can have.

> *Being willing to laugh at yourself and at life's ups and downs may be one of the greatest gifts you can have.*

We've all known people who throw fits when they make mistakes. Some throw golf clubs. Others throw their bats and helmets. A few throw punches. How much fun are they to be around? But the person who laughs at mistakes, flubs, and goofs is someone people want to share their time with.

When we first moved into the former Compaq Center, the security folks gave me a key to the back area where we park our cars. This was a very strange-looking key. It was small and oblong, kind of fat, and plastic. I had never seen anything like it before. I went to try it on the door, but I could not figure out where to insert it. There was no slot for it. I tried to fit it in the doorknob key slot, thinking maybe it would open up more and take it. No luck.

After ten minutes of trying, I gave up and went to the security station and told the guard I couldn't figure out how to open the door.

He offered to go to the parking area and show me. So I gave him the key and back we went. When we arrived at the door, he reached up to the side of it and touched an electronic panel. I didn't even know it was up there!

When he just touched the panel, the door automatically opened because the "key" he'd given me put out an electronic signal to it, like a garage door opener or a remote car key.

When I told the guard how I'd tried to use the key in the doorknob, he laughed and laughed.

I thought, *I'm glad you think it's funny, because we're going to miss you!*

You've heard the saying "If you can't beat them, join them." That really was pretty dumb, so I laughed along with him.

The other day I had breakfast alone in a hotel room and when I was done I wheeled the breakfast cart out into the hallway so they could pick it up. I forgot until the last moment that I only had my shorts on. Not gym shorts, underwear.

I'd already opened the door and had the cart halfway out when it hit me. I peeked my head out into the hall and nobody was out there, so I pushed the cart all the way out, but the back legs got stuck on the threshold.

I had to pick up the rear of the cart, lift it out of the room, step out into the hall, and push it against the wall.

As I did that, I heard a *click*.

That was the sound of my hotel room door closing and locking, with me in my underwear still out in the hallway.

Have you heard the phrase "All dressed up with no place to go"?

Well, I was *not* dressed at all, and there was no place to go!

My heart sank.

I saw a housekeeping cart about five doors down. I ran to it as fast as I could and got a towel and wrapped it around me. The cleaning lady came out, and I asked her if she could let me into my room.

"I need your ID for that," she said.

"It's in the wallet in the pants I'm not wearing," I replied.

I kept smiling, remembering how it had helped with the airline ticket clerk. The housekeeper went for it, too. After a few minutes, she opened the door, stared at me strangely, and said, "You know, you look different on TV."

"Yes, I usually wear clothes for my broadcasts."

To tell you the truth, she laughed some at that, but I laughed louder than she did. It takes a secure person to laugh at himself, especially when he is pants-less in public.

Laugh and Love

People around me tend to laugh a lot. Since smiling attracts people, they probably make many friends on my account, but that's okay. I've spent more than twenty-four years keeping Victoria healthy and surrounded by friends because of my ability to make her laugh—even when I'm not trying.

That's a good thing, because research has also shown that the couples and families who laugh together stay together. They have stronger relationships and tighter bonds. As you might suspect, we are a very tight family.

A few years ago, right before I stepped onto the platform to minister, Victoria told me that my hair was sticking up in the back.

"Put a little hair spray back there," my wife said.

I didn't know where the hair spray was.

"It's back in the bathroom, on the shelf, in a red can."

I was in a big hurry so I hustled back and grabbed the red can off the shelf. Then I sprayed and sprayed that little sprig of stand-up hair, but it would not stay down. So I sprayed it a couple more times and headed out the door.

After the service that day, Victoria said, "Why didn't you spray your hair? It was still sticking up."

"Victoria, I did spray. But that hair spray you gave me doesn't work. I sprayed and sprayed."

She then kindly offered to show me how to use hair spray. I brought the red can out and handed it to her.

She studied it for a second and then broke up laughing.

"Joel, this isn't hair spray. This is air freshener."

I just smiled and said, "You know what? Even if it does stick up, I've got the best-smelling hair around."

House of Humor

Laughter is a great addition to every home. The enemy cannot stand the sound of joyful laughter. He cannot stand the sound of husbands and wives and family members having fun together. He wants there to be so much strife, tension, and pressure that we never have any joy in our homes.

Don't fall into that trap. That's one thing I appreciate about Victoria. She loves to laugh. She keeps a fun atmosphere in our home. When Victoria laughs she doesn't laugh to herself. She doesn't laugh under her breath. When she laughs it fills the whole house with joy.

Her laugh is so contagious I can be sitting on the other side of the house, minding my own business, watching television, but when I hear her laughter, I feel like laughing, too. Before long I find myself laughing just because she's laughing.

Usually, I just have to go find out what's tickling her so much. That happened recently and I found her holding a photograph of our son, Jonathan, when he was just a baby, maybe six or eight months old.

We hadn't looked at that photo in a long time. I'd forgotten about it entirely. But one day we'd put a wig and sunglasses on him, and our son looked like a little baby Elvis. We had a good laugh at that, especially since Jonathan is now a very good guitar player!

If you have small children, there's no reason not to laugh every day, not just at them and their antics, but with them, too. Don't get so caught up in all the pressures of parenting that you don't take time to enjoy your children and see the humor in what they do.

> *Don't get so caught up in all the pressures of parenting that you don't take time to enjoy your children and see the humor in what they do.*

When Jonathan was about two years old, I heard this loud screaming coming from his bedroom. I knew he was having a nightmare. I ran up there as fast as I could, opened the door, and Jonathan was sitting up in his bed, his eyes as big as saucers.

"Jonathan, what's wrong?"

"Daddy," he said, "the Holy Ghost is under my bed."

I assured my son he had nothing to fear from the Holy Ghost.

Our daughter, Alexandra, is equally entertaining. When she was about that same age, I'd work on my weekend messages for church in an office right outside our bedroom.

One day Alexandra strolled in and said, "Daddy, can we go play?"

"No, Alexandra, not right now. It'll be another hour or so before I finish this."

Every five minutes she returned.

"Daddy, is it time yet?"

Again and again, she'd ask me.

I felt a little frustrated with her so finally, when she showed up at my office door again, I said, "Alexandra, listen, I'm trying to concentrate. Please don't come back in. I'll come get you when I can play."

Five minutes later, the door creaks open and this sweet little-girl voice says, "Daddy, are you still trying to constipate?"

"No, honey," I said. "I'm actually pretty regular!"

Couples Therapy

Friends often ask Victoria and me about the secret to a healthy marriage. We always tell them two things: Number one, respect. Always be respectful, even when you disagree. And number two, laughter. Don't ever stop laughing together. Make sure your house is full of joy and happiness. We don't have to work at that; it seems to happen on its own.

The other day I walked into our bedroom and Victoria was over in the corner reading something with her back to me. I had come home much earlier than I had planned. I realized she hadn't heard me walk in. I debated whether to say something, but instead, I decided to just quietly wait for her to notice me. I thought that might be better than startling her.

I thought wrong. When she turned around and I was there, she must have jumped three feet in the air. I know they say white people can't jump, but Victoria got some air.

She had this shocked look on her face, and I could not help but laugh and laugh.

There was one problem with that.

Victoria was not joining in. In fact, she looked upset.

I tried to stop laughing. Really, I tried to zip it, but the harder I tried, the funnier it hit me, and the louder I laughed.

After a minute or so of watching me laugh, Victoria finally gave in and began laughing, too.

But by that time, I was over it.

I was done, but she couldn't stop laughing. So, I joined in for a few more minutes just to keep her company.

If your relationship isn't what you'd like it to be, I recommend a good dose of humor, laughter, and joy. I know the pressures of life can weigh on the best of marriages and test the love of even the most devoted, but it might help you to remember why you fell in love in the first place.

Remember the things you enjoyed doing together, the fun and the laughter that made you always want to be together? Forget what's pulling you apart. Go back to the laughter that made you want to go from being single to being a couple.

If you would bring that joy back into the home, you would see a freshness, a new life in your relationship. That is what some friends of mine did. They were good people who were struggling in their marriage. They loved each other, but they were under a lot of pressure, and it was pulling them apart. They needed a break from their troubles so they decided that once a week, they'd put all the struggles aside and watch a funny movie together.

The first night, they sat there and laughed and laughed some more. It was the first time either of them had shed tears of joy, instead of sadness, in a long time.

The next week, the same thing happened. After a month or so of this, they noticed that their troubles didn't seem quite so heavy. They found that their focus shifted from problems to solutions.

When I saw them next, they marveled at how something as simple as a "Funny Movie Night" could have such a major impact on their relationship and their lives.

Their laughter altered the atmosphere of their home. Their tears of joy washed their relationship clean of its tarnish. They were no longer struggling. They were snuggling.

Free-Flowing Laughter

Laughter will help your relationships, too. Welcome it into your home. Make room for it. Clean out the spare bedroom if you have to. Open the doors and windows and let it fill your house.

In the Old Testament, enemies took over rival cities by clogging the wells that provided water to residents. They filled the wells with stones. This forced the people in the towns to leave the protection of the city walls in search of water. The enemy would then attack them.

You and I have wells of joy inside. As children, those wells flowed freely. We played and laughed and enjoyed each moment. But too often our wells become clogged as we grow older. Stones of disappointment, hurt, unforgiveness, stress, and doubt pile up and block the flow.

Genesis 26:18 says, "Isaac dug again the wells of water,... for the Philistines had stopped them up" (NKJV). It's interesting, in part, because the name Isaac means "laughter." I believe it's significant that Isaac dug new wells. God is saying to unclog your wells with laughter so His goodness can once again live within.

When one of our sinks clogs up at home, I buy some Drano, pour it down the drain, and wait fifteen minutes. When I come back, the sink is unclogged. Laughter works like Drano. It cleans out whatever is clogging our lives. When you laugh regularly it's just like you are cleaning out those pipes.

The instructions on the Drano bottle say to use it on a regular basis to keep the pipes free and clear. The same holds true with laughter. Pour it in, whenever you can. Find the humor in everyday moments. Make laughter a lifestyle choice. Welcome joy into your home as a permanent resident.

> *Welcome joy into your home as a permanent resident.*

Job 8:21 says, "He will yet fill your mouth with laughter" (NIV). God's dream is for you to be filled with laughter. He gave laughter the power to heal your body, soothe your spirits, attract admirers, and mend your relationships.

Don't take humor lightly. Dare to laugh openly, especially at yourself. Give your loved ones the gift of your laughter. When you do all that, you honor God, and He will reward you. You will finish your course with joy!

PART
VI

Be a Dream Releaser

CHAPTER TWENTY-TWO

Help Others to Win

I've heard it said, "You will always have what you want if you help others get what they want." If you want to be happy and joyful, use your influence to help others succeed. Take time to give good advice. Introduce others to helpful people you know. Make a phone call and put in a good word whenever possible.

When you help others to win, you are sowing a seed for yourself to rise higher. Cheryl, who works at a big corporation, told me that her supervisor refused to train her on a new computer program. The company had sent this supervisor to a class so she could learn how to run the program, but when she came back she wouldn't share any of the information. She was afraid if she helped others, they might get promoted over her. So she kept the knowledge and training to herself.

But the truth is, when you hold others back, you are really holding yourself back. If you will live unselfishly and help others reach your level, God will make sure somebody is there to lift you higher, too. Alec, a professional mountain climber, was on his way to the top of a peak when a snowstorm hit. It was very cold and hard to breathe. Even some of the most experienced mountain climbers couldn't make it.

A little farther up the mountain, the storm turned into a blizzard. They were still six hours from the top. Climbing was extremely difficult. Each step was a struggle. Then Alec saw another climber lying along the trail curled up, asleep or passed out. He was in danger of freezing to death. He had a faint heartbeat and was barely strong enough to breathe.

Several other climbers had passed by. Alec's team told him to keep going.

"If you stop and try to help him, you could lose your own life," they said.

Alec could not leave him there to die. He told the team to go on. Alec knelt beside the fallen climber. He massaged the man's arms and legs and face to get the blood flowing and keep him awake. His efforts revived the stricken man enough that Alec was able to get him on his feet and walk him down the mountain, saving his life.

The doctor who examined them both told Alec that he'd done more than save a life. He'd likely saved two.

"Your arms and legs show early signs of frostbite," the doctor said. "You wouldn't have made it much higher before you'd have been in serious trouble yourself. Your efforts to save the fallen climber probably benefited you as much as him because it increased your circulation and forced you to head down the mountain."

It's easy to get so caught up in your climb to the top that you don't want to stop and help someone else. But when you take time to help others in their struggles, you set yourself up for even greater victories.

Share Your Influence

The apostle Paul would never have become such a major figure of faith without the support of another disciple, Barnabas. As you may know, Paul was not always a believer. In fact, he'd once been known as Saul, a persecutor of believers.

Saul's attitude changed dramatically on the road to Damascus when God touched his life and transformed him into the apostle Paul we all know and love.

But it took awhile for the apostle Paul to convince the other followers of Jesus that he wasn't the same old Saul. In Acts 9:26, we are told of this fear and suspicion toward the new apostle.

The next verse says that Barnabas stood up for Paul. Barnabas put in a good word for him. He said, in effect, "Hey, I can vouch for Paul. I know who he is. He is the real deal."

If it had not been for Barnabas using his influence, Paul probably would not have been in a position to write more than half of the New Testament. We don't hear a lot about Barnabas. Paul greatly overshadowed him. But if you were to talk to Paul, he would say, "I succeeded because Barnabas dared to take a risk and opened a door that I could not open on my own. Barnabas believed in me when nobody else did."

Even more powerful is the fact that every life Paul touched later would mean a reward for Barnabas as well. There is no greater legacy than to help someone else win.

> *There is no greater legacy than to help someone else win.*

God has so blessed me, I am constantly looking for ways to use my influence to help others come up higher. I recently received a call from a pastor in another city. He explained that his church was trying to buy a building from their city. I happened to know a person in a position to help, so I put in a good word. This isn't someone you'd find in the phone book. He doesn't have his own business. But I was able to reach him, and I was glad to help someone else secure a win. I've learned that when you do for others what they cannot do for themselves, you will never lack God's favor. You will never lack God's blessing.

After Your Climb, Reach Back

Michael is a talented musician who plays guitar for our services at Lakewood Church. He has performed with great musicians from around the world. He is at the top of his game, yet he is generous with his time and shares his talents with others. I know this well because Michael took our son, Jonathan, under his wing several years ago when Jonathan expressed an interest in playing the guitar.

We never asked Michael to teach Jonathan, and he has never requested payment, even though they've been working together more than eight years now. It's obvious Michael is a great teacher because he's helped Jonathan become a great guitar player.

There is something more to know about Michael and his willingness to help others. Before he came to Lakewood, Michael led a different lifestyle than the one he leads today. He used drugs and partied. That lifestyle led to challenges, but Michael no longer uses drugs. He's not out partying on Friday nights anymore.

Now he is leading worship in our Celebrate Recovery classes. Michael has won, and now he is helping other people get free from addictions.

Our son, Jonathan, will always remember that Michael helped him develop his gifts as a great guitar player. Seventy years from now, he will still remember, *I'm successful in part because of Michael. He helped me to win. He brought the best out in me.* When you help someone win, you become a friend for life. You will always have a special place in their heart.

A letter came to me early in my days as pastor of our church. I'd stepped onto the platform but still didn't feel at home there. I was very unsure of myself on Sunday mornings. I found the envelope on my desk during that period of self-doubt, and when I saw the name on the return address I recognized it immediately.

The letter was from John Maxwell, a former pastor and best-selling author.

I had never met him before. I had only admired his writing and teachings. I opened that letter as quickly as I could, and then I was touched by what he'd written.

"I watched you on television on Sunday and you were outstanding," he wrote. "I've got to tell you, you've got what it takes." He went on to list several things that he liked. "You keep it simple. You've got a good personality." He also offered several suggestions: "Here's some advice. Here's what you can do to be less nervous. Here's what I do when I'm getting prepared."

John Maxwell, a pastor and best-selling author, was sharing his secrets with me. Giving his encouragement. He had forty years of experience, and he was voluntarily pouring it into a young man he'd never even met before. He didn't have to do that. He'd already won. But John understands this principle: True success is when you reach back and bring somebody along with you.

I arranged to meet with John a few weeks after I received his note, which I still have. Because of what he did for me, John will be a friend of mine for life. He spoke encouragement into me at a very critical time on my journey.

Look around this week. Who has God put in your life? They're not there by accident. God brings people across our paths on purpose. We each should live with this awareness: *I am here to add value to people. I am here to help others succeed.*

Don't go around thinking, *I wonder what they can do for me? I wonder what they have to offer?* Your attitude should be to think of what helping hand you can offer others, what you can teach them, and what connections you can share. Like John Maxwell, look for opportunities to call out the seeds of greatness God has planted in each of us.

Be a Dream Releaser

Even as you work to accomplish your goals and build your own happy life, be sure to use your talent, your influence, and your experience to help those around you in need of a lift. There is nothing more rewarding than to end a day with the knowledge that you've helped someone else move closer to a dream. You may have fulfilled your own goals for the day, but even better, you also took time to invest in someone else. It may have been just a two-minute phone call to encourage a friend or a younger person, or five minutes after work to help a co-worker, or lending a hand to help a child with a school project.

When I look back over my life, outside of my family, I can think of four or five dream releasers; people who took special interest in me. A coach in high school spoke faith into me. I was the smallest on the team, but somehow he convinced me that I was the biggest, baddest, toughest player since Michael Jordan.

Another dream releaser, my Sunday school teacher Larry, invested in me. Larry, who still attends Lakewood Church, taught me and the other boys like we were paying attention! He made it fun. He didn't just go by the lesson. He always went the extra mile. I can say now, "I'm successful in part because Larry helped me to win."

You may not see my coach or Larry or my other dream releasers up here on the platform, but let me tell you, they are up here with me. John Maxwell is up here with me, too. I'm happy and successful because so many people reached back to me. They knew the value of helping someone else succeed and find joy.

Being successful doesn't necessarily make you great. What makes you great is when you reach back and help somebody else become great. Greatness is saying, "God has blessed me not to just sit on my throne and let everybody see my accomplishments. No, I know God has blessed me to become a blessing. God has helped me win so I can help someone else win."

> *What makes you great is when you reach back and help somebody else become great.*

Greatness comes to those who say, "God helped me overcome this addiction, now I'll find somebody who's addicted and help them overcome." "God has blessed me with a happy, healthy family. I'll find a family that's struggling and help them get back on track." Or, "God has helped me pass this course in high school. Now I'll go to my friend and help him study so he can pass, too."

Reach Back and Reach Out, Too

Even better than reaching back is reaching out to those who are side by side with you and giving them a hand up. In 1936 the Olympic Games were held in Berlin, Germany. Hitler was in control, and he didn't want any blacks to compete, much less win. One Nazi leader called blacks "nonhumans." There was a young black American athlete by the name of Jesse Owens in the competition. Despite Hitler's wishes, Jesse already had won three gold medals, and he was about to compete for his fourth.

This event was the broad jump, now known as the running long jump. Jesse felt hostility from the haters in the crowd, and he began to lose focus. On his first attempt he faulted. The judges claimed he crossed the line before he jumped. He was faulted again on his second attempt.

One more fault and he would be disqualified. This was very much out of character for Jesse, but he'd let the crowd's boos and name-calling get to him. They were still jeering at him and shouting against him. He was very rattled.

Jesse's main competitor was a tall German athlete named Luz Long. They did not know each other. Jesse may have assumed that Luz Long, who was a sports hero in his country, was his enemy, too.

But in front of tens of thousands of people, Luz Long did what seemed unthinkable in that setting. He walked up, put his arm around Jesse Owens, and offered some advice.

He said, "Jesse, the qualifying distance is only twenty-three feet. You've jumped twenty-six feet many times before. Just move your starting mark back three inches, and that way you'll make sure to jump before the line so they can't disqualify you."

Jesse took his advice, and on the next jump he qualified. The black American went on to break the world record and win his fourth gold medal. He beat out Luz Long on his final jump, but Long was the first to congratulate him.

Jesse Owens later said of his German dream releaser, "It took a lot of courage for him to befriend me in front of Hitler. You can melt all the medals and cups I have, and they wouldn't be a plating on the 24-carat friendship I felt for Luz Long at that moment."

I've heard the saying "No one stands taller on their climb for success than when he bends down to help somebody else." If you will live unselfishly and be willing to give advice as Luz Long did, you will always have God's blessings. When you are a dream releaser, God will make sure your dreams come to pass.

I've found the greatest legacy is not what we leave *for* people, but what we leave *in* people. Luz Long, who died during World War II, left Jesse Owens with a memory of courage and friendship that he never forgot— and neither did the rest of the world.

Invest in the Success of Others

Here's a key: Learn to believe in people before they succeed. Anybody can be a friend after someone is successful, after they win, after they are promoted, after they break the addiction. But when they need us the most is *before* they are successful.

Many people need only a little help, a bit of advice, a word of encouragement. Do for them what you would want somebody to do for you. You may have experiences that could save others heartache and pain. Don't keep your knowledge to yourself. Pick up the phone. Call them. Help someone grow into greatness.

If you want God's continued blessing on your life, you can't be selfish. You must go out of your way to help others. You must make some sacrifices to teach, to train, to share what you know to help others find their happiness and joy.

I have a friend who is black and grew up in poverty in a housing project. His mother raised him on her own. His future looked bleak, even though he was very bright. But he worked hard, and with God's favor he earned a scholarship to an Ivy League college.

Most of his fellow students were from white, well-to-do families. His roommate was a sharp young white man from an upper-income family who had traveled the world. My friend had rarely left his neighborhood. Their lives were very different, yet they became best friends. He told his roommate that his dream was to become a television news journalist. He'd dreamed of that job since childhood.

His roommate supported him but said, "You'll never become a journalist with your vocabulary like it is. It's too limited. We've got to do something about it." The roommate saw his potential and invested in it. They worked on his vocabulary together, studying the dictionary and practicing pronunciation.

This went on day after day, week after week. For four years the roommate taught my friend a new word every day. The roommate was a dream releaser. He'd been blessed with a good upbringing and far more resources. Now he passed on the blessings, investing in the success of another person from a far less privileged background.

Today that young man from the projects, Byron Pitts, is an award-winning journalist seen by millions of people every week on *60 Minutes*, the number one news program in America. He told me, "I would never be where I am if it were not for my roommate. I would have never made it this far if he had not taken the time to invest in me."

Give the Gift of a Dream

True success comes when you unselfishly bring somebody up with you, just as Luz Long and my friend's college roommate did.

Shay was ten years old and both physically and mentally challenged, but he loved baseball. One day he and his father walked by a baseball field where a bunch of young boys Shay's age were playing a game.

"Do you think they would let me play on one of their teams?" Shay asked his father.

Shay's dad knew that he couldn't play at the same level as the other boys, but he didn't want to disappoint his son. The father asked one of the boys in the dugout if Shay could play. The little boy looked around at his friends, trying to get some advice. Finally he said, "Well, sir. There are only two innings left, and we're down by three runs. Sure, he can come play. We'll put him in the outfield."

Shay was so excited. He took the field with joy, just radiating happiness. In the last inning their team was down by one run. There were two outs, with a runner on third, and it was Shay's turn to bat.

His teammates considered using a pinch hitter in hopes of winning the game, but they decided it wouldn't be right to take Shay out. They sent him to the plate with little hope that he could hit the ball. They thought they'd already lost the game. The other team had a very good pitcher.

The star pitcher wound up and threw the first pitch so fast, Shay didn't see it coming. He swung late and missed it by a mile. At that point the pitcher realized that Shay had some physical challenges. The next pitch he threw at about half the speed of the first. But once again Shay swung and missed.

This time the pitcher stepped off the mound and walked closer to home plate. He threw the ball as soft as he could, and believe it or not, Shay hit it. The ball dribbled about five feet and stopped in front of the pitcher's mound. The pitcher ran and picked it up.

Just out of instinct he was about to fire it to first base and win the game, but out of the corner of his eye he saw Shay struggling to run the best he could. The pitcher's heart took over for his instincts. He threw the ball over the first baseman's head into the outfield.

Shay's dad yelled, "Run, Shay! Run!"

The runner on third scored while Shay rounded first and headed toward second. By this time all the other boys knew what was going on. The outfielder threw the ball over the shortstop's head. The player backing up the shortstop let it go through his legs.

Shay rounded third base and the whole crowd was cheering his name. He scored the winning run while his father watched in tears. Shay was nearly bursting with joy when he crossed the plate and was hugged by his teammates.

Shay's team won the game, but all of those boys won God's favor that day. Sometimes you have to give up winning one thing to win something even bigger. In this case, those boys on the opposing team won a friend for life. They gave something to Shay that he will never forget.

Sometimes you have to make sacrifices to let someone else step ahead. Sometimes you have to put your own dreams on hold temporarily so you can help release a dream in somebody else.

> *Sometimes you have to put your own dreams on hold temporarily so you can help release a dream in somebody else.*

What you make happen for others, God will make happen for you. When you live unselfishly and you help somebody else get ahead, God will make sure someone is there to help you get ahead.

My challenge to you is to make every day a Shay day. Find somebody to invest in, a person you can help come up higher. Don't go to bed without knowing you did something for someone to help them win. I'm asking us all to become dream releasers. Believe in people before they succeed. Call out those seeds of greatness.

When you do for others what they cannot do for themselves, you will always have God's favor. You will accomplish your dreams, and then God will take you higher and higher.

CHAPTER TWENTY-THREE

Be a People Builder

Helen, a junior high math teacher in Minnesota, spent most of the school week teaching a difficult "new math" lesson. She could tell her students were frustrated and restless by week's end. They were becoming rowdy so she told them to put their books away. She then instructed the class to take out clean sheets of paper. She gave each of them this assignment: Write down every one of your classmates' names on the left, and then, on the right, put down one thing you like about that student.

The tense and rowdy mood subsided and the room quieted when the students went to work. Their moods lifted as they dug into the assignment. There was frequent laughter and giggling. They looked around the room, sharing quips about one another. Helen's class was a much happier group when the bell signaled the end of the school day.

She took their lists home over the weekend and spent both days off recording what was said about each student on separate sheets of paper so she could pass on all the nice things said about each person without giving away who said what.

The next Monday she handed out the lists she'd made for each student. The room buzzed with excitement and laughter.

"Wow. Thanks! This is the coolest!"

"I didn't think anyone even noticed me!"

"Someone thinks I'm beautiful?"

Helen had come up with the exercise just to settle down her class, but it ended up giving them a big boost. They grew closer as classmates and more confident as individuals. She could tell they all seemed more relaxed and joyful.

About ten years later, Helen learned that one of her favorite students in that class, a charming boy named Mark, had been killed while serving in Vietnam. She received an invitation to the funeral from Mark's parents, who included a note saying they wanted to be sure she came to their farmhouse after the services to speak with them.

Helen arrived and the grieving parents took her aside. The father showed her Mark's billfold and then from it he removed two worn pieces of lined paper that had been taped, folded, and refolded many times over the years. Helen recognized her handwriting on the paper and tears came to her eyes.

Mark's parents said he'd always carried the list of nice things written by his classmates. "Thank you so much for doing that," his mother said. "He treasured it, as you can see."

Still teary-eyed, Helen walked into the kitchen where many of Mark's former junior high classmates were assembled. They saw that Mark's parents had his list from that class. One by one, they either produced their own copies from wallets and purses or they confessed to keeping theirs in an album, drawer, diary, or file at home.

Helen the teacher was a "people builder." She instinctively found ways to build up her students. Being a people builder means you consistently find ways to invest in and bring out the best in others. You give without asking for anything in return. You offer advice, speak faith into them, build their confidence, and challenge them to go higher.

I've found that all most people need is a boost. All they need is a lit-

> *All most people need is a boost.*

tle push, a little encouragement, to become what God has created them to be. The fact is, none of us will reach our highest potential by ourselves. We need one another. You can be the one to tip the scales for someone else. You can be the one to stir up their seeds of greatness.

Draw Out the Best in Others

Reggie Jackson, the Hall of Fame baseball player, said, "A great manager has the ability to make a player think that he is better than he is. He convinces you to have confidence in yourself. He lets you know that he believes in you, and before long you discover talent that you never knew you had."

That's what happens when we believe the best in someone. We draw out the best. The Scripture says in 1 Thessalonians 5:11, "Encourage one another and build each other up" (NIV). The word *encourage* simply means "to urge forward." Every one of us should have someone we believe in, someone we're urging forward, someone we're helping to achieve goals and dreams.

How do you encourage someone? You study that person and identify what he or she does well. What excites him? What are her strengths? An encourager sees things in others that they often can't see in themselves. A simple compliment, a single word of encouragement, can give a person the confidence he or she needs to take that step of faith.

A young man who'd been struggling with finding direction in his life was home for a visit from college in 1975. He visited his mother's beauty shop and found a regular customer, Ruth Green, was having her hair done. He greeted her and sat down, but grew nervous because she was staring so intently at him.

Finally Ms. Green lifted the hairdryer off her head and said, "Somebody get me a pen and a piece of paper."

She wrote down a vision she'd had about the young man when he walked into his mother's shop. She handed it to him and it said: "Denzel, you will speak to millions. You will travel the world and you will make a positive difference."

Young Denzel Washington put that prophecy in his wallet and in his heart. In the years that followed, whenever he became discouraged in his acting career, he pulled out Ms. Green's prophecy. It reminded him that someone believed in him.

To this day, the Academy Award–winning actor carries around that prophecy. Who knows where he would be if Ms. Green hadn't taken the time to bless his future. Who knows if he would have been such a success if she hadn't planted those seeds of faith in his heart. You never know the impact a small note, a kind word of encouragement, can have.

We can either draw out the best in people or we can draw out the worst. I read that 75 percent of people in prison reported that either their parents or their guardians had predicted in childhood where they would end up. The wrong seeds were planted. Low expectations were set.

When a child is told to expect the worst, the child becomes the worst. I often wonder what would have happened if somebody would have told those people in prison that they might one day be doctors or entrepreneurs or great teachers. There's no telling where those inmates might have ended up if only they'd had people builders in their lives.

If only someone had believed in them and taken the time to draw out their gifts, to listen to their dreams, to see what they were good at, and then encourage them to be the best they could be. If only someone had given them permission to succeed instead of a prediction that they would fail.

Permission to Succeed

A friend of mine, Robert, had an uncle who set him on a path to success early in life. This uncle had been in China since his birth, but when he returned they met on the front porch of the Iowa farm where Robert grew up.

He'd watched the uncle's car driving toward the family's home on their dusty lane and Robert was so excited to finally meet this uncle. When he pulled in the gate, little Robert ran out there to meet him. The uncle got out, gave him a big hug, and swung him around and around.

"You must be Robert. I've heard so much about you," the uncle said.

Then the uncle stepped back and looked at him. And out of the blue he said, "You know what, Robert? I think one day you will be a minister. In fact, I think one day you will be a great minister."

Why did the uncle say this? There were no ministers in this family. He simply felt something inside, and he was bold enough to speak it out by faith. He planted a seed in little Robert's heart. That night as Robert lay in his bed he secretly prayed, "God, let what my uncle said be true. Let me be a minister one day."

As you may know, Robert Schuller, who grew up in Alton, Iowa, became one of the great ministers of our time. Isn't it amazing what a simple word of encouragement can do? Look what it did in his life.

You have the ability to stir up someone's dreams by giving them permission to succeed. You can light a fire on the inside that glows joyfully for a lifetime. When you take time to believe in someone, and you speak faith into the heart of another, your words can become the seed God nourishes.

I'm asking you to grant others the permission to succeed. Be a seed planter. Be a people builder. Don't become so focused on your own dreams, your own goals, that you grow only yourself. Be on the lookout for those you can urge forward. Learn to speak faith into them. Give them a greater vision. Speak the blessing over others' lives.

I know an older gentleman who is great at this. Any time he sees a small child, he'll ask the parents' permission to call them over and say, "Young man (or Young lady), I have a very special talent, something only a few people can do. I have the ability to pick a winner."

The child's eyes usually grow big. He'll ask the child if he can do an evaluation. Of course, the parents are playing along. He'll stand back and look at the child, walk around very slowly, saying, "Uh-huh. Yes. Okay. I see..."

When he finishes the "evaluation," he'll say, "I have great news. I've never been wrong. I'm right every time. You, my friend, indeed, you are a winner!"

The child lights up with a smile, runs back to the parents, and says, "Hey, Mom. Hey, Dad. Guess what? I'm a winner."

My friend is building up those children, urging them forward, bolstering their confidence, and instilling self-esteem.

This is such a simple thing to do, yet so many people benefit. I'm sure there are many in your life—people you work with, play sports with and live near—who could use an encouraging and approving word. Someone around you is craving your blessing.

You can't imagine what it will mean to those you affirm when you give them your approval and let them know in no

> *Everyone needs to be valued.*
> *Everyone needs to be appreciated.*

uncertain terms that you are proud of them and you think they are destined to do great things. Everyone needs to be valued. Everyone needs to
be appreciated. Every person needs that blessing.

Cast Your Votes of Confidence

Even Henry Ford benefited from encouragement in his early days, and one
of his boosters was none other than Thomas Edison. The pioneering auto-
maker was introduced to Edison as "the man trying to build a car that ran
on gasoline." When Edison heard this, his face lit up. He slammed his fist
on the table and said, "You've got it. A car that has its own power plant;
that's a brilliant idea."

Up to that point, Henry Ford had dealt with many naysayers and dis-
couragers. He had just about convinced himself to give up, but along came
Edison and spoke faith into him. That was a turning point in Henry
Ford's life.

"I thought I had a good idea, but I started to doubt myself," he once
said. "Then came along one of the greatest minds that's ever lived and
gave me his complete approval."

A simple vote of confidence helped launched the automotive industry.
We don't realize the power we hold. We don't always realize what it means
when we tell somebody, "I believe in you. You've got what it takes. I'm
behind you 100 percent."

Cast your vote. Step up and volunteer to be someone's number one fan.
Encourage them. Lift them up when they are down. Celebrate when they
succeed. Pray when they are struggling. Urge them to keep pressing forward. That's what it means to be a people builder.

We all need someone to believe in us more than we believe in ourselves,
to see our potential, to look beyond where we are now and guide us to
what God has planned for us.

Jesus didn't focus on the faults of those around Him. He saw their
potential. His disciple Peter, in particular, was rough around the edges,
hot-tempered and foulmouthed. Yet Jesus looked beyond all that and saw
Peter's potential. Jesus spoke faith into Peter and helped him form a vision

of himself rising higher and overcoming obstacles. His encouragement helped Peter become what he was created to be.

It says in Proverbs 12:25 that a word of encouragement works wonders. When you help people expand their thinking to create a real vision of victory for their lives, they will accomplish things that they never could have before. Their success will come, in part, as the result of your faith, your confidence in them, and the seeds you planted to help them grow.

We Rise to Expectations

The principal in a California high school conducted an experiment in which he told three teachers that they'd been judged the brightest and most effective educators in their school district. As a result, they'd been selected for a new program.

"We are giving you the top ninety students, the smartest students with the highest IQs, and you will teach them accelerated courses," the teachers were told.

The students and the teachers naturally were excited and proud to be selected as "the cream of the crop." Their performances improved dramatically in the new program. At the end of that school year, those three classes had learned 30 percent more than the other students. They were 30 percent further along in their educations.

Imagine their shock when the principal informed the teachers that this was only an experiment, and in reality their students had been randomly selected and were not high achievers. Still, the teachers were amazed at how well the students had performed and they congratulated themselves. Then the principal broke the rest of the news.

They were not the top three teachers in the district. They, too, had been randomly selected. The principal's experiment confirmed that we rise to the level of our expectations. When you build up those around you, they rise to your expectations.

You may not realize it, but my books are sold to only the smartest, the brightest, the most creative, the most talented, the most generous, and the happiest readers in the world! You, too, are the cream of the crop. I have incredible confidence in you. I know you will do great things. You will fulfill your God-given destiny.

Now that I've built you up, pass it on. Look around and see whom God has put in your life to inspire and motivate. Even small gestures like a kind word, a note of encouragement, or recognizing a person's gifts can make a difference to someone in need of a boost.

Kind Words Can Change Lives

A teen girl struggled with anorexia. She stood nearly six feet tall but weighed less than one hundred pounds. She wouldn't eat but a couple hundred calories a day. She became depressed and disillusioned. She cut off ties to friends and family. Starvation seemed like a reasonable option to her because she felt she had no purpose.

One day a longtime friend from school called and asked if she would help her with math homework. She pleaded for help, so the anorexic teen agreed to help her. They worked together on the problems and afterward the friend said, just in passing, "You are so smart and you have such a way of explaining things. You would make a great math teacher one day."

That simple comment planted a seed within this troubled teen. The encouraging words gave her a sense of purpose. She realized that she had talent, and that she had something to give others. Her perspective changed, and so did the course of her life. Twenty years later, she is a healthy and happy mother of three and an award-winning math teacher who works with underachieving children. She credits the turnaround in her life to the words of the girl she'd helped with her math homework.

A simple affirmation, an encouraging comment, or a bit of praise can make a huge difference. When you bless people with your words, you speak faith into them.

Growing up, we had a tradition my mother began on our birthdays. Before we could eat any birthday cake, we each had to come up with one nice thing to say about the birthday boy or girl. In my younger days, I dreaded that tradition. For one thing, I could never think of anything good to say about my brother, Paul. The only thing I came up with was, "You sure have a good-looking brother!"

As I grew older, though, I began to realize the importance and the value of not only hearing those words but saying them, too. Simple affirmations can do so much for our confidence and our self-esteem. Even just a few words of praise can make someone's day or plant a seed of hope. "Your drawings are amazing." "You have such a way with words." "Your voice has so much character."

One thing you can be certain of, people never grow tired of hearing compliments and encouragements. You can go on and on about how wonderful they are and they'll never be bored! That's proof of just how much we hunger for praise and direction in our lives.

John Wooden, the late basketball genius, told his players, "After you score a basket, always look for the player who made the pass to you and acknowledge them. Nod your head. Smile. Point your finger. But do something to express your appreciation."

One of the players said, "What if he's not looking?"

Wooden replied, "Don't worry. He'll be looking."

The point is, we all love to be appreciated. We love to be valued, to feel encouraged.

Mark Twain said, "I can live for a whole year off of one good compliment." Who can you give the gift of encouragement to? Don't leave out even those who seem to have accomplished more than most. Everyone wants to be

> *Who can you give the gift of encouragement to?*

appreciated. Abraham Lincoln was carrying several things when he was killed that are on display now at the Smithsonian Institution in Washington, D.C. He had a handkerchief with his initials on it. He had a five-dollar bill, and he had a newspaper article folded up. The headline read "Abraham Lincoln—One of the Greatest Statesmen That's Ever Lived."

Why would he carry around an article like that? Lincoln served during difficult times of civil war and upheaval over slavery and other major issues troubling our young country. He was criticized, ridiculed, and constantly put down. So even this great man needed to be reminded now and then that someone appreciated and believed in him.

I don't know about you, but I want to be a dream releaser and a wallet filler. I want to speak much vision, much faith, and many blessings to inspire others and give them encouragement. You have the power to help someone go to a higher level. The people in your life are not there by accident. Are you believing in them? Are you urging them forward? Are you speaking the blessing?

I have an assignment for you. Find at least one person you can build up. You may have four or five different people. Write their names on a sheet of paper. List what you like about them, their strengths. Pray over that. Ask God to show you ways to bless them. And then speak favor into their lives. Write them encouraging notes. Let them know you believe in them.

As they succeed, so will you. Your bringing out the best in others will also bring out the best in you. Remember, an encouraging word works wonders. Be free with your compliments. Tell people what they mean to you. Get in the habit of building up those around you. When you sow those seeds, God will make sure you go higher, too.

CHAPTER TWENTY-FOUR

Living as a Healer

A well-dressed man stopped me on a busy sidewalk not long ago. From his appearance, you'd think he was on top of the world, but behind the facade, he was in much pain. He and his wife had separated. He was so discouraged.

"I don't have a reason to live anymore," he told me.

He sobbed and sobbed. My coat was wet with his tears. I didn't have all the answers. I couldn't solve all of his problems right there on the sidewalk. But I could pour in some healing oil. I offered words of encouragement.

"God has you in the palm of His hand," I said. "Our meeting is not an accident. That's God's way of saying, 'Everything will be all right.'"

That's all some people need to hear. You don't have to preach a sermon. You don't have to quote twenty-five Scripture verses or counsel them for eight hours. Just a few kind words can start the healing process.

After I prayed with the man on the street, he noticed how wet my suit was from his tears. He was embarrassed. "Oh, Joel. It looks like I've ruined your jacket."

I didn't tell him, but I wore those tears like medals on my jacket. You're never more like God than when you're helping those who are hurting. One of our assignments in life is to help wipe away the tears.

Everywhere we go there are people in need. There may be smiles on the outside, but on the inside there is pain. Many are quietly hurting and they need healing. We all have a ministry. It may not be in the pulpit, but God is counting on each of us to reach out to others and bring healing wherever we go.

Are you sensitive to the needs of those around you? Your friends? Your neighbors? Your co-workers? Many times, like the man who stopped me on the street, someone may be hurting, but they hide it because of shame or embarrassment. Often, they don't know how to reach out for help, so be prepared to reach out to them. Be a healer. Be a restorer. Take time to wipe away the tears.

Your job is not to judge. God wants you to lift the fallen, restore the broken, and heal the hurting.

Too often we focus on our own goals and our own dreams, hoping for a miracle, but I've learned that I can become someone's miracle. There is healing in our hands. There's healing in our voices. We are containers filled with God's love.

You are full of encouragement, mercy, restoration, and healing. Everywhere you go, dispense the goodness of God. You can say to those in need:

- "You may have made mistakes, but God's mercy is bigger than any mistake you've made."
- "You may have wasted years of your life making poor choices, but God still has a way to get you to your final destination."
- "You may have had an addiction, but the power of the Most High God can break any addiction and set you free."

That's what it means to dispense good. You lift the fallen. You encourage the discouraged. You take time to wipe away the tears.

Give Up Your Comfort to Comfort Others

Jesus told about the good Samaritan who was riding his donkey and saw a man who had been beaten and left for dead on the roadside. He lifted the injured man onto his donkey and took him to a place where he could recover. I love the fact that the good Samaritan let the injured man ride while he walked because sometimes to comfort others, you may have to give up your own comfort. Sometimes you have to trade places with those who are hurting.

To be a healer, you will be inconvenienced. You might have to miss dinner in order to wipe away a tear. You might have to skip a workout to help a couple work through their challenges. You may even have to drive across town and pick up that co-worker struggling with an addiction and then bring him to church.

A true healer doesn't mind inconvenience, or taking risks in the course of reaching out to those who truly need a hand up. Jim Bakker, the fallen minister and cohost of *The PTL Club* television show, went to prison for five years on fraud convictions. When he was about to be released, Franklin Graham,

> *A true healer doesn't mind inconvenience, or taking risks in the course of reaching out to those who truly need a hand up.*

Billy Graham's son, contacted him and said his family had rented him a house and provided a car for him.

"Franklin, you can't do that," Bakker told him. "I have too much baggage. You'll be criticized. Your ministry can't be associated with me."

Franklin said, "Sure we can, Jim. You were our friend before, and you will be our friend afterward."

The first Sunday after his release, Jim Bakker was living temporarily in a halfway house as a condition of the court. Ruth Graham, Billy Graham's wife, called the place and asked the man in charge if Jim could have permission to leave and come to church with the Grahams that Sunday. The judge agreed. When Jim entered the church, they ushered him right down to the very front row and sat him next to Franklin Graham.

The Grahams had ten or fifteen family members there. There were two vacant seats next to Jim Bakker before the service started. He didn't know who they were for. But when the music kicked up, a side door opened and out walked Billy and Ruth Graham. They sat right next to Jim Bakker. He had been out of prison only forty-eight hours, but the whole world was put on notice that the Grahams still considered Jim Bakker a friend.

What were the Grahams doing associating with a convicted criminal? They were loving him back into wholeness. They were acting as healers.

I heard somebody say, "A true friend walks in when everybody else walks out. A true friend doesn't rub it in when you make a mistake. They help rub it out."

That's a question to ask yourself when someone you know falls off the path. Are you rubbing the mistake in or rubbing it out? Are you a healer and a restorer, or are you critical and judgmental?

Healing God's Children

The Scripture says that Jesus was a friend of sinners (see Luke 7:34). I don't know about you, but I'm determined to live as a healer. When someone falls and makes a mistake, I'm showing up to help rub it out and not rub it in.

That doesn't mean you overlook wrongs and act as if they never happened. But you understand if it were not for the grace of God, you, too, could be in need of healing. When you show mercy to the guilty, when you encourage the discouraged, when you lift people up as everyone else is pushing them down, your actions touch the heart of God in a very special way.

As a parent, I appreciate it if someone helps me, but if someone helps one of my children in a time of need, there is nothing in the world I wouldn't do for that person. It's the same way with God. When you make it your business to help His children, His sons, His daughters, by wiping their tears or lifting them when they are down, be prepared: You will not be able to outrun the goodness of God.

Singer Tammy Trent went to Jamaica with her husband, Trent Lenderink, shortly after their eleventh wedding anniversary. They rock-climbed and went to the beach for several days and then, just before they were supposed to leave, Trent decided to check out the blue lagoon, a favorite diving spot on the island. Trent was an avid scuba diver, but he didn't have his gear this time. Instead, he dove into the lagoon with just fins and a snorkel while Tammy watched. She didn't worry because Trent often dove like this. He could stay underwater for up to ten minutes free diving.

Ten minutes or so went by and Tammy began looking for her husband. He had not yet come up for air, and she grew worried. Fifteen minutes— still nothing; twenty minutes...panic set in. Tammy called the authorities. Trent had drowned, tragically. They recovered his body the next day.

Tammy, who had been with Trent since high school, was in shock, totally devastated, and she was alone in this foreign country. She called her parents and they said they would come immediately. The first available flight was the next morning, which just happened to be September 11, 2001, the day the terrorists struck in the U.S. All flights were grounded. Tammy's parents could not go to her, and she could not leave Jamaica.

Tammy was so distraught. She prayed, "God, if You're up there anywhere, please send somebody to help me, somebody to let me know that You care."

A little later there was a knock on her hotel door room. It was the housekeeper. She was an older Jamaican woman. She said, "I was cleaning the room next door. I don't mean to bother you but I couldn't help but hear you crying, and I was wondering if there is anything that I could pray with you about."

Tammy told her what had happened. That older Jamaican woman put her loving arms around Tammy and held her like she was her very own daughter. That moment, thousands of miles from home, Tammy Trent knew that God was still in control.

The Jamaican housekeeper was living as a healer. She was sensitive to the needs of those around her. She heard the cries for help coming from another room. She could have thought, *Oh, I've got a lot of work to do. I'm busy. I've got problems of my own.* Instead, she dropped what she was doing and embraced one of God's children. She knew her assignment in life was to help wipe away the tears. That moment, she poured the healing oil onto Tammy's wounds.

She simply let her know that she cared. She was the first step in Tammy's long period of healing.

Follow the Flow of Compassion

The Scripture says that one day God will wipe away all the tears (see Revelation 21:4). There will be no more tragedy, no more sickness, and no more pain. But in the meantime, God is counting on you and me to wipe away the tears. It's great to go to church and celebrate God's goodness. But your work continues when you step outside. Always be ready to step up and offer healing.

You can sense when someone is hurting. All of a sudden, you feel a flow

> *It's great to go to church and celebrate God's goodness. But your work continues when you step outside.*

of compassion and you think, *I need to go pray for them. I need to go encourage them.*

Don't ignore those instincts. That's God wanting you to bring healing. There's a tear that needs to be wiped away.

Victoria called a friend named Shannon awhile back. A young lady answered and seemed somewhat troubled. Victoria said, "Shannon, is this you?"

The voice was muffled and said, "Yes, this is me and I'll be okay."

Confused, Victoria gave Shannon's full name and asked again if she had the right number. The young lady said, "No, you must have the wrong number. This is a different Shannon."

Victoria was about to hang up, but she felt this flow of compassion toward the person on the line.

"Shannon, I know this may sound strange, but can I pray with you about something?" she asked.

The woman began to weep.

"Would you please? My father just died, and I'm so depressed I don't know what to do."

Victoria prayed and spoke faith to her. She comforted her as best she could, assuring her that God was at her side. Before she hung up the young lady said, "You're my angel. Now I know that God still has a plan for my life."

God will bring people across our paths so we can restore. Be sensitive and follow that flow of compassion.

I was at the hospital visiting with a friend when a mother and daughter recognized me in the hallway. They asked if I would go down the hall and pray for the woman's husband, father of the young woman.

I agreed, and when we arrived at his room they said they would wait outside.

I thought that was a little strange, but I went in. The man was about sixty years old. I did not know him, but we visited for ten or fifteen minutes. Then I prayed over him. I gave him a big hug.

When I walked out, the mother and daughter were grinning from ear to ear.

"What is so funny?" I asked them.

"We can't believe he let you pray for him," the mother said. "He doesn't even like you."

I thought, *Oh, thanks a lot. That's why I went in by myself.*

"When we watch you on television, he always makes fun of you and tells us to turn you off," she added.

I thought: *If I had known that, I might have prayed a little bit differently.*

But when you take time to care, you never know what God will do. That was years ago, and today, do you know that man and his family come to services at Lakewood every week? They never miss a Sunday!

When you live as a healer, you break down the walls. You soften hard hearts. Love never fails. Come to find out, that man used to be a deacon in another church, but he'd been mistreated and hadn't gone to any church in thirty years!

Healing Faith

The book of James talks about how we need to go after the prodigals (see 5:19–20). We need to go after those who have fallen away. If you know of people who were once strong in faith but have weakened, go after them. Write them a letter. Track them down. Call them. Stop by their houses and say, "Hey, where have you been? We miss you. We need you. Why don't you come back home?"

Go after the prodigals. They need healing, too. They need their happiness and joy restored. Your attitude should be: *I'm on a mission from God. If you fall away, you're on dangerous ground because I will track you down. I will help bring you back into the fold.*

Years ago, my father went to a service across town at a friend's church. He arrived late so he sat in the back row. After a few minutes, a young man walked in looking very troubled. My father felt that flow of compassion and made a note to reach out to him after the service.

But midway through, the young man walked out. My father felt so strongly that he went after him. He looked in the lobby and couldn't find him. Daddy went out into the parking lot, searched and searched. Still nothing. He came back in and checked the restroom, and sure enough, there he was.

My father looked the young man in the eyes and said, "I don't know you, but I want to tell you God's hand is on your life. He's got a destiny for you to fulfill. Don't give up on your future."

The young man wept.

"My life is so messed up," he said. "I'm addicted to so many drugs. I decided to come to church one more time, and then I was going home to take every pill I could find."

Later, this young man recalled that when he walked into the church, one of the first things he noticed was my father's shoes. Then, when he'd walked out, he'd seen my father following him, and "Everywhere I went I saw those shoes following me."

My father wore the shoes of a healer. The shoes of a restorer. The shoes of a minister tracking down prodigals and healing hearts.

That night was a turning point in the young man's life. Today, more than thirty years later, he's the pastor of a very successful church. But I wonder where he would be if my father had not been living as a healer?

A hundred years from now, if someone were to remember me, I don't want them to say, "Oh, yeah. Joel, he's the guy that had a big church. He wrote some nice books. He was kind of popular."

No, I want them to say, "That man was a healer. He was a restorer. He lifted the fallen. He encouraged the discouraged. He gave mercy to the guilty. He spent his life wiping away the tears."

I received a letter just recently from a lady who said that for more than forty years she'd felt beaten down by life and abandoned by her religion. She was told that God loved her only when she kept all the rules and followed all the man-made laws.

"I suffered under religion," she said. "I could never be good enough."

She ended up dropping out of church depressed and confused. Twelve years later she was flipping through the channels, and she heard me talking about God's unconditional love and how God has a great plan for all of us.

For the first time, she felt a freedom on the inside, she said. It was like God had breathed new life into her spirit.

"Joel, sometimes, because you don't condemn people, others criticize you and say you're just preaching 'Christianity lite,'" she said. "But let me tell you, I lived under 'Christianity heavy' for forty-two years. I was broken. I was defeated. I was depressed. But today I am healthy. I'm happy. I'm whole. I'm helping others.

"I will take 'Christianity lite' over 'Christianity heavy' any day of the week," she said.

Religion likes to beat people down. Religion will criticize you because you're not hard enough on others. But I love what Jesus said: "My yoke is easy and My burden is light" (Matthew 11:30 NKJV).

I don't see the need to beat anyone down. Life does that enough to people. I encourage you to be a healer and a restorer of dreams. Look for those you can lift up instead. Help them reclaim their happiness and joy.

> *I encourage you to be a healer and a restorer of dreams.*

You are a container filled with God. Release His healing wherever you go, and I can assure you, God's face will always shine down upon you.

PART
VII

Celebrate Yourself

CHAPTER TWENTY-FIVE

Encourage Yourself

One of the battles we all have to fight is the battle with discouragement. Our dreams don't always come true on our timetables. We go through disappointments and adversities. It's easy to lose enthusiasm, happiness, and joy and zeal for life. In those times, it's good to have family and friends who encourage us. It's good to have a coach, a teacher, or a pastor to cheer us on.

But one thing I've learned is that other people cannot keep us encouraged. Other people cannot keep us cheered up. They may give us a boost. They may help us from time to time. But if we really want to live in victory, that encouragement has to come from the inside. We must learn to encourage ourselves.

This is especially true when times get tough and things aren't going your way. At those moments, you may not feel like pursuing your dreams. Your mind may be telling you, *It's not worth it. It's never getting any better. You might as well just settle where you are.* Deep down in your spirit there has to be a resolve, a strength on the inside that says, *I refuse to settle where I am. I know God has a great plan for my life, and I'm pressing forward and becoming everything that He's created me to be.*

This is what King David had to do, according to Scripture. He had just suffered a major setback. It was one of the most difficult times of his life. His city had been destroyed. His family had been kidnapped. And now his own men had turned against him. The situation looked impossible.

He could have easily just given up and faded off into the sunset, defeated and depressed. But the Scripture says, "David encouraged himself in the LORD his God" (1 Samuel 30:6 KJV).

David understood this principle. He wasn't depending on his family, his friends, or his colleagues. He knew how to draw strength and encouragement from within. Sometimes when you need encouragement the most, those you're counting on to cheer you up won't be there, unfortunately. The friend who normally calls may be out of town. Your spouse may be having a tough month. Your co-workers and your parents may be preoccupied with their own challenges. But when you learn to dig down deep and encourage yourself, there is a real freedom.

This is one of the secrets to David's success. He knew how to draw encouragement and strength from the inside. How did he do it? He began to replay the victories God had given him in the past. He remembered how God chose him from the other brothers when he was a shepherd boy. He remembered how he killed the lion and the bear with his bare hands. He remembered how God helped him defeat Goliath and how God protected him when King Saul was trying to kill him.

As David rehearsed over and over in his mind the goodness and faithfulness of God, strength began to fill his heart. He created a new vision of victory. He thanked God for what He had done. He thanked God that He could turn the situation around. David went from being depressed and defeated to rising up with a warrior mentality.

A Hall of Fame Encourager

When you look at how successful and celebrated Emmitt Smith is today, you might be tempted to think that he never needed to encourage himself. The former Dallas Cowboys running back holds the record for most yards rushing in NFL history. He has three Super Bowl rings. He was inducted into the Pro Football Hall of Fame in 2010. A few years before that, he won the *Dancing with the Stars* competition! And he's married to a beautiful woman, a former Miss Virginia.

But Emmitt grew up in a low-income family and spent his first few years living in public housing. He made a name for himself as a football player in high school and college. But there were many who thought he'd never make it in the National Football League. Many scouts and coaches felt he was too short at five feet nine inches tall. Others said he wasn't fast enough to play in the pros.

On his NFL draft day, Emmitt waited with his family and friends for his name to be called. But after fifteen others were chosen in the draft, he still had not received a call. Emmitt began to doubt himself. He questioned his decision to leave the University of Florida before his senior year. Nervous and discouraged, he went for a walk on the beach outside a friend's Florida condominium.

As Emmitt walked alone, he didn't let himself think of the fifteen other players who'd been called before him. Instead, he encouraged himself by thinking of all that he'd accomplished so far. In high school, he'd led his football team to two state championships and set the state record for rushing yards. In just three seasons of college football, he'd set fifty-eight school records and was named an All-American.

After raising his spirits by remembering his victories, Emmitt prayed, "God, it's all in Your hands." Then he returned to the condo where everyone was gathered. They informed him that he hadn't been the sixteenth pick in the NFL draft either.

Just then the phone rang. It was Jimmy Johnson, then the coach of the Dallas Cowboys.

"Emmitt, would you like to wear a star on your helmet?" said Coach Johnson.

"Yes, Coach, I would love to wear a Cowboys star," said Emmitt.

Maybe you are discouraged and doubting yourself right now. Maybe you've lost your fire and your enthusiasm because of a disappointment or setback.

Encourage yourself as Emmitt did. Encourage yourself as David did. Look back on past accomplishments and victories and draw inspiration from them. Stay focused on encouraging thoughts—thoughts of hope and thoughts of faith.

> *Stay focused on encouraging thoughts—thoughts of hope and thoughts of faith.*

Replay the Victories

When you're in difficult times and you're tempted to get down—whether it's a bad medical report, a relationship problem, or you are struggling in your finances—don't dwell on the negative and replay over and over all the reasons why things won't work out and how impossible your situation is. Instead, change the channel. Get the remote control. That's not the only channel. Start replaying in your mind, like David and Emmitt did, all the times that God helped you, the times God protected you from those accidents, and the times God gave you a promotion even though you weren't the most qualified.

You were disappointed when it seemed doors were closed to you, but looking back now, you know things worked out for the best. How about the time you lost a loved one? You could have felt defeated. You didn't think you could make it through. But eventually you felt a peace and a strength like you've never felt before.

Every one of us has seen the hand of God at work in our lives. A key to encouraging yourself is to replay your personal trials and accompanying victories. As you remember the great things God has done, faith will fill your heart. Strength and courage will come from the inside. No matter what you're facing, no matter how difficult it looks, you'll know deep down, *God did not bring me this far to leave me here. If He did it for me in the past, He'll do it again for me in the future.*

You can get your joy back if you just change the channel. If you are remembering only the negative, remembering what didn't work out, and who hurt you, and how unfair it was, then it's not surprising you're feeling down. You are watching the wrong channel. God has done something great for every one of us. Maybe God has given you a child. The day that little baby was born you were so excited. Why don't you replay that miracle in your mind? Maybe God has given you a house, He's given you a promotion, or maybe you received a good medical report. You were so thrilled. You were on cloud nine. Learn to replay those victories in your mind.

To keep yourself encouraged, make sure you're watching the right channel. You cannot stay down and defeated as long as you're thinking about the goodness of God. I try to do that, in fact, every time I drive near Lakewood Church. Whether I'm driving by on the freeway or pulling up to a service, I always say, without fail, "Thank You, Lord, for our beautiful building."

I'm still amazed at what God has done. Whenever I see our church, I don't even have to think about it anymore, my thank-you to the Lord just comes out of me naturally. I guess I've developed a habit. I've probably said that phrase ten thousand times. Every time I do, you know what's happening? I'm encouraging myself. My faith is increasing. I can feel strength on the inside. I know if God gave us this building, He can do anything.

Our son, Jonathan, was in a car driven by our friend Johnny when they passed Lakewood Church on the way home one day. As they were driving by, Jonathan said to Johnny, "Let me say it for my dad: 'Thank You, Lord, for our beautiful building.' " He's heard me say it so often, now he's saying it. The Scripture says we should tell our children and our grandchildren the great things God has done!

Every Setback Is a Setup for a Comeback

I see too many people today who have just settled where they are. Giving in to the spirit of discouragement steals dreams. The attitude of those who settle for less is: *It's not worth it. My marriage is not worth fighting for. It's never working out.* Or, *I'm tired of dealing with this child. It's not worth the struggle. I'm tired of doing what's right; I'm never getting ahead.* No, don't believe those lies. That is the spirit of discouragement trying to steal your dreams and keep you right where you are.

Let me tell you something you already know deep down in your spirit. Every promise God has put in your heart, every dream He's planted on the inside, is well worth the fight. Your child is worth it. Your marriage is worth it. Your health is worth it. Your dreams are worth it.

Don't you dare settle where you are. You may have suffered a setback. Like David in the Bible, you've been through a disappointment. Maybe a relationship didn't work out. Maybe you're facing a major health issue right now. Remember this: Every setback is a setup for a comeback.

You may have been knocked down, but you weren't knocked out.

You've got to get back up, dust yourself off. God has you in the palm of His hand. He said if you would stay in faith, He would not only bring you out, He would bring you out better off than you were before.

This is what David had to do. He was down, but he didn't stay down. He mentally replayed his victories. He thanked God for what He had done in the past. When he changed the channel and took on an attitude of faith and expectancy, David went from being a victim to being a victor. He said to his men, "Get up, guys. We're attacking the enemy."

The Scripture says they not only recovered everything that had been stolen from them, but they came out with more than they had before (see 1 Samuel 30). That's what God wants to do for every one of us. But it all started when David encouraged himself. He recognized the main battle wasn't taking place on the outside. It was taking place on the inside.

When all the odds were against him—his family wasn't there, his friends had turned on him, the news wasn't good, the economy was low, gas was high—his attitude was, "I'm not worried about any of that. I know the God I serve is well able to deliver me."

David said, in effect; "I've seen God lift me out of the pit before. He set my feet on a rock, put a new song in my heart. And if He did it for me back then, I know He'll do it for me right now." That's the kind of attitude that gets God's attention.

I know you can look back in life and say with David, "If it had not been for the goodness of God, where would I be?" In other words:

- "I should have had a nervous breakdown when I went through that divorce, but God filled me with His strength."
- "I should have given up and been depressed when my loved one died, but God gave me a new beginning."
- "I shouldn't be here today, according to the medical report, but because of the goodness of God, I'm still alive and well."
- "My business should have gone bankrupt a long time ago, but because of God's favor it turned around."
- "I should be messed up in my mind because of all the addictions I had. But because of the mercy of God, my chains are broken and I'm totally free today."

- "My family should be torn apart, but because of God's goodness we're still here together."

You cannot stay down and defeated as long as you're meditating on the goodness of God! Switch off the Defeat Channel. Switch off the Who Hurt Me Channel, the I Come from the Wrong Family Channel, and the Gloom and Despair Channel.

Turn them off and switch to the Victory Channel, to the All Things Are Possible Channel, to the God Is Well Able Channel, to the My Best Days Are Ahead of Me Channel. Remember the good things God has done, and faith will fill your heart.

> *Remember the good things God has done, and faith will fill your heart.*

Create an Encouragement File

Another thing that can help you stay encouraged is creating an "Encouragement File." Whenever someone sends you a kind note or a compliment, put it in a file in your home or office. Then when you're tempted to be down, pull out those letters and notes and read them again. Let those words lift your spirits. Many times, after just five minutes of being reminded how much people love you and of remembering some of the good things you've done, your attitude will totally change.

I started an Encouragement File when I first began ministering. Whenever someone sent me a kind note, a nice letter, or even when someone just gave me a compliment, I'd put it in the file. Back in those days, if someone said something even halfway encouraging, I put it in there. I remember this elderly man I'd see at the gym was always kidding me about something. But one day he wrote me a note that said, "I watched your sermon on television yesterday. All I can say is, 'Better luck next time.'"

I was so happy that he at least watched the sermon; I put his note in my Encouragement File. Sometimes you can't be picky. Thank God, today his note is in "File 13." I don't need that one anymore.

Shortly after I became a minister, this little boy about five years old came up after my sermon and said: "I really love listening to your stories."

I was feeling so good.

Then he said, "But if I were you, I'd leave out all that other boring stuff."

You need an Encouragement File, too. In my file I have letters, compliments, and birthday cards. Not long ago one of my third-grade teachers wrote my mom a note about what a good student I was, and how friendly I was, and how I smiled so much even back then. That encouraged me. I put my teacher's note in my file. And now, at least every couple of months, I'll pull out that file and flip through some of those letters.

What am I doing? I'm encouraging myself. It's like being on a good maintenance program. Be encouraged on a regular basis.

Self-Encouragement Works

If you are worried that no one has sent you nice notes, given you credit, or offered a compliment that you can put in an Encouragement File, I have a solution. Write yourself some nice letters. Write down what you like about yourself. List your strengths. List your accomplishments. List some of the good things you've done for others.

When nobody else celebrates you, learn to celebrate yourself. When nobody else compliments you, compliment yourself. It's not up to other people to keep you encouraged. It's up to you. It should come from the inside.

This is what God did. He praised Himself. We're told in the book of Genesis that God created the waters and He said, "That was good." He created the sky and He said, "That was good." He created the fish and the animals and He stepped back and said, "That was good." He created you and me and said, "That was really good."

I love the fact that God praised Himself. Most of the time we are so critical of ourselves, and so focused on what we've done wrong, we never even think about complimenting ourselves.

I've got these faults. I'm struggling with this addiction. Or, *I'm not nearly as talented as my co-workers.*

That's not the way to think. Find something that you're doing right so you can say, "You know what? That was good."

Even when you walk out of church, you can pat yourself on the back and say, "I did something right today. I took time to honor God by coming to church. I must say, 'I did good.'"

When I walk off the platform at Lakewood Church each week, I look at myself in the mirror and say, "You did good today." I may not have done as well as somebody else, but I did the best that I could do, and that's all that really matters.

Here's my point: If you don't compliment yourself, you will never become everything God created you to be. Feel good about who you are. I'm not talking about being arrogant and going around thinking you are better than everybody else. I'm talking about learning to accept and approve yourself. Happiness is an inside-out proposition. If you aren't happy with yourself, you will never be able to find joy in each and every day.

Instead of always catching yourself doing something wrong, I want you to get in the habit of catching yourself doing things right. I hear people who are always condemning themselves. "There I go again—spent too much money." "There I go again. I ate something that I shouldn't have." "There I go again—lost my temper."

They always see the wrong, never the right.

"I'm just down on myself 'cause I didn't work out one time last week."

Maybe not, but you did take the stairs instead of the elevator. That was good.

"Well, I didn't clean my house yesterday like I wanted to."

Maybe not, but you did go to your child's ball game. That was good.

"Well, I didn't take my friend out to lunch like I promised."

No, but you sure were kind to that security guard. Quit catching yourself doing something wrong and start catching yourself doing something right.

Change the Channel

Some of you have never once said out loud to yourself, "I'm a good mother." "I'm a good father." "I'm talented and creative." "I'm kind and considerate."

I don't say this arrogantly, but I like who God made me to be. I love to compliment other people, but I've learned even to compliment myself. I like the gifts God has given me. I like my personality. I like my height. I like my age. I like what I'm able to do.

One of the recordings playing in my mind all through the day is: *You're a good father. You're a good husband. You're talented. You're creative. You're kind. You're fun to be around.*

It is easy to stay encouraged when you learn to compliment yourself. Sometimes we think it's humble to compliment somebody else while putting ourselves down.

"Man, you're so good at that. I could never do anything like you."

No, you can do exactly what God has created you to do.

People often tell me, "I could never speak in front of large crowds like you do."

Maybe not, but I could never fly an airplane like you do. I could never design houses like you do. I could never teach children like you do. The fact is, every one of us is good at something. We shouldn't look at somebody else and think, *Man, they are so talented. They are so creative. They are so disciplined. They are so good-looking. I don't know what in the world happened to me.*

No, start looking in the mirror and saying, "You are so talented. You are so creative. You are so disciplined. You good-looking thing."

You've got to compliment yourself. Try it. It may work. It didn't for my brother, Paul! But you try it anyway.

A young lady named Brittany moved to a new school in junior high. Most of the students had grown up together and been friends for years and years. She was having a tough time breaking in and really connecting with anybody.

This school had a tradition that during the week before Valentine's Day, students could buy 25-cent carnations to send to one another. The carnations were all delivered during homeroom on Valentine's Day in front of the whole class. So it was a big deal to see how many carnations everyone received.

Well, Brittany knew she would not receive any carnations. She was new to the school and didn't have any friends. She was dreading that day, thinking she'd be left out and embarrassed.

But then Brittany came up with a great idea. Instead of just sitting back and watching everybody else get flowers, she decided to send some to herself. She took five dollars down to the school office where she asked for twenty carnation delivery forms. Then she filled them out in private so nobody would know she was sending them to herself.

On Valentine's Day, most of the young ladies received three or four carnations. The real popular girls might have five or six or seven delivered to them. But in Brittany's homeroom, it seemed every other carnation came to her. Her homeroom classmates looked at her, thinking, *Who in the world is this girl? She has so many friends.*

One after another carnation was delivered to her. Her classmates would ask, "Who's that from?" And Brittany would look at the note and say, "Oh. They are so special. They love me so much. I can't wait to tell them thanks."

They had no idea she was talking about herself. You would have thought Brittany was the most popular girl in school. By the end of Valentine's Day, she was the envy of the whole class. She had more carnations than anybody else.

You need Brittany's attitude: *If nobody else is celebrating me right now, I'm celebrating myself. If nobody is asking me out to dinner, I'm dressing up and taking myself out to dinner. If nobody is sending me a birthday gift, watch out. I'm buying myself a present.*

If you've lost your happiness, your joy, your fire, and your enthusiasm, maybe it's because no one is celebrating you, cheering you on, or encouraging you. So do as David did in the Bible and encourage yourself. Draw that line in the sand and say, "That's it. This is a new day. I am done living negatively, discouraged, and with no enthusiasm. I know this is the day the Lord has made. I'm choosing to live this day with faith and with expectancy."

You may have gone through a setback, but prepare for a comeback. God did not bring you this far to leave you where you are. He has you in the palm of His hand. He had the solution before you ever had that problem. He already has a way out. God knows the end from the beginning. Everything you're facing right now is subject to

> *You may have gone through a setback, but prepare for a comeback.*

change. That means one touch of God's favor can turn any situation around. You've got to dare to do like David. Shake off that spirit of discouragement and say, "I may be knocked down, but I'm not staying down. I'm rising back up and going again."

Encourage yourself so that you can find happiness in every day. When the negative voices start up and say, "Well, the economy is bad. Aren't you afraid?"

Say, "No, I know God is my provider. He supplies all of my needs."

"Well, gas is high."

"Yes, but God is well able to take care of me."

"Well, your child is not doing right."

"That's true, but I know he's subject to change."

"Well, you were laid off. I heard you lost your job. Aren't you frustrated?"

"Not at all. I know God is about to open up another door. I know He has something better in store for me."

"Well, you look like you're not feeling well. Somebody said you received a bad report from the doctor."

"Yes, I did, but I know God is in complete control. He said that nothing would snatch me out of His hand. So I believe I will live out every second He's planned for me."

That's what it means to encourage yourself. Get up every morning thinking about the goodness of God. Replay in your mind the victories that He's given you in the past. Don't remember the negative. Change the channel and remember all the times God has brought you through.

If you don't have an Encouragement File, start one. When you're tempted to get down, go get those letters out. Let them lift your spirit. And don't wait for others to compliment you. Compliment yourself. Learn to celebrate who God made you to be.

It's up to you to keep yourself encouraged. Don't put pressure on your friends and family to encourage you all the time. You can draw strength from the inside. When you learn to encourage yourself, that's your faith at work. By encouraging yourself, you will enjoy your life more and you will overcome every obstacle. You will restore your happiness and your joy. You will help every desire, every promise put in you come to pass.

Even when you do get knocked down and suffer a setback, just as God did for David in the Bible, He will make sure you not only come back but that you come back better off than you were before.

CHAPTER TWENTY-SIX

The Voice of Victory

There are all kinds of thoughts and all kinds of voices we can tune in to just like with a radio station. There are hundreds of different frequencies in the air right now all around you. If you had a receiver, you could tune in to station after station. In the same way, you can tune out a station. You've been in your car when a song or a talk show that you don't like comes on the radio. It's no big deal. You don't make yourself listen to it. You don't sit there and endure it. You just push a button and switch over to a different station. The same principle works with your thinking.

All through the day there are thoughts coming into your mind. Many of these are negative and discouraging thoughts like *You'll never be healthy. You'll never accomplish your dreams. You'll never be married. You'll never overcome your problems.*

Many people are unaware that you don't have to stay on that station. Just because a thought comes doesn't mean you have to dwell on it. If that thought is negative, discouraging, or depressing, you simply need to tune out that frequency and find a different station or channel.

There's a channel I recommend called the "Voice of Victory." It originates from God's Word. It says, "You have a bright future." It says, "You are blessed. You are healthy. You are forgiven. You have favor. You can overcome any obstacle. You can accomplish your dreams."

If you want to live in victory, in happiness and joy, stay tuned to the right channel. You can't go around all day thinking things like *I can't stand my job and I'm so overweight and I'm never getting out of debt.*

Thinking those thoughts is draining your energy, your joy, your happiness, and your zeal. You are losing all the good things God has put in. You would be amazed at how much better you would feel if you got up each day and went on the offensive instead of being passive and entertaining every negative thought that comes to your mind. Think positive thoughts on purpose. Get up in the morning and make a declaration of faith. Say out loud to yourself, "This will be a great day. God is directing my steps. His favor is surrounding me like a shield. I'm excited about this day."

When you do that, you will be stronger and happier, and you will see God's favor in a greater way. Pay attention to what you're thinking. Some people have been tuned in to the Worry Channel so long they could be lifetime members. They could own stock in that channel they are so full of worries.

"I'm just worried about my child, worried about my health, worried about my finances."

There is a better way to live. When those negative thoughts come, you have to make a choice to not dwell on them. Instead, use the arrival of negative thoughts as a reminder to thank God that He's at work. Just switch the channel and thank Him for changing things in your favor.

You Control the Doorway to Your Mind

When somebody does you wrong, there's a voice inside that says, *Get even. Hold a grudge. Never speak to them again.* If you dwell on those thoughts, they will poison your life. But there's another mind frequency you can tune in to. It says, *God is my vindicator. He'll make my wrongs right. What was meant for my harm, He'll use to my advantage.*

That's the Voice of Victory. When you make a mistake one voice says, *You blew it. You'll never be blessed. Don't expect anything good.* Another voice says, *I'm forgiven. God's mercy is bigger than any mistake. My best days are still ahead.* It all depends on what voice you choose to tune in to. Our thoughts set the direction for our lives. What station or channel are you tuned in to?

I'm just an average person. I'm just ordinary. I'll never do anything great.

No, you're on the wrong channel. If you'll switch over to the Voice of Victory, you'll hear, *I am one of a kind. I'm a masterpiece. I have seeds of greatness. I will leave my mark on this generation.*

Pay attention to your thoughts. Make sure you're tuned in to the right channel. Maybe you're driving through a nice neighborhood and you see a beautiful home and that thought tells you, *I will never own a nice house like that. I will never get ahead. I'm so in debt. Nobody in my family is really successful.*

Change the channel. You've got to guard your mind. If you believe those lies long enough, your own think-ing will keep you from God's best. Just switch over to the Voice of Victory in

> *You've got to guard your mind.*

your thoughts: *God, You said if I keep You first, You will give me the desires of my heart. You said no good thing will You withhold when I walk uprightly. You said in due season I would reap if I didn't give up, so I want to thank You that my due season is on its way. I know my time is coming.*

That is what it means to be tuned in to the Voice of Victory.

Some people are so trained to expect the negative that when a thought comes telling them something discouraging about themselves or their future, they just swallow it hook, line, and sinker. It drags them down and they go around defeated.

But then there are others who train themselves to latch on to positive, hopeful thoughts. They can have a thousand negative thoughts bombard-ing their minds, but then one positive thought comes—one little phrase that says, *Everything will be all right*—and they weed through all those other thoughts and choose to latch on to the one faith-filled thought.

Train Your Ears

That's the way to be, so disciplined in your thoughts that you can weed out discouragement and grab hold of encouragement. You have to train your ears to do that.

We have two shih tzu dogs, Daisy and Spirit, who are amazing pets. Spirit has supersensitive hearing. She is so tuned in to her surroundings, she can hear people coming to the front door long before they get there. She'll start barking ten or fifteen seconds before they ring the doorbell. She has trained herself to hear what she wants to hear.

Spirit loves cheese, and she can hear when we're opening a bag of it, even if she's out in the yard. Spirit immediately comes running into the kitchen, sits at our feet, and waits for her piece of cheese.

When the whole family is in the kitchen, there are all kinds of noises, all kinds of sounds. Jonathan is pouring cereal. Alexandra is opening chips. I'm using the blender. Victoria is wrapping up food. Spirit sits as calm as can be; she never even flinches. But the moment anyone touches the cheese, she goes on alert.

Her attitude is: *It's my time now. I am ready for my snack.*

There have been times when I have tried to sneak a piece of cheese out of the refrigerator without her hearing it. I've told my children, "Watch this." I'll open the refrigerator. I don't even pull the cheese out. I leave it there so it won't make any noise. Very quietly and delicately I open that ziplock bag. Spirit is in another room, thirty feet away, sleeping, but you cannot fool that dog. She either has supernatural revelation or she has superdog hearing.

It is impossible to keep her away. Why is that? She has trained herself to hear what's important to her. She doesn't care if I get the bread out. She doesn't care if I open the chips or unwrap the lettuce. Everything else goes in one ear and out the other. All she's concerned about is the cheese, and she is keenly aware of that sound.

Selective Hearing

What sound are you tuned in to? Some people have a habit of tuning in to the negative. They're drawn to it, almost like they feed off it. If a thought comes that says, *It's a lousy day*, they just take the bait. "Oh, yeah, it is a lousy day."

They wake up and the thought comes, *You're depressed today.*

"Oh, yeah, I am depressed."

Don't let that be you. You've got to retrain your ears. You're hearing the wrong things. Tune out the negative and start listening for faith-filled thoughts. When you wake up after you ignore all the negative thoughts, eventually you will hear, "This is the day the Lord has made. This will be a great day."

If you trained yourself to hear the bad, you can train yourself to hear the good. Next time a negative thought comes just say, "No thanks, that's not for me."

Well, it's not getting any better. You've reached your limits.

"No thanks. I'm not dwelling on that."

You've made too many mistakes.

"No thanks. I hear another sound. It says I'm forgiven."

You're never getting well. It's over.

"No thanks. I believe I hear something else. It says God is restoring health to me."

You're never paying off that house.

"No thanks. That's not for me. I will lend and not borrow."

You may have to weed through a thousand negative thoughts until you hear another positive sound. The Voice of Victory channel saying, "You can do all things through Christ. Your best days are ahead. This situation is about to turn around."

Latch on to the good. When you hear those faith-filled thoughts, act like Spirit our dog and come running. "That's for me. I believe. I receive. I'm well able." Play those thoughts over and over. The battle is taking place in your mind.

Let the negative thoughts bounce off you like water off a duck's back. Just like Spirit sat there unfazed by the sound of the chips and the cereal and the bread. Dismiss those thoughts that are not productive and positive.

Eventually you will hear the right sound. Something will open up positive thoughts like *I'm talented.* It will be just like an alarm going off in your spirit. Rise up and say, "Yes, I'll take that one. I am talented."

The thought will come up, *I am blessed.*

"Yes, that's for me. I am well able. I am more than a conqueror."

Focus on the Good

I watched a television documentary about a jungle bat that eats certain small frogs, but not all small frogs. Some of the jungle frogs are poisonous.

They look just like the nonpoisonous frogs. But this bat can tell the difference by the sounds made by the frogs. The bat tunes in to only the sound made by the nontoxic frog.

At night all the frogs make this high-pitched chirping sound, but the poisonous frogs chirp in a slightly higher pitch than the nontoxic frogs. These bats have hearing so keen, they just listen intently for five or ten minutes, and then they tune in.

The documentary showed twenty jungle frogs packed into a little bitty area. Then the jungle bat tuned in and swooped down. For its dinner, the bat picked out the one nonpoisonous frog from the midst of all its poisonous cousins. How could the bat do that? He had trained his ear to tune in to the right frog frequency.

That's the way to be when selecting which thoughts to tune in. Be so trained in your thought life that you don't take the enemy's bait. You tune in to only hopeful, positive, faith-filled thoughts.

> *Be so trained in your thought life that you don't take the enemy's bait.*

When a jealous thought comes saying, *Why do they get everything? They're so smart? That's not fair*, recognize that thought is making the wrong sound. It may look good, you may be tempted to dwell on it, but your instincts should tell you that's a toxic thought.

If a thought comes telling you, *You're so sloppy. You're undisciplined. You can't do anything right*, it may be tempting to get down on yourself, but don't take that bait. Recognize those are poisonous thoughts. They will keep you from your destiny.

I'm asking you to be extremely aware of what you're dwelling on. What thoughts are you allowing to take root? Poisonous or nonpoisonous? Helpful or hurtful? Have you trained your ear like little Spirit the dog to have selective hearing? Are you being perceptive like those bats to leave the poisonous thoughts alone?

Guard Your Mind

You control what you think about. The Scripture tells us in Philippians to "fix your thoughts on what is true, and honorable, and right, and pure, and lovely, and admirable. Think about things that are excellent and worthy of praise" (4:8 NLT).

You have to program your mind with the right software. If you'll keep your mind filled with the right thoughts, there won't be any room for the wrong ones. Purposefully think good things about yourself and your future. It's not enough to just avoid negative thoughts. If you don't fill your mind with these faith-filled thoughts, the negative ones will try to take over. It's much better to stay on the offensive.

The Bible says, "You will keep him in perfect peace, whose mind is stayed on You" (Isaiah 26:3 NKJV). Meditate all through the day on what God says about you: *I'm strong. I'm talented. I'm forgiven. Good things are in store for me. My best days are in front of me.* When your mind is full of positive thoughts, negative thoughts will find a NO VACANCY sign when they try to enter. They won't be able to get in.

That is a powerful way to live. You decide the direction of your life. You decide your moods. You determine your attitudes.

You may need to clean house to rid your mind of all the negative condemning thoughts so you have room for the *can do* thoughts, the *all things are possible* thoughts, the *I am well able* thoughts. There's not room for both the negative and the positive.

Deuteronomy 30:19 says to choose blessings or choose curses.

When you keep your mind filled with positive thoughts, you choose blessings; you are choosing to live with happiness each day. You choose joy and victory. But when you are passive and accept whatever negative thoughts come to mind, that's when you miss out on God's best.

I want you to get in the habit of filling your mind with praise and thanksgiving. I want you to go out expecting good things. When you have setbacks and disappointments, you have to be especially on guard. Instead of complaining and being depressed, just say, "I know God is about to turn this around. It may be difficult, but this, too, shall pass. It's only temporary."

Keep that NO VACANCY sign up to lock out negative thoughts. Your thoughts control your life. You lock your house because you don't want strangers coming in. That's your home. That's where you live. Have the same attitude with your mind. "This is who I am. This is my future. I'm not letting just anything come in. I will make sure my thoughts are positive. I'm staying tuned to the Voice of Victory."

I heard somebody put it this way: If you owned an apartment complex and you rented 80 percent of the apartments to drug dealers and thieves and cheaters, and then you rented the other 20 percent to normal law-abiding citizens, after a few months the drug dealers and cheaters would run off all the normal people. It's the same way in controlling what lives in your mind. If you dwell constantly on your problems and what you don't have and how the future looks tough, all those negative thoughts will run off any positive thoughts.

Quit renting space in your mind to your problems. Don't rent that valuable space to self-pity. Don't rent it out to *can't do it, not able to* thoughts, or *never going to happen* thoughts. You have only so much space. Take inventory of what's occupying your mind.

Serve an eviction notice to negative thoughts: *I'm sorry, but your time here is up. Your stay has officially ended. I've rented to you long enough, and now I've got a new renter coming in. It's called the Voice of Victory, and it needs all the space that's available.*

Detox Your Mind

We hear a lot about detoxing our bodies and how there are chemicals in our food that can be harmful, certain hormones and bacteria that can build up, even pesticides in the air. Many people don't realize their bodies are full of harmful toxins and that's what's causing them to feel bad. Most experts recommend you go through a deep cleansing where you put yourself on a fast and then eat a certain diet, staying away from things that are harmful. They say over time you'll rid yourself of those toxins and begin to feel better.

In the same way, there are all kinds of toxins that can build up in your mind. When you dwell on what you can't do and the hurts you've felt and the challenges you face, you are focusing on toxic thoughts that can do as much damage as toxins in your body.

Toxic thoughts build up and become like toxic waste that will eventually contaminate your whole life. They affect your attitude, your self-esteem, and your confidence. They become part of who you are. That's why the Scripture says in Proverbs 4:23, "Above all else, guard your heart, for everything you do flows from it" (NIV). Make guarding your mind a priority, put it at the top of your to-do list. If your mind is polluted, your whole life will be damaged.

You probably know someone who is bitter, cynical, and has a sour attitude. They expect the worst. Why is that? They've allowed toxic thoughts to take root. These negative thoughts are poisoning their future.

What's the solution? They need to go through a detoxification—not a physical cleansing but a mental cleansing. The only way they will be free, the only way they will return to who God made them to be, is to detox the mind.

You may need to detox the bitterness, the low self-esteem, the negative words spoken over you, the condemnation from past mistakes, and the discouragement that's trying to become a part of you.

How do you detox? You make a decision that you will not dwell on those thoughts anymore. You starve those toxins. Every time you dwell on that negative thought, that condemnation, that bitterness, that low self-esteem, you are feeding it. You're giving it new life, making it stronger.

Those thoughts come saying, *You will never get well. You heard what the doctor said. You will never be happy. You've been hurt too many times. You will never accomplish your dreams.* But instead of dwelling on them, just say, "No, I'm not going there. I'm not dwelling on my hurt, or what I don't have, or my mistakes. I'm dwelling on what God says about me. He says I'm forgiven. He says He will pay me back double for every wrong. He says I am well able to fulfill my destiny. He says my best days are still in front of me."

If you ignore toxic thoughts and keep your mind filled with thoughts of hope, thoughts of faith, then those toxic thoughts will grow weaker, and before long they won't have any effect on you.

Cleanse Your Mind

I know people who go on fasts so they can detox their systems. They won't eat for a period of time or they just won't eat a certain type of food. I have a friend who is trying to be healthier and he won't eat any kind of meat. He's not drinking anything but water. He won't eat after a certain time at night. I saw him the other day and offered him a soft drink and he didn't think twice.

"No, that's not a part of my eating program," he said.

He was on a strict diet. That's the way to be when toxic thoughts come to mind, those thoughts of worry, low self-esteem, and *not able to* thoughts. When they arise, just say, "Thanks, but no thanks. That's not a part of my plan. I don't dwell on thoughts of fear. I don't dwell on thoughts of defeat. I don't dwell on thoughts of inferiority. Toxic thoughts are not a part of my program."

If you don't have the joy, the happiness, or the victory, maybe it's because of an unhealthy diet. Not physically, but mentally. There is too much mental junk food polluting your mind.

I'm just average. I've reached my limits. I've missed so many good opportunities. I've been too hurt to ever really be happy.

Cleanse your mind and put it on a healthier diet. Those toxic thoughts are not a part of your program. I'm asking you today to go on a fast. Not a fast from food (although that probably wouldn't hurt you), but a fast from negative thinking, a fast from condemnation, a fast from resentment, a fast from *can't do it* thoughts, a fast from undernourished dreams.

> *Cleanse your mind and put it on a healthier diet.*

Starve those toxins. Do not give them any power over you. Every morning when you wake up, go through a mental cleansing. Release any bitterness, forgive the people who hurt you, and let go of every disappointment. Start the day in faith. Start the day believing. Don't let those toxins build up.

When you're lying in bed in the morning before you get up, just say to yourself, "This will be a great day. I'm expecting God's favor. I know I'm well able to fulfill my destiny. I've been empowered to overcome every obstacle. I have the strength to overlook every offense. I have the grace to rise above every disappointment. Even if things don't go my way today, I know God's in control, and I'm making up my mind right now to be happy and enjoy this day."

You are cleansing your mind. You are cleaning out all the toxins, all the negativity, and all the condemnation. During the day when opportunities arise to be offended, to be upset, to be discouraged, don't accept those thoughts. Banish them from your daily mental diet.

If somebody is rude to you or offends you and negative thoughts arise, instead of dwelling on them, learn to say, "I'm not getting upset. I know this day is a gift from God, and I'm making a decision to stay in peace."

When you do that, you are staying with a healthy mental diet. That toxic thought can't poison you if you don't dwell on it.

Detox Negative Things People Say to You

Don't accept their hurtful words about what you can't do and what you can't become and that you aren't as smart as someone else. Don't allow those lies to take root. You are not who other people say you are. You are who God says you are. And He says, "You are talented. You are creative. You are anointed. You are strong. You are determined. You are confident. You are a victor and not a victim."

A woman told me recently about the negative environment she grew up in. The people who raised her were constantly putting her down, and she didn't feel like she measured up to her sister. She couldn't seem to catch any good breaks and couldn't keep any good friends. She finally said, "It's like these people have cursed my future. It's been one disappointment after another."

I told her what I'm telling you: Before anyone could put a curse on you, God put a blessing on you. And no matter what they've said about you, no matter how they've tried to make you feel, the blessing always overrides the curse.

Get in agreement with God and start shaking it off. Just say, "Thanks, but no thanks. That's not on my diet. I know who I am. I'm a child of the Most High God. I am blessed and I cannot be cursed. I am surrounded with favor. I'm wearing my crown of honor. I'm equipped with everything I need to succeed."

If you go around thinking and speaking like that, those toxic thoughts won't have a chance. Always remember, you are not who people say you are, you are who God says you are. People may say you'll never be successful. God says whatever you touch will prosper.

People may say you'll never get well. God says with long life He will satisfy you. People may say you will never overcome that challenge. God says He will always cause you to triumph. People may say your family will never get on the right track. God says that you and your house will serve the Lord.

I believe there's a cleansing taking place as you read this book. I can see through my eyes of faith right now that your toxic thoughts are starting to dissipate. I can see strongholds that have held you back for years being broken. I can see you stepping into a new freedom, rising to a new level.

I see you shaking off negativity and coming into faith. I see you breaking free from condemnation and stepping into confidence. I see a mind-set of poverty and defeat giving way to an abundant life mentality. As you get rid of those toxic thoughts, God will take you places you've never dreamed of.

You Are a Child of God

I read about this young boy raised by a single-parent mom in the hills of Tennessee. Back then, especially in that area, children born to unwed mothers were subject to extreme discrimination. In fact, when this boy was just three years old, the neighbors wouldn't allow him to play with their children. They said things like, "What's he doing in our town? And who is his father, anyway?"

They treated him like he had some kind of plague. On Saturdays he would go with his mom to the local store and invariably people would make disparaging comments. They would say hurtful things loud enough on purpose so they could hear: "There they are again. Did you ever figure out who his dad is?"

This little boy grew up insecure, ridiculed, always feeling that there was something wrong with him. When the boy turned twelve, a new minister moved into the town. He was a young man, very gifted and very passionate. He created quite a stir. People were excited.

The boy had never been to church a day in his life, but one Sunday he decided to go hear a sermon by this new minister everybody was talking about. He got there late, snuck in, and sat toward the back so no one would notice him. As the boy listened that day, he felt a love and an acceptance that he had never felt before. He had planned to leave early, but he was so engrossed in what the minister was saying that the service was over before he knew it.

The boy was caught up in the crowd. As the young minister greeted everyone who was leaving, he saw the boy. He had never met him, and he didn't know anything about him. But the minister noticed the boy wasn't with anyone. He was by himself.

The minister said to him in a very friendly tone, "Young man, whose child are you?"

The room grew completely silent. The minister had asked the question everybody else wanted to ask. The boy didn't know what to say. He had heard all the talk that he was the outcast and a child with no dad. So he just put his head down.

The minister noticed something was wrong, something he obviously didn't know anything about. But God gave him wisdom. He was quick on his feet. He looked at the boy and said, "Oh, I know who your Father is. I can see the resemblance so strongly; why, you're a child of almighty God."

That day was a turning point in the boy's life. Those who had been talking about him put their heads down and walked out of the room. The stronghold of insecurity and inferiority was broken. He began to see himself not as the inferior outcast people said he was but as a child of almighty God.

The boy went on to become very successful and live a blessed and happy life. Many people grow up without fathers. I wish it were not so, but if that's the case for you, let me tell you what the young minister told the boy. Your Father is almighty God. You have been

> *You have been chosen and set apart before the foundation of the world.*

chosen and set apart before the foundation of the world. You didn't get here by accident. You didn't just happen to show up. God breathed His life into you. He put seeds of greatness on the inside. You have a destiny to fulfill, an assignment, something that no one else can accomplish.

Don't let what people say about you or what they don't say about you cause you to feel less than whole. Your earthly father may not be around as much as he should; maybe you don't even know him. But your heavenly

Father says, "I am proud of you. You have a bright future. You will do great things."

Feed Your Mind God's Thoughts

I remember after the service a couple of years ago this young lady came up with two small children, a girl and a boy. They were so loving. The little boy hung on to me and didn't want to go. He was about five years old. I hugged him back and we talked for a little while and finally we high-fived and they walked away.

A couple of minutes later, the boy came back and said he wanted to whisper something in my ear. I leaned down, and I'll never forget what he said.

"I wish you were my dad."

That almost broke my heart. I told him what I'm telling you: Every morning, look up and just imagine your heavenly Father is smiling down on you. He's saying, "You're the apple of My eye. You're My most prized possession."

The Scripture says God is "a father to the fatherless" (Psalm 68:5 NIV). Many people are not reaching their full potential because of a lack of identity. Their minds are full of thoughts that say, *You're not from the right family,* or *You don't even have a father. No wonder you can't succeed.*

Don't believe those lies. Those thoughts are not on your program. Stick with your diet. It's found right here: "I am who God says I am. I may not have an earthly father, but I have a heavenly Father. People may have spoken negative things over me, but I know before anybody could curse me, God put a blessing on me. That's what I'm dwelling on."

If you have had these negative things spoken over you and they are poisoning your future, go back to the roots of those thoughts. Who said you were not smart enough to go to college? Who said you would never be successful? Who told you that you don't have what it takes? Who said you would never be married? Who told you that you would never overcome this obstacle? Who said your best days are behind you?

I can promise you it was not God who put those thoughts in your mind. Detox that garbage. Detox what your ex-husband said about you. Detox what that teacher said you couldn't do. Detox what that manager said you would never become. Detox what those critics said about your ability.

I'm putting you on a new diet today. This diet will clear out all the toxins. It will free you from all the negativity, all the *can't do it* thoughts, all the *not good enough* thoughts. This is faith food. When you eat this food, it's like Popeye eating spinach. It's like Clark Kent stepping into the phone booth and coming out as Superman. A transformation takes place when you get rid of negative condemning thoughts and feed your mind what God says about you.

Treat the Root

We have a couple of rabbits at home, and awhile back we noticed one of them looked like he wasn't feeling well. He kept rubbing the side of his face like something was bothering him. We checked it out and didn't see anything. He looked fine. A few days later that area had really swollen up. It looked like he had a big growth on his face.

So we took the rabbit to the vet. They gave him some antibiotics and said he should get better. We tried that for a week, but he didn't improve. In fact, he looked really bad. We took him back and they examined him again. This time they discovered the real problem was that a fly egg had somehow entered the rabbit's nasal passage. The fly larva was growing and about to hatch. That's why the rabbit's face was so infected.

No matter how many antibiotics the vet gave the rabbit, they didn't work. They had to get to the root of the problem. Once they found the source of the infection and removed it, the rabbit was fine.

This is the way the enemy works. He tries to plant these lies in your mind that infect your thinking. So often we deal with the surface problem and try to have a good attitude and a good self-image, but it's a constant struggle, like we're always going uphill.

Could you be like our vet and the rabbit, treating the symptoms but not dealing with the real issue? Are you treating the outside but missing the root cause, a negative mind-set toward yourself? Your thinking in some area may be infected.

Maybe you are trying to break an addiction, but deep down you still hear the words, *You'll be an alcoholic just like your father.* Maybe you are trying to make your marriage work, but that thought keeps playing: *You'll get a divorce just like your parents.*

Maybe you want to step out and start a new business, or you want to take a promotion, but something inside you says, *You don't have what it takes. You will fail. You remember what the high school counselor told you. You remember what those ladies said about you.*

Those are lies, and they are infecting your thinking. The way to get rid of those thoughts is to meditate on what God says about you. The Scripture says to "meditate on [God's Word] day and night" (Joshua 1:8 NIV). In other words, *continuously* have positive thoughts playing in your mind: *I am talented. I am creative. I am anointed. I am equipped. I am empowered. I am blessed. I am prosperous. I am disciplined. I am free from every addiction. I walk in divine health. I have the favor of God.*

When you play thoughts like that, the toxins can't stay. Your mind is being renewed. Imagine a glass of cloudy water with all kinds of dirt and sand particles in it. If I pour clean water in it continuously and just keep letting it overflow and overflow with this new clean water, eventually all the dirty water will be gone and the water will be perfectly clear.

I didn't have to try to get rid of the dirty water. I simply had to keep putting the right thing in, and before long the wrong thing was gone. It's the same way in our thinking. If you'll develop a habit of putting the right thoughts in, thoughts of faith, thoughts of hope, encouraging thoughts, *can do* thoughts, eventually your mind will be transformed. You will find yourself positive, hopeful, strong, and courageous.

> *If you'll develop a habit of putting the right thoughts in, thoughts of faith, thoughts of hope, encouraging thoughts, can do thoughts, eventually your mind will be transformed.*

Focus on Your Best

I just read about this child whose parents moved from Germany to the United States a few years before he was born. The father was an international businessman and very successful. He wanted the boy to join him in business one day.

But the boy struggled terribly in school. He tried and tried, but he had great difficulty in reading and writing and arithmetic. His mother and father were hard on him. In German, they called him a "*dumm hund*," which translates to "dumb dog."

The boy, whose severe dyslexia would not be diagnosed until he was in his thirties, was devastated by their harsh words. He grew up insecure, thinking he was stupid. The only thing that saved him in school was a sense of humor. He was good at making the other kids laugh.

He told jokes about himself. He became popular with the other kids. He really shone in his speech and drama classes so he pursued those subjects, much to the horror of his parents.

They thought he'd never amount to anything. Of course, they changed their minds when their son Henry became a huge television star. They couldn't believe it when their insecure boy, a graduate of Yale Drama School, became the star of a hit television show by playing a tough high school dropout.

It was ironic that the name of his first big show was *Happy Days*, because Henry Winkler, now a famous actor, writer, director, and producer, really does remember those days on his first hit television show as some of the happiest of his life.

Those were the days when he finally rejected the toxic thoughts of others and became the talented and creative man that his heavenly Father intended him to be. He focused on God's best within him, not on what others said about him.

In the Bible, God called Gideon a mighty man of (fearless) courage.

Gideon looked around and said, "Who's He talking to? That's not me." God had an assignment for Gideon, something great for him to accomplish, but Gideon had not renewed his mind. He had these toxic thoughts. God saw him as strong, but Gideon saw himself as weak, defeated, not able to.

God wanted him to lead the people of Israel and to defeat an opposing army, but Gideon said, "God, I can't do that. I'm the least one in my father's house. I come from the poorest family. I don't have the education, the skills, the courage."

Notice how Gideon perceived himself compared to how God saw him. God said he was a mighty man of fearless courage. If God were to call your name today, He wouldn't say, "Hello, you weak worm of the dust. Hello, you failure. Hello, you ol' sinner. How's My loser doing today?"

God would say the same sort of thing to you that He said to Gideon: "Hello, Mary, you mighty woman of fearless courage." Or "Hello, Bob, you mighty man of fearless courage."

I wonder if you would be like Gideon and say, "God, who are You talking to? Don't You know what family I come from? Haven't You seen the mistakes I've made? Let me remind You of some of them. God, You know I'm not that talented. Why are You calling me a mighty man?"

The problem is, you have allowed these wrong thoughts to infect your thinking. But thank God this is a new day. You are beginning a new diet. You are starting a fast by cutting out every negative, discouraging, *can't do it* thought.

When those wrong thoughts come up, instead of saying like Gideon, "I'm not able. Who am I?" Turn it around and say, "I know who I am. I am well able. I'm ready for my assignment. God, I am who You say I am."

I believe in the coming days God will present you with new opportunities. New doors will open. New people will come across your path. Maybe there will even be a new career opportunity. If you are to reach a new level, you must have a new way of thinking. You have to clean out the old so you'll have room for the new. I'm asking you to detox all the garbage telling you what you're not and what you can't do. Remove all those strongholds. Detox little dreams. Detox low self-esteem. Detox the negative words. Stay on your diet.

Every morning go through a good cleanse. Start the day off in faith. If you'll guard your mind and instead of letting it get toxic keep it full of faith-filled thoughts, God promises you'll overcome every obstacle, you'll defeat every enemy, and every dream and every desire God has put in your heart will come to pass.

CHAPTER TWENTY-SEVEN

Wear Your Blessings Well

A few years ago, a well-known reporter referred to me as "the smiling preacher." That story caught on and went all over the world. But some people use that term in a derogatory sense, as in, "Why does he smile so much? What's wrong with him? He couldn't be that happy."

I was young and new to the ministry, and at first I thought, *Well, maybe I shouldn't smile so much. People are making fun.* Then I realized I don't have to hide God's blessings. I don't have to apologize because I smile all the time. I'm wearing my blessings well.

When you keep God in first place and do your best to honor Him, the Scripture says, "all these blessings shall come upon you and overtake you" (Deuteronomy 28:2 NKJV). That means you will come into happiness, increase, promotion, and good breaks, even some that you didn't necessarily deserve. That's God rewarding you for walking in His ways.

We see this principle in the Old Testament with Ruth. She was out in the fields following behind the workers and gathering up the leftover wheat they had missed.

One day the owner of the fields, Boaz, told those workers to leave handfuls of wheat on purpose for Ruth. Now Ruth didn't have to struggle anymore. She didn't have to work night and day. Ruth came into blessings that were simply dropped at her feet.

Every one of us can look back and see times where God has left us handfuls of blessings on purpose, something we didn't deserve, we didn't have to struggle for, we didn't even ask for it. We just stumbled into it. Now here is my challenge: Don't apologize for God's goodness. Don't downplay what God has done in your life. Don't make excuses because a

> *Don't apologize for God's goodness.*

friend might be jealous. Don't try to hide God's blessings because a co-worker might judge you and think it's not fair.

One key to happiness is to wear your blessings well. You may not feel you deserved a blessing, but favor is not always fair. It's just the goodness of God. The moment you start apologizing for what God has done and downplaying His goodness, God will find somebody else to favor.

I'm not saying you should show off and brag on what you have and how great you are. But you should brag on how great God is. We used to sing a song growing up called "Look What the Lord Has Done." That's the song to sing. All through the day, praise God's goodness. When you're bragging on God's goodness, when you're giving Him all the credit, you are wearing your blessings well.

David said in Psalm 118:23, "This was the LORD's doing; it is marvelous in our eyes" (NKJV). That is a great attitude. Give Him credit for every good thing that happens: "This was the Lord's doing."

"You know what this beautiful building is? It's the Lord's doing."

"My mother is still enjoying life thirty years after being diagnosed with terminal cancer. You know what that is? That's the Lord's doing. It's marvelous in our eyes."

If you always see the promotion, the good break, the healing, the new, and the opportunities coming your way as the Lord's doing, you won't have any problem wearing your blessings well.

I used to feel kind of guilty that God has given me such a great life. I've always been happy and blessed to have great parents and grandparents, a beautiful wife, and wonderful children. Again and again Victoria and I have seen these handfuls of blessing on purpose.

We've just been blessed, and it's the Lord's doing. But when I used to see people dealing with hardships and struggling to overcome, I tried to downplay how God has blessed me so they wouldn't feel badly. But I've learned that doesn't bring any honor to God. God wants us to be an example of His goodness. I don't have to apologize if I get a handful of blessings on purpose and somebody else doesn't.

No Apologies Necessary

You don't have to hide your happiness, your peace, your victory, or your possessions. You don't have to dress down and look poor and pitiful and depressed to show people you are humble. When you wear your blessings well, giving God all the credit, talking about His goodness, thanking Him for what He has done, that's what really brings honor to our God.

If God has blessed you with financial success or helped you through a challenge in a relationship, a job, your health, or your finances, wear that blessing well. Tell everyone what God has done for you. If they make fun of you like they make fun of me and ask why you are so happy, just tell them, "I'm wearing my blessing well. God has been so good to me I can't keep it to myself. I've got to tell somebody. I once was lost, but now I'm found. I should be dead, but I'm still alive. Look what the Lord has done."

Some critics and doubters may tell you to calm down or chill out on the happiness stuff. Let that go in one ear and out the other. Keep wearing your blessings well, and over time, instead of them affecting you, you will infect them. You will help them come up higher.

When you dress your best, you're wearing your blessings well. When you step up and take that promotion, you're wearing your blessings well. When God opens the door and you move into that new house you've been believing for, others may be critical. But don't allow those who are negative, jealous, judgmental, bitter, angry, and nonsmiling to bring you down.

If you want to please God and live in happiness, don't drag around broke, defeated, or depressed. Wear your blessings well. Step up to a new level. Enjoy God's favor. Be proud of who you are and of what God has done in your life.

Live for the Most High God

The Scripture says, "Let the LORD be magnified, who has pleasure in the prosperity of His servant" (Psalm 35:27 NKJV).

I say this respectfully, but we have to fight the religious spirit that says we're supposed to be poor, broke, and defeated to prove to everyone that we're really humble. When we're poor, broke, and defeated, all that proves is that we're poor, broke, and defeated. Nobody will want what we have. I can be poor, broke, and defeated without serving God. We're supposed to be examples of what it means to live for the Most High God.

We should be so blessed, so prosperous, so kind, so generous, so happy, and so peaceful that people will want what we have. If you think you're showing God how holy you are and how humble you are by not wearing your blessings and not taking that promotion, your own thinking is what is keeping God from doing something new in your life.

Enlarge Your Vision

You have to enlarge your vision. God owns it all. God's blessing you in a greater way will not bankrupt heaven. God makes streets out of gold. If you want to bring a smile to God's face, embrace an abundant-life mentality.

Victoria and I found these two acres we wanted to buy for a home some day. It was a great piece of property close in to the city. God has blessed us through our books and other avenues. We tithe our income and we give generously, but we also believe in making good investments. I was praying and debating whether we should buy this property. I thought, *You know what? We don't really need two acres to live on. We're fine where we are.*

But deep down I wanted it. It was a desire of my heart, but I felt guilty, like it was more than we needed. Then one day I was on an airplane thirty-five thousand feet in the air. It was a clear, beautiful day. I was sitting by the window looking out toward the ground.

I heard God say something to me, not out loud, but just down inside me; an impression. He said, *You wonder if it's okay to buy that property. What do you think those two acres look like to Me? What do you think it looks like from My point of view, from My perspective?*

Well, from where I was, thirty-five thousand feet in the air, two acres looked like a little dot, just like you took your pen and touched the earth.

It was nothing. I felt God say, *I give you permission. It's okay to have enough land the size of a pinhead from My viewpoint!*

Wear Your Blessings Well

Sometimes, we think so small. We limit our possibilities and our potential. God owns it all. "The earth is the LORD's, and the fullness thereof" (Psalm 24:1 KJV). We have to enlarge our vision.

So often we think, *Is it wrong for me to want to live in a nice house? Is it wrong for me to want a bigger piece of property? Is it selfish for me to want to drive a nice car? Is it okay for me to want to bless my children and leave them an inheritance?*

God says, "It's okay. Wear your blessings well." As long as you're keeping God in first place and you're not living selfishly and you're not making material things your idols, then God wants to give you the desires of your heart. He takes pleasure in blessing His children.

> *God says, "It's okay. Wear your blessings well."*

A young man in our congregation came to me after he was promoted to a high position at a major retail company. He was the youngest ever to hold the job overseeing a large region. He was very excited. He knew it was God's favor.

But he was promoted over co-workers who had been there much longer and were more experienced. They had been his friends, but he felt they were avoiding him since his promotion. He sensed that they were trying to make him look bad by talking about him behind his back.

"I know you've quoted Ephesians 3:20 in situations like this," he said to me. "This is just what you've been talking about, but I feel guilty, like I've done something wrong."

I told him what I'm telling you: That is the goodness of God. Wear it well. The Scripture tells us that promotion doesn't come from people; promotion comes from the Lord (see Psalm 75:6–7).

If you don't step up and wear that blessing well with a grateful attitude, do you know what will happen? God will give it to somebody else! Don't worry if others are jealous or turn against you. I've learned some people will be your friend until you get promoted. Co-workers may go to lunch with you as long as you're at the same level, but the moment you see increase, the moment you come into a handful of blessings on purpose, jealousy takes hold and they try to make you look bad. Don't worry about it. God will take care of your enemies. Be grateful for the goodness of God.

We see an example of this in the Scripture when Isaac was in the famine. There had been a great drought in the land for some time. It didn't look like there was any end in sight. Isaac went out to his land and he planted crops, right in the middle of the famine. It didn't make any sense, but somehow in that same year, without the proper amount of water, Isaac received one hundred times what he had sown because the Lord blessed him (see Genesis 26:12).

Notice where the blessing came from: almighty God. It was a handful of blessings on purpose; supernatural increase. But what's interesting is when Isaac's crops came up, when God blessed him, the people he was living around, the Philistines, his friends, all of a sudden became jealous of him.

They were fine as long as Isaac was hungry, too. As long as they were at the same level it was no big deal, but when he stepped up to a new level, when he began to wear his blessings well, the Scripture says, "the Philistines envied" Isaac (Genesis 26:14 NIV)

Don't Worry About the Backbiters

If you worry constantly that not everyone likes you, you'll have a long-term problem with being blessed because when you're blessed, the haters come out. When you step up to a new level, the backbiters show up. When you wear that blessing well and you take one of those handfuls of blessing on purpose, don't be surprised if it draws jealousy out of people.

When they come at you, simply say, in a humble way, "I'm wearing this blessing well, despite criticism and jealousy. If my friends aren't happy for my blessings, then it's time to find new friends who will celebrate with me as I celebrate with them."

A friend of mine is pastor to a small church that meets in a high school auditorium. Every Sunday they have to move their equipment in and out. It's a lot of work. His dream is to one day build his own auditorium.

When he visited us at Lakewood Church, I had some concerns about showing him around because it is so big. I didn't want to seem like I was bragging and I didn't want him to feel badly. I was tempted to downplay the size of our church, even to apologize for it.

Then I realized I would not be bragging on anything we've done. I'd be bragging on what God has done. I had to shake off that guilt and when we toured Lakewood, I said, "Here it is. Look what the Lord has done."

Before he left I reminded him, "If God did it for us, He can do it for you as well!"

Don't Apologize for God's Goodness

My parents sowed seeds for forty years before I ever took over the Lakewood ministry. I'm reaping the rewards of a generational blessing. My paternal grandmother made ten cents an hour washing clothes for other people during the Great Depression. She worked twelve hours a day and made $1.20. My father went to school with holes in his pants. He would put cardboard in the bottom of his shoes because the soles were so torn up.

My grandparents and parents made great sacrifices to get us where we are today. So I'm wearing my blessings well. People may criticize us. They may judge. They may find fault, but they don't know what it took to get where we are today.

They weren't there when the kids in our family would sweep out the old church and clean buildings. They weren't there when my father traveled for weeks doing missionary work around the world while my mother took care of five children on her own. They weren't there when my mom was diagnosed with terminal cancer and we fought the good fight of faith. They weren't there when my father went to be with the Lord and I stepped up to pastor the church practically scared to death.

Some people come in after the struggle and they see you as you are now: blessed, prosperous, healthy, sober, free, and happy. They want to judge you and criticize, but the problem is, they missed seeing the years of struggle. They didn't see the sacrifices made. They didn't see the battles fought—the times you felt like giving up but you kept pressing forward, the nights you stayed up and prayed and believed and gave and served. They didn't see the price that was paid to get you to where you are.

A blessing may look free, but the truth is it cost you something. Ruth's blessing, her handful on purpose, came after she had buried her husband and after her father-in-law had died. She had suffered great heartache and pain.

I'm sure some of those workers said, "Hey, it's not fair. Why is this lady getting all this free wheat when we have to work?" They didn't realize Ruth had paid the price. She had proven herself as being faithful. She was taking care of her loved ones. God was rewarding her.

Don't let anyone make you feel guilty for the favor, the honor, the joy, the peace, the victory that God has given you. Somebody paid the price. The Scripture talks about this: "I have given you a land for which you did not labor and cities you did not build, and you dwell in them; you eat from vineyards and olive yards you did not plant" (Joshua 24:13 AMP). Those are generational blessings; God rewarding us for seeds other people have sown.

Just last week a gentleman stopped me and told me about bumping into my father on a street in downtown Houston back in the 1970s. My dad didn't know this young man, but he was at one of the lowest points in his life. He had just dropped out of school and didn't have any direction. My father came up to him and gave him one hundred dollars and said, "Young man, I don't know you, but God has got a great plan for your life. You keep moving forward."

That was a turning point in the young man's life. He went back to school and earned a degree. Today he is a medical doctor with a very successful practice.

When I wear my blessings, I'm not only honoring God, I'm also honoring my earthly father who spent his life helping others. I'm honoring my mother, who has cared for so many. I'm honoring my grandmother, who worked tirelessly. I'm honoring my grandfather, who gave and served.

> *God takes pleasure in the prosperity of His children.*

When you see me happy, healthy, blessed, and living well, I make no apologies. It's the goodness of God being passed from generation to generation. I won't downplay it. I won't make excuses. I know God takes pleasure in the prosperity of His children.

Brag on the Goodness of God

Our attitude should not be *Look how great I am. Look at what all I have.* No, turn it around: *Look at how great God is. Look at what the Lord has done in my life, in my family."*

All through the day we should be bragging on the goodness of God. We may not have deserved it. We didn't earn it. Many times it's just another handful of blessing on purpose. Now, don't let some negative, judgmental, jealous person, or even your own thoughts try to convince you to not wear the blessings God has given you.

If you will wear your blessings well, being quick to always give God the credit, then there is no limit to where He will take you. God will make you an example of what it means to live a joyful, blessed, prosperous, and abundant life.

As I noted in the opening chapter, we all have the power to choose happiness each and every day. That doesn't mean we ignore our challenges or that we can always control everything that happens to us, but it does mean that, with God's help, we can choose to respond to life's inevitable setbacks and hard times with a positive attitude. You have the power to focus on solutions, to surround yourself with supportive people, to rise above criticism and discouragement, and to put your faith in God and trust His plan for your life. Be happy with who God created you to be and enjoy each day you are given as His gift. If you do this, I believe you will make every day a Friday.